PREVENTING CRIME IN AMERICA AND JAPAN

PREVENTING CRIME IN AMERICA AND JAPAN

A Comparative Study

Robert Y. Thornton
with Katsuya Endo

M. E. Sharpe, Inc.
Armonk, New York
London, England

Available in the United Kingdom and Europe from M. E. Sharpe,
Publishers, 3 Henrietta Street, London WC2E 8LU.

Library of Congress Cataloging-in-Publication Data

Thornton, Robert Y.
Preventing crime in America and Japan : a comparative study / by
Robert Y. Thornton, with Katsuya Endo.
p. cm.
Includes index.
ISBN 0-87332-788-8
1. Crime prevention—Japan—Kawagoe-shi. 2. Criminal justice,
Administration of—Japan—Kawagoe-shi. 3. Crime prevention—Oregon—
Salem. 4. Criminal justice, Administration of —Oregon—Salem.
I. Endo, Katsuya. II. Title.
HV7115.K38Y46   1991
364.4′0952′134—dc20
91-3511
CIP

Printed in the United States of America

MV   10   9   8   7   6   5   4   3   2   1

Contents

Preface

Anyone familiar with the world's major industrial countries may be well aware that crime rates in Japan are far lower in almost every category than those in the United States. Given this fact, it is natural to wonder if the example of Japan can offer some new approaches to preventing crime and delinquency in America.

To explore this question, we undertook a study of the crime prevention strategies used in America and in Japan. The result is this cross-cultural comparison of crime and delinquency prevention methods and techniques, which includes a special focus on two cities: Salem, Oregon, and Kawagoe, Japan. Material was collected during forty-eight months of study and field research in the United States and Japan. Our method of investigation included participant observation and in-depth interviews, and we worked directly with city officials and employees, police officers, educators, students, family court judges and personnel, civilian attendees at neighborhood meetings, youth counselors, mental health professionals, crime prevention trainers, public and private welfare agencies, parole and probation officers, youth corrections personnel, and volunteers in many areas. After an initial feasibility study, we became convinced that the proposed investigation would produce a number of innovative approaches to the prevention and control of crime and delinquency in the United States, as well as in Japan and other countries. We completed our research by conducting in-depth studies and interviews in Salem, Oregon, and Kawagoe, Saitama Prefecture, Japan.

Aware that foreign observers and writers may be accused of over-emphasizing the effectiveness of traditional crime and delinquency controls in Japanese society, and to guard against possible bias, we decided upon joint American-Japanese authorship and we interviewed members of both the pre–World War II generation and the generation born after the war, including a representative sampling of youth under twenty-one years of age. We have also endeavored to recognize the effect of the drastic socioeconomic changes Japan has undergone since the Second World War.

The purpose of our research was to survey and report on crime prevention methods and techniques presently in use in America and Japan and in the sister cities of Salem and Kawagoe, to assess their role and effectiveness in control and prevention of crime and delinquency, and, finally, to compare the methods and techniques. As will be explained later in considerable detail, Japan has a unified crime prevention system, as well as a national police system and a national criminal justice system. Thus, crime prevention as devised and implemented in Kawagoe is substantially the same as that generally found in urban areas throughout Japan. Salem's population, police, educational, court, juvenile, and correctional systems and social problems are in the main typical of middle America. Salem was named an All America city in 1962–63.

To the best of our knowledge, Japan's crime prevention programs have never before been the subject of a comprehensive and integrated study published in English.[1] And, according to Sister Cities International, a worldwide organization of sister city affiliates, this is the first time two sister city affiliates have been the subject of a cross-cultural comparative study of this type.

Note

1. A booklet dealing with the topic of "Crime Prevention in the U.S. and Japan" and containing copies of a series of papers presented at a conference held in Tokyo in 1988 has recently (1990) been released by Transnational Juris Publications, Inc., Dobbs Ferry, New York.

Acknowledgments

This manuscript was prepared with the helpful assistance and cooperation of James Heuser, Diane Craven, Shirley Evenhus, Kathryn Ann Farr, Nobuko Sato Marion, Carolan Gladden, Marjorie Napper, Mayor Kiichi Kawai, former Mayor Sue Harris Miller, Hugh Wilkinson, George Joseph, and the Salem, Oregon, and Kanazawa, Kawagoe, Japan, police and crime prevention agencies. Our study of Salem and Kawagoe was made possible in part by a grant from Tokyo International University. My wife, Dorothy, offered constant advice and encouragement and deserves special thanks.

Many of those listed read all or parts of the manuscript, offered suggestions, gave valuable insights, and in dozens of ways made significant contributions to the finished product.

Robert Y. Thornton

PREVENTING CRIME IN AMERICA AND JAPAN

1

Introduction and Overview

What Is the Benefit of a Comparative Research Project?

Professor Charles R. Fenwick, of Trenton State College in New Jersey, in speaking of the values of cross-cultural comparative research in the criminal justice field, has perceptively observed that by studying the experiences of other nations, one should be able to see one's own system in a new light, which can lead not only to higher levels of understanding/explanation but also to informed policy decision making.

The experiences of these other countries can provide valuable information and research/policy implications for nations in search of answers to their respective crime, law, and justice concerns.[1]

It is not surprising that some Japanese criminal justice scholars have also expressed similar views of the value of cross-cultural comparative research. For example, Professor Nobuyoshi Araki, professor of criminology at Rikkyo University in Tokyo, has observed:

> Comparative study of law usually generates new points of view and suggestions for improving the system and its function. This is one of the reasons why so many Japanese scholars are studying American criminal law and procedure and why some American scholars have been interested in the Japanese criminal justice system.[2]

A cross-cultural comparative study is like "holding up a mirror" to oneself for a frank self-examination. In this case, the purpose of the self-examination is to permit federal, state, and local criminal justice

3

and law enforcement leaders to examine and reassess their own crime prevention strategies to discover how those strategies may be improved.

Those studies of Japan's police system that have appeared have already had a significant impact on police systems in America.[3] The city of Santa Ana, California, adopted a modified form of the Japanese police substation (*kōban*) system and instituted foot patrolling in its urban sections; the results in Santa Ana have been dramatic. In 1986, San Francisco Mayor Dianne Feinstein established a kōban in the center of San Francisco's Chinatown after she witnessed how Tokyo's kōban police recovered a purse that had been snatched from a member of her party on a trade mission. San Francisco's Chinatown merchants were delighted with the results, and reported that the incidence of street crime in the area dropped substantially. In fact, the system has been so successful that three more kōban have been established, one in the Japantown tourist area, one at the terminus of the cable car line, and another in a predominantly Hispanic area of the city.

There have been other success stories, both in the United States and elsewhere. Most extensive adoption of the kōban system in America by far has been in Detroit, Michigan. A total of ninety-two kōban have been established in that city. This was the result of the experience and recommendation of a local police officer who had observed the effectiveness of this policing technique while serving in the U.S. Army in Japan. Singapore, Hong Kong, and areas in South Korea have also adopted the Kōban system, and have reported good results. According to press reports, the Los Angeles Police Department has instituted foot patrolling in at least one high-crime housing project area. Other cities that are using new community-based approaches to crime control include Oakland, California, Flint, Michigan, and Denver, Colorado. Among the approaches used are increased citizen involvement, foot patrols, and more intensive crime prevention programs.

What we undertook in this study was to learn at first hand the successful innovative approaches developed and now in use in Salem, Oregon, and Kawagoe, its sister city in Saitama Prefecture, Japan. The variety of crime prevention methods and techniques in use, with varying degrees of success in these two cities on opposite shores of the Pacific Ocean, are discussed in this book. Many municipalities will find a host of crime prevention techniques worth careful study, and possibly even worth borrowing or adopting. Although Salem has the higher crime rate of the two sister cities, we feel confident that many of its methods and techniques, such as Citizen Neighborhood Crime Watch, Anti School Dropout Program, and Youth Service Teams in schools, will be of particular interest. Similarly, Kawagoe's foot and bicycle patrols, the kōban system, early intervention through the school system, and the *Hodōin* program are also of considerable interest.

This study provides something else of equal value: it offers a fund of experience relevant to the control and prevention of crime and delinquency. From this experience, both citizens and governments may obtain a deeper understanding of the underlying causes of crime, as well as of which techniques work and which do not. We believe that it will provide new insights and contribute to solving problems on both sides of the Pacific Ocean by looking in the mirror and reevaluating the effectiveness of both systems.

Are Crime Prevention Programs Cost-Effective?

What exactly is the cost of crime? No one knows for sure. According to the National Institute of Justice, U.S. Department of Justice, direct expenditures due to crime and crime prevention were approximately $100 billion in 1983.[4] During 1986, according to the Oregon Law Enforcement Data Systems report, the estimated value of property stolen in Salem totaled $5,504,156. The value of recovered property was $1,889,351, leaving the estimated net loss at $3,614,805.

During 1985, the estimated overall cost of operating the Oregon Criminal Justice system—police, prosecutors, courts, parole and probation, jails, and prisons—was $416,316,000, or approximately $155 for every man, woman, and child living in the state. In 1965 the cost of the national criminal justice system was estimated by the President's Commission on Law Enforcement and the U.S. Administration of Justice at 3 percent of our gross national product (GNP). By 1985, the cost had increased to approximately 11 percent of the GNP for that year. In fiscal year 1985, federal, state, and local governments spent $45 billion for civil and criminal justice: $22 billion for police protection; $13 billion for jails, prisons, probation, and parole; $10 billion for courts, prosectuion, and public defense of accused offenders.[5] These figures, of course, do not take into account the human cost to the victims of crime.

The Cost of Incarceration and the
Effectiveness of Preventive Education
versus the Cost of Crime

According to a study released in July 1988 by the U.S. Department of Justice, new crimes committed by 1,000 released repeat offenders in California, Michigan, and Texas cost society an estimated $40,000 a year for each offender in victim losses, police work, court work, and private security expenses. The study concluded that the $8.6 billion cost of operating the nation's prisons and jails in 1987 was a mere one-tenth of the overall cost of crime. According to information supplied by the Oregon Corrections Division on August 1, 1990, the cost of maintaining one inmate in the Oregon correctional institution for one year is currently $15,732. At the same time, the study estimated the cost of other programs such as police, courts, and probation at about $25 billion.

Clearly, with the staggering cost of operating our national criminal justice system—$45.6 billion per year—local crime prevention programs will be cost effective if they divert even a handful of young offenders from a life of crime. For every single youth who embarks on a life of crime, it is estimated that society faces a total cost of at least $200,000. Thus, successful crime prevention programs are most definitely cost effective, in terms of both victim and property costs and the enormous cost of operating our overburdened criminal justice system.

Often cited to support this conclusion is the Perry Pre-School Project carried out in Ypsilanti, Michigan, from 1962 to 1966.[6] This was a Head Start preschool program designed to improve the school performance of disadvantaged (by race and class) African-American children. The project also examined the impact of Head Start on criminal conduct. The experimental group of fifty-eight children received training beginning at age five. By age fourteen, they showed less self-reported criminal conduct than the sixty-five children of the control group. Altogether, 40 percent of the control group had been involved in criminal conduct during the intervening period, but only 25 percent of the training group had been. The project was subsequently taken over by the High/Scope Educational Research Foundation. High/Scope tracked the same students to age nineteen. Again, the preschool training group had significantly fewer dropouts, arrests, or welfare recipients, and appreciably more literacy, employment, and postsecondary enrollments.

Law-related education programs in schools are another form of crime prevention shown to be successful. A study conducted under the auspices of the Office of Juvenile Justice and Delinquency Prevention of the U.S. Department of Justice verified that properly implemented law-related education programs in schools can reduce delinquent behavior and promote prosocial behavior.[7] A similar study was conducted in 1987 in a mix of inner-city, suburban, and rural schools in eastern Colorado by the Social Service Education Consortium and the Center for Action Research. This study reaffirmed other, earlier findings: students who participated in high-quality law-related education programs were less likely to be truants, to smoke marijuana, to cheat on tests, or to commit felonies.[8]

Definition of Crime Prevention

The term "crime prevention" as used in this study means all measures of any kind or description taken by government or the community to keep crime and delinquency from occurring within its boundaries.

Crime prevention generally takes one of three forms:

1. Measures to reduce the opportunity for crimes to be committed, such as neighborhood crime watches, home security devices, and "safe homes" for children going to and from school.
2. Measures designed to reduce the individual's desire to commit crime; these range from character education, including self-discipline, to youth recreation programs.
3. Swift and certain punishment for criminal conduct.

The approach taken in our study is interdisciplinary; it covers not only the crime and delinquency prevention role of law enforcement agencies, but also citizen crime prevention programs and the crime prevention activities of schools, court counseling services, parole and probation agencies, and youth correctional institutions.

Notes

1. Charles R. Fenwick, *Internal Criminal Justice Systems,* Vol. 1, New York Academy of Criminal Justice Sciences (1984), p. 24.

2. Nobuyoshi Araki, "The Flow of Criminal Cases in the Japanese Criminal Justice System," *Crime and Delinquency* 4 (October 1985): 601–29.

3. David H. Bayley, *Forces of Order* (Berkeley: University of California Press, 1976); Walter L. Ames, *Police and Community in Japan* (Berkeley: University of California Press, 1981); William Clifford, *Crime Control in Japan* (Lexington, MA: Lexington Books, 1976); L. Craig Parker, *The Japanese Police System Today* (New York: Kodansha International, 1984).

4. *Making Confinement Decisions* (Washington, DC: National Institute of Justice, U.S. Department of Justice, 1987).

5. *Sourcebook of Criminal Justice Statistics—1987* (Washington, DC: Bureau of Justice Statistics, U.S. Department of Justice, 1987).

6. *Changed Lives: The Effects of the Perry Pre-School Program on Youths through Age 19,* Monographs of the High/Scope Educational Research Foundation, no. 8 (Ypsilanti, MI: High/Scope Press, 1984).

7. "Law-Related Education Evaluation Project Final Report: Phase Two, Year Three" (Boulder, CO: Center for Action Research, Inc. and the Social Science Education Consortium, 1984).

8. "Using School-Based Programs to Improve Students' Citizenship in Colorado." Report to Colorado Educators from the Colorado Juvenile Justice and Delinquency Prevention Council Action Research Project, University of Colorado, Boulder, October 1987.

2

General Description of
the Two Target Cities

Salem

Salem is the capital city of the state of Oregon and the county seat of
Marion County. It is located on Interstate Highway Five some forty-
five miles south of Portland, the largest city in the state. Salem's
boundaries encompass 40.8 square miles with a population of 106,942
at the 1990 preliminary U.S. census. Residents within the Salem metropolitan area, however, total 276,450. It has a charter form of government, an appointed city manager, an elected mayor, and eight elected
council members.

The economy of the Salem area is highly diversified. With more
than 100 different agricultural products grown for market and processing,
Salem is one of the largest food processing centers in the nation. The
largest employer in the area, however, is the state government, which
employs approximately 14,553 individuals full time in the Salem–
Marion County area.

The school system has 24,877 students at thirty-seven elementary
schools, six two-year middle schools, and five four-year high schools.
Twenty-eight elementary schools also serve the community after regular school hours as community schools. Five private high schools,
mostly church-related or church-oriented, cover kindergarten to grades
six to eight. There is one university, Willamette, the sister university of
Kawagoe's Tokyo International University. There is also one community college, Chemeketa, and one church-affiliated college, Western
Baptist.

State correctional institutions located in or near Salem include the Hillcrest School, for both male and female emotionally disturbed and socially maladjusted juveniles; Oregon State Correctional Institution, originally built for younger criminal offenders; Oregon State Penitentiary, for older offenders requiring maximum security confinement; and Oregon Women's Correction Center, for adult female offenders. A recent study showed that while only 9 percent of the inmates sentenced to state correctional institutions were from Marion county, approximately 18 percent remained in the Salem area after their release from the institution. This phenomenon has a definite bearing on Salem's crime prevention problem.[1]

The police department consists of 148 sworn officers and 100 civilian support personnel. It operates under the direction of the mayor, the city council, and the city manager. (It may be worth pointing out that, according to the U.S. Constitution, the United States is a federal system in which the responsibility for criminal justice is shared among national, state, and local governments.)

Kawagoe

Kawagoe is located approximately thirty miles northwest of Tokyo and is a leading commercial center of Western Saitama prefecture. During its long history, it was a castle town during the Edo Period (1615– 1868). Kawagoe encompasses about forty square miles within its boundaries and has a population of 272,433. It has an elected mayor, a deputy mayor, forty-four elected city council members, and an elected chairman of the city council. Because of its proximity to Tokyo, a large number of residents commute to work there daily, and the city is sometimes described as a bedroom community. In this respect it is distinctly different from its sister city of Salem.

The Kawagoe economy is highly diversified, with agriculture and light industry existing almost side by side. According to recent statistics, 6,336 people are engaged in primary industry; 43,927 in secondary industry; and 63,313 in tertiary industry.

The school system includes thirty-eight kindergartens with a total of 8,097 pupils, all privately owned and operated, some by religious organizations. There are thirty-two elementary schools with a total of 31,284 students; twenty-one junior high schools with 15,398 students; seventeen senior high schools, including seven private schools, with

16,317 students; and four colleges and universities with a combined registration of 9,014. The city's superintendent of education (*Kyoiku Cho*) is appointed by the mayor with the approval of the city council.

An integral part of the national police system—rather than the local city unit we find in Salem—Kawagoe's police department is a branch of the Saitama Prefectural Police Agency, which falls under the general supervision and direction of the National Police Agency of Japan in Tokyo. The National Police Agency in turn is under the supervision of the National Public Safety Commission (*Kokka Kōan Iinkai*), a civil body. In the same manner, each prefecture police agency is under the supervision of its prefectural public safety commission.

Although Japan can be said to have a quasi-national police system, operation and control are largely decentralized, with funding supplied by both the prefectural and the national governments; the bulk of the funding comes from the prefectural government. Japan's system of justice is unitary as well, roughly analogous to the U.S. Department of Justice, where judges are under the supervision of the Supreme Court and prosecutors supervised by the Ministry of Justice.

To be sure, a national police system has certain inherent advantages, including overall coordination, centralized planning, and more efficient, more cost effective operation; standardization of procedures, equipment, and training; better communication between geographical areas and political subdivisions; and speedier and more efficient transfer and concentration of police in times of disaster or other national emergencies. It has been suggested by one leading American authority that the United States adopt a type of national police system.[2]

Notes

1. Karen Seidel and Carol A. Henkel, "Salem Area Institutions: Correctional and Mental Health Institutions and the Ex-Institutional Population," Bureau of Governmental Research and Service (Eugene: University of Oregon, 1987).

2. L. Craig Parker, Jr., *The Japanese Police System Today* (Tokyo: Kodansha International, 1984).

3

Crime Differences

Wide differences in cultural heritage and value systems have a direct impact on rates of crime, and it is obvious that there are many cultural differences between the United States and Japan. This does not mean, however, that Japanese approaches to crime prevention cannot work in the United States, or vice versa.

Crime Rates

The crime rates listed in Table 3.1 are typical of the data available for several years in the early-to-mid-1980s. In almost all instances, the crime rate in the United States far exceeds that in Japan: the incidence of rape was eighteen times higher in the United States; the homicide rate was essentially eight times higher. According to statistics gathered in 1982,[1] the incidence of murder was four times greater in London than in Tokyo; the incidence in New York was a staggering twelve times that in Japan's largest city. Tokyo's robbery rate was a mere one-thirty-fourth that of London; New York's robbery rate—in another telling comparison—was 270 times that of Tokyo. As the table reveals, the only specific area where Japan comes anywhere near the United States is in the incidence of organized crime and juvenile offenses.

Incarceration Rates

A statistical comparison of the number of people in penal institutions in the two nations reveals a similar disparity. According to the Bureau of Justice Statistics,[2] as of 1986 the U.S. prison population was

Table 3.1

**Crime Rates in Japan and the United States, 1984,
per 100,000 Population***

	Japan	United States
Overall**	1.204	4,890
Homicide	0.8	7.9
Rape	1.6	35.7
Burglary	231.2	1,263.7
Drug-related offenses	32.0	281.0
Juvenile offenses	22.9	31.3

*Based on Interpol data for 1984.
**U.S. Department of Justice and Interpol, "Study on Criminal Victimization in the United States," 1983.

546,659 men and women inmates, while the Research and Training Institute of the Ministry of Justice reports that the average daily prison population in Japan in 1986 was only 55,223 inmates.[3] In short, although the total 1986 population of the United States (estimated at 242,200,000) was approximately twice that of Japan (estimated at 121,402,000), the United States had nearly ten times as many offenders in its prisons as Japan. This translates into an incarceration rate in Japan of just 45.5 per 100,000 population, while the ratio in the United States was a striking 225.7 prisoners per 100,000 population.[4]

Why should America have nearly ten times as many offenders behind bars as Japan? Even when put on a per-population basis (i.e., allowing for the difference in population of the two countries), the U.S. incarceration rate is five times greater than Japan's. Are Americans inherently that much more inclined toward crime?

Although that could be one conclusion drawn from this comparison of crime statistics, taking a closer look at U.S. prison populations in the recent past shows an interesting phenomenon. In 1979, for example, there were an estimated 274,563 inmates. By 1986, the number had nearly doubled to 450,416; and according to a study of prison overcrowding sponsored by the National Judicial College in Reno, Nevada, and completed in June 1989, over the past twenty years U.S. prison populations have increased two-and-a-half times, and since the end of World War II have tripled. According to the study, the number of incarcerated individuals in the United States "now stands at 228 per

100,000 population, the highest rate of imprisonment among all nations."[5]

Some observers of the dramatic increases in the number of people incarcerated have attributed most of them to increases in penalties for criminal violations by legislative bodies and more severe sentences being imposed by criminal court judges. But it is reasonable to question whether crime actually has increased enormously or whether lawmakers and judges are simply responding to citizen alarm over crime in their communities.

The fact that, on a per-population basis, a higher proportion of the U.S. population is incarcerated for criminal offenses than is the case in other Western democracies does not necessarily mean that the United States is more punitive in its treatment of offenders. As the U.S. Bureau of Justice Statistics pointed out in a Special Report, "Comparing only population-based incarceration rates ignores the impact that higher crime rates in the United States may have in accounting for higher incarceration rates."[6] In other words, higher crime rates can result in higher incarceration rates for a given country.

The same report goes on to point out that the United States, Canada, and England have similar rates of imprisonment for adults arrested for robbery. For theft, imprisonment rates range from 14 percent in Canada and England to 18 percent in the United States. For burglary, Canada has the lowest rate (23 percent) followed by England (30 percent) and the United States (35 percent). Because of a number of statistical reporting differences, exact comparisons with West Germany were not possible. The authors estimated, however, that in general the German criminal justice system relies less on incarceration than do the three English-speaking countries.

Penal Sentences

As several writers have pointed out, sentences for imprisonment imposed in Japan tend on the average to be shorter than in the United States.[7] Japanese judges prefer to sanction offenders with a fine and/or a minimum term, believing that lighter sentences encourage rehabilitation and that long sentences only plunge the offender deeper into the criminal subculture and more criminal behavior.[8] Surprisingly, about 90 percent of all penal code offenses are punished by the imposition of a fine. Of offenders, about 80 percent receive sentences of not more than three years, with 50 percent receiving sentences of less than one year. Prisoners may be paroled (by a regional parole board) after serving one-third of their term.[9] The 1981 study in which these statistics were presented also reviewed sentencing practices and crime rates in the Netherlands, Japan, Pennsylvania, and Texas,[10] and reported that the average amount of time served in Dutch prisons during 1975 was thirty-five days. From 1964 to 1973, the Netherlands sentenced only two offenders to life imprisonment and none to death.

In 1981, in the state of Florida, which has half the population of the Netherlands, there were 140 persons on death row and more than 2,000 individuals serving life sentences. The state of Pennsylvania, which has been strongly influenced historically by the rehabilitation philosophy of the Quakers, had a significantly lower crime rate than Texas, where the influence of the frontier concept of justice has prevailed and where Texans have reportedly led the nation in expanding their prison system.

According to Nagel's study, Texans are 15 percent more likely to be mugged, twice as likely to be raped, and twice as likely to be murdered as Pennsylvanians. The author attributes the decrease in Japanese crime to less harsh sentencing policies, a ban on private ownership of handguns, full employment, and job security. Nagel concludes that corrections professionals should promote public policies that reduce the harshness of sentencing; promote job security for all Americans, but especially for the poor and for ex-offenders; punish nonpredatory offenders by nonconfinement alternatives; reduce the opportunity for and incidence of gun violence; and stimulate safe, therapeutic environments within correctional facilities.

Although the U.S. prison population nearly doubled in the seven years from 1979 to 1986, the nationwide crime rate during approximately the same period (1977 to 1986) showed an increase of only 7.9 per 100,000 inhabitants. It follows that, while the increase in the crime rate was certainly a contributing factor, the bulk of the enormous increase in incarcerations was due to stiffer sentencing; i.e., more offenders were sentenced to prison and for longer periods of time.

Do more severe sentences have the desired effect of reducing crime? Or do they have the opposite effect? Or do they have no effect whatsoever? The data we have seen are, in our opinion, still insufficient to suggest a categorical conclusion, and it is doubtful that any amount of research will result in a satisfactory answer to these questions, although a good case can be made for the argument advanced by Nagel and others that harsher sentences may increase rather than decrease crime.

Although the recent trend of many American lawmakers to increase penalties and of criminal court judges to sentence more offenders to prison terms may or may not have affected U.S. crime rates to any appreciable extent, it has obviously exacerbated greatly the problem of prison overcrowding. And, because an estimated 75 percent of all U.S. offenders classed as "under correctional control" are supervised in community-based corrections programs, sentencing practices have probably had an even greater adverse impact on the workloads of virtually all community supervision/treatment programs. (In Japan, approximately 60 percent of offenders are supervised in community-based programs. See Chapter 10 for a discussion of Japan's voluntary probation and parole officer system.)

Law Enforcement Profiles of Salem and Kawagoe

Tables 3.2 and 3.3 present comparative data on various aspects of law enforcement in the sister cities of Salem, Oregon, and Kawagoe, Japan. When we analyze the 1986 crime statistics for the two cities, a horrific picture emerges. The following are some salient comparisons:

• Although Salem's population is only one-third that of Kawagoe, there were nearly nine times more reported crimes.
• Computed on a per-population basis, the contrast between crime rates is even greater, with 37.8 times as many crimes committed against persons in Salem as in Kawagoe.
• There were 25.7 times as many property crimes in Salem as in Kawagoe.

A comparison of crimes cleared by arrest is also startling:

• In Kawagoe, 97.7 percent of crimes against persons were cleared by arrest, compared to only 67.8 percent in Salem.
• As Table 3.2 shows, the rate for all crimes was 41 percent in Salem and 69 percent in Kawagoe.

The term "police clearance rate" has slightly different meanings in the United States and in Japan. In the United States it means the proportion of all offenses that the police can attribute to an identifiable

Table 3.2

Salem and Kawagoe Statistical Profiles*

	Kawagoe	Salem
Population	290,148	94,600
Police personnel		
Sworn officers	238	128
(male)	(231)	(124)
(female)	(7)	(4)
Civilians	13	68.5
Ratio of police to population	1:1,261	1:739
Annual number of calls for police service**	10,773	55,649
Average police response time (mins.)		
Emergency calls	5:49	4:00 or less
Nonemergency calls	depends on circumstances	20:00
Common service calls	depends on circumstances	45:00
Police patrol vehicles	10	59
Motorcycles	41	7
Bicycles	91	0
Land area (square miles)	42.25	40.8
Population density (per square mile)	6,908	2,309
Total police budget	$2,972,761	$8,956,680
Salaries	$1,354,206	$7,461,240
Cost per capita	$10.20	$94.68
Cost of crime prevention services	$59,454	$191,825
Cost of school police liaison unit	NA	$187,665
Cost of special crime prevention patrols	NA	$355,982
Number of crimes reported (1986)		
Against persons	130	1,604
Against property	2,037	17,091
Proportion of arrests involving juveniles (in percent)	68	26.2
Arrests and clearances (1986)		
Against persons	127	1,088
Against property	1,368	6,657
Proportion of crimes cleared (in percent)	68.98	41.4
Traffic accidents reported	1,077	2,321

*All data were obtained from the Salem and the Kawagoe police departments, with the exception of the Kawagoe police budget. This information could not be obtained from official sources and should therefore be considered unofficial.

**This figure includes 110 (all) emergency telephone calls only. The total number of calls is approximately twice this number.

Table 3.3

Breakdown of Calls for Police Service in Kawagoe and Salem

Kawagoe		Salem	
1,085	relating to crimes	18,326	relating to crimes
4,504	traffic accidents	2,455	traffic accidents
88	relating to drugs	424	narcotics/drug offenses
160	disasters	4,548	animal problems
527	neighborhood complaints	13,423	neighborhood complaints
500	requests for information	3,068	burglar alarms
1,287	informers	1,483	lost or found property
1,355	duplicate calls	2,042	criminal vandalism
100	false reports/hoaxes	9,231	miscellaneous/noncriminal
1,064	neighborhood/domestic disturbance	55,649	total
103	miscellaneous		
10,773	total		

suspect, while in Japan the clearance rate reflects the number of crimes the police report to the prosecutor as solved. Not counted are certain lesser cases, such as petty larceny, fraud, embezzlement, etc., which the Japanese police are specifically authorized, by general order of the local prosecutor, to dismiss summarily at their discretion.

Obviously, there was a wide disparity in clearance of crimes, to which many salient factors no doubt apply. But, considering Salem's nine times as many reported crimes and five times as many calls for police service, it would appear that the substantially lower crime clearance rates are due to the sizable handicaps under which Salem's police struggle, including an excessive number of crimes, and a much larger number of calls from citizens for police services. The bottom line, then, is this: When there are fewer crimes and fewer calls from citizens for service, the police have more time to spend on solving crimes.

There are other factors that affect comparative clearance rates. Under Japan's penal code, police may detain a suspect for questioning for up to twenty-three days, or more under certain circumstances. This practice, as well as occasional accusations of forced confessions extracted by police using so-called "third-degree" methods (prohibited by article 38 of Japan's constitution), have recently come under sustained attack by Japan's Federation of Bar Associations and by defense lawyers, as well as by a number of international human rights organizations and experts. "Stopping for questioning" (*shokumu shitsumon*) needs no special judicial authorization. The Police Duties Law of 1948 (article 2) allows police to stop and question suspects or potential witnesses, but the person stopped has no legal duty to respond to questions.[11]

It is also relevant that more than 80 percent of all suspects are handled without formal arrest in Japan, and more than 90 percent of criminal defendants plead guilty. In 1986, prosecutors disposed of 69.5 percent of all cases by summary proceedings. Less than 4 percent went to trial. We might also note that Japanese law does not embody a "presumption of innocence"; but under an equivalent Roman law principle, in all criminal trials the courts are supposed to resolve all doubts in favor of the accused.[12]

In the United States, on the other hand, a Department of Justice study for the year 1986[13] of the typical outcomes of felony arrests in 28 selected major cities reported: 5 percent of the cases were diverted or referred to another court immediately; 24 percent were rejected for various reasons at the initial screening stage; 18 percent were dismissed for various reasons in felony court.

Of the 55 percent that were carried forward, 52 percent were disposed of by a guilty plea; 3 percent went to trial; 2 percent were found guilty. In 1 percent of the cases, the defendant was acquitted.

This leads us to the question of how we can explain Japan's successful record on crime. Could it be due to better prevention programs? Better police training? An almost totally homogeneous population? Stricter gun controls? Or could there be better informal social controls woven into the fabric of Japanese society, cultural values that reach back centuries in Nippon's history?

After thirty-plus years of traveling and working in Japan, and observing that society, I believe that all of these factors, and a few others, play a part in the remarkably lower crime rates. In only two areas do Japanese crime and crime rates approach those of the United States: one, as pointed out earlier, is juvenile crime; the other is organized crime. In all probability, Japan has more active gangsters (*yakuza*, discussed in Chapter 13) per capita than the United States, although as far as we can learn, American agencies do not keep separate statistics on gangs, as Japan does. For example, *jiageya* are *yakuza* who intimidate small landowners to sell their real estate at a low price so that it can be traded on Tokyo's speculative real estate market.[14] This is not to say, however, that federal and state law enforcement agencies in the

United States have not been active in moving against organized crime. In fact, many agencies have special task forces that maintain crime files and keep a close watch on organized crime. These agencies make cases against criminal gang members, including the so-called Mafia and Cosa Nostra, as well as African-American and Asian gangs, where evidence warrants prosecution.

Notes

1. *Nippon: The Land and Its People* (Tokyo: Nippon Steel Corp., 1984), p. 369.

2. U.S. Department of Justice (Washington, DC: 1986). The U.S. figures do not include persons on probation, parole, or incarcerated in jails or juvenile detention facilities.

3. Government of Japan, Ministry of Justice, Research and Training Institute, "Summary of the White Paper on Crime" (Tokyo: 1988). Statistics used in this portion of the study were also obtained from the "Annual White Paper (*Hanzai Hakusho*)" and the "Summary of the White Paper on Crime," both publications of the Research and Training Institute of the Ministry of Justice (*Hōmo Sōgō Kenkyūsho*). These publications summarize and analyze statistics of the National Police Agency, Supreme Court, and Ministry of Justice, and present some editorial studies; they are a good general resource for scholars. A summary is available in English. Various statistics are also summarized in such publications as *Japan Almanac;* published by *Mainichi Newspapers; Japan Statistical Yearbook* (Prime Minister's Office); *Nippon: A Chartered Survey of Japan,* Kokuseisha (National Administration Tokyo); *Statistical Handbook of Japan* (Prime Minister's Office).

4. U.S. Department of Justice, Bureau of Justice Statistics, Washington, D.C., 1986.

5. Report of the Commission to Advise the Nevada Legislature on the Question of Prison Overcrowding, Reno, Nevada, June 1989. Dr. Gerhard O. W. Mueller, Chairman.

6. "Imprisonment in Four Countries—United States, Canada, England, and West Germany" (Washington DC: U.S. Bureau of Justice Statistics, February 1987).

7. Richard J. Terrill, *World Criminal Justice Systems* (Cincinnati, OH: Anderson Publishing, 1984), p. 280.

8. *Encyclopedia of Japan*, vol. 2 (Tokyo: Kodansha International, 1983), p. 172.

9. Ibid.

10. W.G. Nagel, "Balancing Offender Needs and Public Safety," Proceedings of the American Corrections Association (College Park, MD: 1980), p. 243.

11. *Encyclopedia of Japan,* vol. 2 (Tokyo: Kodansha International, 1983), p. 49.

12. Ibid., p. 51.

13. "The Prosecution of Felony Arrests, 1986" (Washington, DC: U.S. Bureau of Justice Statistics, NCJ–113248 June 1989), chapter 1, p. 2.

14. Chalmers Johnson, "The People Who Invented the Mechanical Nightingale," in "Showa: The Japanese Hirohito," *Journal of American Academy of Arts and Sciences* 119, 3 (Summer 1990): 81.

4

Factors Affecting the Crime Rate

Japanese Social Structure

First and foremost among cultural factors that have a bearing on the incidence of crime is the traditional social structure. Japanese society is oriented around the family and the group to an unusual degree. Informal crime controls begin in the family, where every Japanese automatically assumes a set of obligations to family and to society. A sense of collective responsibility for individual behavior and family responsibility for the behavior of its members has always been a fundamental precept. The result is that threat of exclusion from the group, rather than fixed punishments, is the most effective social control. It is a cultural system that has survived remarkably well.

While there was a sense of shared responsibility for the actions of any member in prewar Japanese families, according to some Japanese criminal justice system professionals, the feeling of shared responsibility is gradually decreasing. As in the West, urbanization has brought about a decline in solidarity of the community and an increase in apathy, anonymity, and egocentricity. Recently, volunteerism has also decreased because of increasing materialism within modern Japanese society.

In Japan, as in China, Korea, and most Asian cultures, the family name always comes before the individual's own given names wherever and whenever a name is used, including in school, business, and the press. This is but one example of the primacy of the family over the individual.

Maintaining the family honor and good reputation is a top priority in every Chinese, Japanese, and Korean family. If a family member steals, he disgraces the whole family. This Asian culture pattern is sometimes referred to by Westerners as "face," as in the importance of not "losing face," or of "saving face." The family also may be shunned in the community (*mura hachibu*).

A similar cultural pattern is found in Western societies but it is nowhere near as important as in Far Eastern societies where the desire to avoid morally reprehensible or antisocial behavior that would bring ridicule or shame (*haji*) to the family is extremely important. Thus, through community sanctions, Japanese society is often the primary enforcer—before formalized laws—of societal norms.

Interestingly, this trait was brought to the United States and the Hawaiian Islands by the first Japanese immigrants in the early 1900s. Even today, crime is virtually unknown among Japanese-Americans (*Issei*—Japan born; *Nisei*—second generation; *Sansei*—third generation) living in the United States.

Cultural Continuity among Oregon's Japanese-Americans

That Japanese immigrant parents were highly successful in transmitting their Japanese value orientations to their Oregon-born children was evident from our interviews with a representative sampling of these offspring, all of whom are now middle-aged adults.

Answers to our question, "Why is it that Japanese Americans rarely if ever violate the law?" were most revealing. Here are some noteworthy examples:

Harold "Bones" Onishi, a Portland high school teacher:

> I would attribute it to the upbringing of the children by the *Issei* parents—the training and nurture of the children and the values they instilled in us.
>
> Ours was a very strong, cohesive family. We talked over our problems at home. Our parents instilled in us a large measure of pride in our Japanese ancestry. We children had a great respect for our parents.

James Sugimura, a retired owner of a Portland barber shop:

> Our parents taught us to avoid bringing shame on the family and to the family name.

Mary Nakadate, prominent cultural leader:

> I would attribute our generally lower crime rate to the moral values instilled in us by our parents. Our willingness to obey without question the relocation order issued by the government during World War II was an example of that. I would also mention the element of *haji*.
>
> There was also the element of Shinto beliefs. This is not religion per se. I believe that similar attitudes were to be found among all pre–World War II Asian immigrants. This unfortunately is not the case with postwar Asian immigrants. In my case it was largely the influence of my mother that instilled these values. My father was usually busy earning a living and keeping food on the table.

Percy Loy, a prominent successful Portland businessman of Chinese descent, expressed very similar feelings with respect to Portland's substantial Chinese community, once the second largest on the West Coast, after San Francisco.

> In my view it was our immigrant parents that instilled in us children respect for authority. It was a family tradition. We were expected to meet the hopes and expectations of our parents. While our father was at all times the head of the family, our mother exercised a great amount of influence in her own quiet way in molding our characters.

Tatsuru Yada, a retired Salem-area truck farm operator and Willamette University graduate, expressed a similar point of view:

> We were brought up, taught to be honest, respect our elders, work hard and do what's right. Our parents encouraged us to get a good education. Both mother and father imparted this training.
>
> During the Great Depression [1930s], the Japanese community in Salem helped each other if in need, rather than going on welfare. Our parents also brought us up to be proud of our Japanese ancestry and heritage. We were taught that we should not be just as good as the other kids in school; that we should be better.

His wife, Masako Yada, also college educated and a former journalist:

> Our parents taught us to be considerate of others, respectful to our elders and older people. Constantly we heard the terms duty [*giri*], obligation [*on*], and shame [*haji*]. We were admonished not to do anything to bring shame to the Japanese community.

In my youth there were several organizations for Japanese-Americans—Nikkeijin Kai [Japanese Ancestral Society], Kenjin Kai [Native Prefectural Society]. We met frequently, such as at Fujin Kai [Women's Society] meetings. We were taught that we were responsible for and to look out for each other. In many ways it was simply the application of the "golden rule."

We were a close family unit starting with my parents. They had great consideration and respect for each other. This was repeated in the attitudes of the children to our parents and by the parents toward each child. I remember how my first *Nisei* friends always treated their parents with such wonderful kindness and respect.

As far back as 1933, a study in Seattle found the delinquency rate in the Japanese-American community, which was located in a very deteriorated area where there was generally a high delinquency rate, to be lower than in the best residential areas of the city.[1]

That the same qualities and traits—duty, obligation, honor, respect for elders, etc.—were found in members of both the Chinese and the Japanese communities in Oregon might suggest that these cultural patterns may actually have originated with the Confucian teachings of ancient China brought to Japan possibly by early Buddhist monks. (The influence of Confucianism in Japan is discussed briefly later in this chapter.)

When I served on the Oregon Court of Appeals (1971–83), the court considered a great number of criminal appeals. In checking back, I discovered that out of more than 2,000 criminal cases, only three involved offenses committed by persons with Japanese surnames. All were third-generation Japanese-American youths accused of using or dealing in marijuana.

The traditional respect for constituted authority and deference to the father, the emperor, laws, courts, police, school, teachers, and the like is thoroughly instilled in every Japanese child practically from the cradle. Clearly, the net effect of all this in-home family training is to equip these children with an unusually strong sense of self-discipline. Another aspect of this character trait is the social stigma that often attaches to a person who has been convicted of a crime.

The Haji Factor

The *haji* factor was at work during a Kawagoe juvenile court hearing we attended by permission of both the family court judge and the juvenile offender and his parents. The father became so embarrassed and so emotional in recounting the incident for which his son was being tried, that his voice broke, tears welled up in his eyes, and he was unable to continue for some moments.

Tsuneo Matsumura, a prominent Kawagoe businessman, described one aspect of *haji*:

> Not only is the unfortunate ex-offender stigmatized, so is his entire family. Even a daughter may be unable to find a husband to marry her. No prospective husband wants his family name sullied by marriage to an ex-offender's family.

Such facts are normally discovered during the searching premarital examination by the go-between (*baishakunin* or *nakōdo*), whose background investigation is a vital part of the Japanese arranged marriage system (*miai kekkon*). In some respects, marriage in Japan is as much a union of two families, as it is of two individuals. Doubtless this accounts for the low divorce rate (currently 12 percent), compared with the United States (currently more than 50 percent), which may in itself be a factor in Japan's low crime rate.

The Role of Apology

If the reader is to gain a basic understanding of the major factors behind Japan's phenomenally low crime rates, we must describe the prominent and long-established role that "apology" plays in Japanese culture and in the crime prevention process.

In Japan, there is a widely acknowledged ethical obligation on the part of the citizen who has acted unlawfully to acknowledge his or her guilt. This concept is, of course, foreign to the Anglo-American criminal justice process, with its presumption of innocence of the accused and the duty of the prosecution to prove guilt beyond a reasonable doubt. The Japanese responsibility of the citizen to acknowledge guilt stems in all probability from the teachings of Confucius concerning honesty, uprightness, and duty. It may also reflect a fundamental teaching of Buddhism—the necessity of first achieving mental and moral purification in order to attain nirvana, the state of spiritual liberation.

This behavioral norm manifests itself in a number of ways. For example, the large percentage of guilty pleas entered by the accused in criminal cases in Japan—usually over 90 percent—may reflect this norm. Second, prosecutors and even the courts often require a formal apology as part of the imposition of a lighter sentence before granting probation, or in suspending the execution of sentence in a criminal case. In a law violation setting, an apology is more than an admission of guilt—it is a solemn pledge by the apologist not to offend again.

In some minor violations, the Japanese police frequently allow guilty offenders to go free without paying a fine, if they show the requisite degree of genuine regret and contrition for their violation and have no criminal record. They are, however, required to write an appropriate apology to the victim. If there is no victim, as in illegal parking for instance, then the apology is made to the local chief of police, showing that the individual is truly remorseful for his or her behavior. The police recognize the difficulty of maintaining parameters but feel that such discretionary tactics toward essentially upright citizens contribute to building good public relations. This exercise by police is called *ninjo*, or "human feelings."

Americans, particularly law enforcement professionals, might counter this Japanese approach by asserting that police in the United States sometimes exercise a similar discretion. However, in the United States, a formal apology—particularly a written apology—is seldom, if ever, required by the police. Moreover, in America the apology is not deeply embedded in the cultural patterns of a people, as it is in Japan, where the tradition reaches back centuries.

There are many examples of public apologies by the presidents of major Japanese companies for corporate malfeasance. They may even resign their position to atone for their dereliction of duty when, in fact, they may not have had anything directly to do with the misconduct. Similarly, though less frequently, a high-ranking public official may issue an apology for his official malfeasance, or a member of a social or business organization may issue an apology to the group for personal acts that may have reflected adversely on the group.

We may offer a final example: in 1972, when several young Japanese terrorists calling themselves the "Red Army" perpetrated an exceedingly brutal massacre of innocent passengers at the Lod Airport in Israel, the Japanese government issued a formal letter of apology to Israel and to the families of the victims. The apology was also released to the press and published worldwide. To the Japanese people, this letter was profound—it represented the entire nation doing penance for the injuries and deaths caused by these young Japanese extremists.

It is not uncommon for certain crimes and interpersonal civil wrongs to be settled between the concerned parties without intervention by the police, the prosecutor's office, or the courts. The family of the offender is anxious to make amends, and often pays considerable damages to make matters right with the victim. This is invariably accompanied by a formal apology to the victim and his or her family. In this manner, all parties are satisfied and a potential blot on the offender's family escutcheon is avoided.

It should be noted that some of the younger Japanese we interviewed felt that cultural factors were no longer all-powerful deterrents to crime. They cited as reasons the rapid and massive urbanization of Japan's population; the emergence of large-scale housing complexes (danchi) with apartment-type living and its attendant anonymity (tokumeisei) effect; the effect of both parents working outside the home; lack of parental supervision; and the absence of grandparents living with the family unit as in former times. Others disagreed, feeling that although the five family neighborhood associations of old Japan (tonari gumi, go-nin gumi) had all but disappeared, the ancient customs were continuing. They asserted that people still had mutual concern for each other, and concern for maintaining the family honor and good reputation. Even those who played down the importance of the haji factor acknowledged that it exists today in a new form, as peer pressure not to commit any act likely to bring dishonor upon one's employer and the company for whom one works.

In the United States, individualism has a stronger influence on cultural norms, with emphasis on standing alone free of both formal and informal group ties. This lessens the stabilizing influence of networks of individuals, as experienced in Japan. From this difference it has long been persuasively argued by Sutherland and Cressey,[2] Taft,[3] and others, that when social controls are reduced, there is a greater likelihood of criminal behavior.

Perhaps the diversity of opinion is but another indicator of changes occurring in Japanese society due to industrialization and increasing urbanization. There are many factors and strengths behind Japan's low crime rate, but the unanswered question is whether the remarkable value system will continue to survive the impact of these continuing changes into the next century.

Of particular interest in this same connection is an editorial in the

Tokyo Mainichi Daily News for July 29, 1984.[4] The editorial writer was commenting on the fact that emergency calls (similar to our 911 calls) for police service had more than doubled in the last decade. Speculating on some of the reasons behind this increase the paper declared:

> The phenomenon [increased emergency calls] both in urban and rural districts resulted from the alienation of human relations and the collapse of time-honored regional social orders. In other words, the solving of various problems automatically, the mutual-help spirit and the ability to prevent crime, which were inherently rooted in households and regional society have decreased or have been lost.
>
> According to a survey of 1,606 persons conducted last December by the Tokyo Metropolitan Police and the Osaka Prefectural Police, the sense of alienation had deepened as 69.1 percent said that they just ignore or chat briefly with their neighbors, indicating that their relations are not close. Only 13.7 percent said they seek advice from their neighbors.

Other Reasons behind Japan's Low Crime Rate

Homogeneity

The low crime rate in Japan may be due in part to the extreme homogeneity of its population of 121 million people. Chinese residents number less than one-tenth of one percent of the population, and only about 840,000 are Korean-Japanese, most descendants of workers, most of whom were brought to Japan involuntarily after 1910 after Japan annexed Korea. According to the latest information, only 140,000 of these Korean-Japanese have acquired voting rights by gaining Japanese citizenship.[5] Despite an occasional report of complaints of racial discrimination and alienation by members of this minority group, particularly with reference to the fingerprinting requirement for aliens, this requirement does not appear to have resulted in triggering a crime problem.

Japan's is a closely knit society with a strong sense of community, although unfortunately this sense of community seems to be undergoing considerable erosion—a process occurring to an even greater extent in all other industrialized countries, including the United States. In Japan, it is still routine to help one's neighbor. This tradition probably goes back to the country's agrarian roots. As a result, there is an unusually high level of citizen involvement (*shimin sanka*) in crime prevention activities. In fact, the entire criminal justice system is based largely on volunteers.

Hierarchy

Contributing to Japan's special social cohesiveness is the deeply rooted hierarchical system that governs all interpersonal relations (*sempai kōhei seido*). Even today, the relative rank and status of the individual is an important part of society. For example, the exchange of business cards (*meishi*) between two business people when first introduced is partly for the purpose of establishing their rank and status relative to each other. As Professor Takie Sugiyama Lebra (Associate Professor of Anthropology, University of Hawaii) has observed, "The slightest difference in age, graduation time, time of entry into a company, and so on makes one person higher than another."[6]

The element of hierarchy or seniority in action is often observed by foreigners in the course of their dealings with Japanese. Juniors in the government and in business invariably defer to senior officials and employees. Hierarchy is even observed among students, with underclass students deferring to those in upper classes, both on campus and off. Lower-graders are expected to remove their caps, bow, and say, Good morning or Good afternoon when they meet upper-class members.

Work Ethic

Most Japanese possess an unusually strong work ethic and apply themselves with dedication and diligence to any job they are doing. Coupled with a very low unemployment rate, this work ethic creates a society that is 98 percent gainfully employed. A definite correlation between unemployment and criminal behavior has been shown in numerous studies both in the United States and abroad, but recent public opinion surveys have shown that wage earners' attitudes are changing. The so-called new breed (*shinjinrui*) are turning away from the philosophy of "all work and no play" to less work and more enjoyment of life's pleasures.

A recent comparative study by Priscilla Blinco of Stanford University proposes a novel theory regarding the source of the Japanese work ethic.[7] Studying the task persistence of first-graders in Japan and the United States, Blinco found that Japanese children demonstrated a higher task persistence under noncompetitive conditions and received more family and teacher reinforcement than their peers in the United States. Further, she identified a significant correlation between home and family attitudes and student task persistence. Japanese mothers played a major role in alerting children to the importance of persistence in life. In fact, said Blinco, "The importance of persistence and hard work is inculcated from infancy."

Respect for Law

Japanese people habitually and historically obey laws, rules, and customs and cooperate with the police, not because they fear authority, but because they perceive of this as a social obligation. Unlike the United States, where jury trial in criminal cases is constitutionally guaranteed, in Japan all criminal trials are by a judge. Not widely known is the fact that Japan did institute jury trials for a time beginning in 1928. Under the law that established these trials, the court was not bound by the jury's verdict. According to some anecdotal reports, criminal defendants and defense attorneys objected strenuously to the jury trial provision because—again unlike in the United States—Japanese juries were more severe and punitive in their verdicts than the judges! In any event, this "noble experiment" was abandoned in 1943.

It is interesting to note that the police-community relationship was not always as it is today. Until after World War II, the police held invasive powers, and frequently used them. As a result, they were often feared by the citizenry. There are stories of when the military (*Gumbatsu*) virtually ruled Japan, and of "thought police" arresting citizens for having "dangerous thoughts."[8] A past and all but forgotten chapter, today the police receive a measure of public confidence, respect, and cooperation that is seldom exceeded anywhere in the civilized world. (See Chapter 5 for a discussion of Japanese police public relations.)

We should also note that, as Japan's population increased after the war, the government had the foresight to proportionately increase the number of police officers. On the other hand, according to Emil Brandaw, superintendent of the Oregon State Police, in the state of

Oregon there were 300 *fewer* deputy sheriffs and state police officers in 1987 than in 1980, despite substantial increases in population. In Salem, according to Chief of Police Brian Riley, there are eighteen fewer police officers on duty today than there were five years ago.

In Japan, more than 50,000 voluntary probation officers and more than 200,000 women's associations are engaged in crime prevention activities. To determine the underlying reasons for this exceptionally high level of public cooperation and support, an experimental study was undertaken by the Japanese government in 1980 in its four largest cities. The police tested three different approaches:

- Mass media.
- Police informational bulletins and fliers.
- Small meetings.

The results of public opinion surveys were revealing:

- The most successful means of bringing about public cooperation was through small meetings. This method apparently produced the largest number of crime prevention volunteers.
- The efforts of various agencies within the criminal justice system in physically meeting with citizens and talking with them brought about positive results.

As we have already indicated, the Japan criminal justice system is in many ways markedly different from the American system. For example, after a suspect is apprehended by the police, no money or property bail is available or permitted. The person arrested is either released without bail or is held. More surprising, if the penalty for the crime includes a fine up to approximately $1,000, the Japanese summary criminal procedure (*Ryakushiki Tetsuzuki*) provides that upon a prosecutor's petition and with the defendant's consent, a public hearing and appearance by the defendant may be waived. The summary court judge then makes a determination of guilt based upon the police report and imposes a fine without anyone—defendant, prosecutor, complainant, or witnesses—ever appearing in court. A similar procedure is authorized in several European countries, notably Germany and Sweden. If the accused changes his mind, he or she may apply for a formal trial within fourteen days. As a practical matter, this seldom occurs.[9]

Not to be overlooked is the effect of integration of the Japanese bench and bar, by virtue of the national bar examination and provisions requiring that all future lawyers, judges, and prosecutors go through the National Legal Training institute (*Shihō Kenkyūsho*),[10] which produces a criminal justice system thoroughly schooled in the role of each segment of it.

Mention should also be made of the rate of conviction of criminal defendants. In 1980, for example, the national conviction rate was 99.9 percent. It is also worth noting that the public prosecutor has broad discretion, regardless of the nature of the crime, to suspend prosecution and frequently exercises it. Under this provision, an average of about 30 percent of those cases referred to prosecutors are not prosecuted. Instead, the public prosecutor often calls in not only the offender but also family members, neighbors, and even workplace superiors. All are given admonitions so that they will understand their responsibility for supervising the offender in order for prosecution to be suspended.

The Education System

Japan's children attend school an average of forty days more a year than do Americans. In addition to a full schedule of the standard academic curriculum (reading, writing, arithmetic, etc.), they receive training in "character education" (*Dōtoku Kyōiku*) from first grade through middle and high school. This "character education" is not only a separate course of study but a component of other subjects as well, and one of its critical aims is to inculcate a strong sense of self-discipline in the youth of Japan, which, we have suggested, is a basic element in any crime prevention program.

Schoolchildren spend the last twenty minutes of lunch hour sweeping and cleaning classrooms and hallways. A similar practice, yielding salutary lessons in cooperation, personal responsibility, and the importance of cleanliness, has long been followed in Chinese schools. This custom also provides an antidote to school vandalism and thoughtless disfiguring of public property.

Most elementary school children go to calligraphy school, abacus school, piano school, English school, or sports clubs nearly every afternoon, after the regular school day. With alot of homework and a much shorter summer vacation, Japanese schoolchildren have little idle time in which to become involved in antisocial behavior.

Confucian Ethic

Another infusion from China is the Confucian ethic. Historically, it has been fostered mainly by Japan's Buddhist clergy. The teachings of Confucianism place a strong emphasis on the cardinal virtues of filial piety, kindness, righteousness, propriety, intelligence and faithfulness, and have historically formed the basis of much of Chinese and Japanese ethics, education, statecraft, and religion. One wonders how many of today's Japanese realize how profound and far-reaching the Confucian influence has been in shaping the Japanese character.

Drug Traffic Control

Traffic in illegal drugs is on the increase in Japan. Though not yet as serious a problem as it is in the United States, it is nevertheless a major problem and is being met head-on with a combination of tough enforcement policies and severe penalties.

Not to be overlooked is a high standard of living and an unusually broad and even distribution of income. The great majority have shared in the country's remarkable economic boom. As for Kawagoe, its citizens appear to be enjoying as high a living standard as the majority of the residents of Salem.

Geographic Insularity

The fact that Japan is an "island nation" should not be overlooked; this insularity has contributed not only to the racial and cultural homogeneity of Japan's population, but it has made policing borders a much easier task than that faced by nations such as the United States whose land and sea borders are far-flung. This truth has been brought home increasingly with dramatic effect as law enforcement officials in the United States struggle desperately to stem the flow of illegal drugs over America's coastal and southern borders.

America—The Comparison Is Obvious

Without indulging in detailed comparisons between Japanese and American life and culture, it is obvious to anyone that the United States is definitely not a homogeneous society. In fact, it is precisely the opposite.

With the exception of native Americans (misnamed "Indians" by

Christopher Columbus), all Americans are immigrants or descendants of immigrants who came to the United States initially from Europe, but ultimately from all over the globe. It is essentially a pluralistic immigrant society, most of whose citizens are but two or three generations removed from some other country.

More important, American society is individualistic rather than group oriented. The average citizen thinks that crime prevention is the job of the police, not the citizen. "That's what we pay them for" is a typical American attitude. Strangely enough, this same attitude is also prevalent among public officials, which may account for the lack of interest in crime prevention and a preventive approach to crime control frequently encountered. An important breakthrough took place, however, in Oregon in July 1989, when for the first time in the state's history the legislature created a Crime Prevention Resource Center to "develop, plan, and carry out a comprehensive crime prevention program implemented by local crime prevention councils." The law provides, among other things, that the Crime Prevention Resource Center act as a clearinghouse for crime prevention efforts and provide a means to acquire resource materials, technical assistance, and training for local programs.[11]

Most Americans do not take kindly to being "called on the carpet" by a traffic police officer. The average American resents receiving a ticket for speeding or overparking, sometimes remonstrating, occasionally with indignation or even truculence. Historically, a Japanese simply would never do such a thing, although the younger generation appears to be changing. When one Kawagoe youth was told by an officer to stop blocking traffic at their popular huge autumn street festival (Kawagoe Matsuri), he replied, "Shut up!" This is definitely not traditional behavior!

Americans, on the other hand, have traditionally stressed and valued self-expression. Children are taught to stand up for their rights. Individual freedom is the watchword of society. An example of this individualistic streak is illustrated by a readiness to resort to litigation. Not only does it seem to many that Americans delight in suing one another, they frequently sue governmental agencies, challenging some rule, regulation, ordinance, or statute that they feel infringes upon their constitutional rights.

This tendency toward litigiousness may explain the large number of attorneys in the United States: there are more practicing lawyers in some major American cities—New York, Chicago, Los Angeles, San Francisco, or Philadelphia, for example—than in all of Japan (less than 13,000 at last report)!

Little social stigma attaches to bringing a lawsuit against someone else in the United States, whereas in Japan, the average citizen shrinks from contact with courts and lawyers, preferring to settle controversies informally without recourse to law. The Japanese are baffled by the frequency with which Americans go into court whenever controversies arise in business transactions, property disputes, adverse decisions by public agencies, and even arguments with neighbors.

The Japanese approach is to hold everyone involved in a conflict responsible for it. The usual practice in such cases is to work out a satisfactory compromise among the parties, including a mutual apology. The entire mediation process is known as *jidan*. Sometimes the negotiations are handled through a lay intermediary, not a lawyer. Resort to the courts in such cases is extremely rare.

America's extreme individualistic attitudes extend to the claim by some of the right to possess firearms freely, without the necessity of registration or a permit. Some sociologists attribute this to the Revolutionary War, when the American colonists took up arms against England, and to the heritage of the frontier, where law enforcement officials were seldom seen or even available, where the pioneers had to look out for themselves and their loved ones in protecting life and property.

The American philosophy of inalienable rights, fundamental freedoms, individualism, and the right to privacy may well go back in American history to the colonial period, where it became manifest in the Boston Tea Party, the American rebellion against English rule, the Declaration of Independence, and the Revolutionary War, in which the colonies won their independence from England. If that is in fact how and where the American philosophy of freedom and individualism began, then certainly it was nurtured and became a truly national philosophy as rugged settlers struggled westward and carved homesteads and farms out of a vast wilderness inhabited by scattered native American nations and wild game. Many illustrations of the primacy of individualism, of privacy and rights of the individual, are to be found in constitutional restrictions on the powers of federal and state governments:

• The "Bill of Rights" found in both the U.S. Constitution and in virtually every state constitution, including Oregon's.

• State constitutional prohibitions against the enactment of certain local and special laws by the legislature.

• The preservation of states' rights found in Amendment IX to the U.S. Constitution.

• The preservation of municipal home rule contained in the Home Rule Amendment (XI) of the Oregon Constitution.

• The retention of a large measure of local control of the public schools through locally elected school boards.

The same contrasting cultural patterns are apparent when we compare the criminal prosecution patterns of the two nations. In 95 percent of the cases in Japan, the defendant confesses and pleads guilty. In 80 percent of American prosecutions, cases are disposed of by a so-called "plea bargain," where the defendant agrees to plead guilty to a lesser charge. In Japan, on the other hand, plea bargaining is expressly prohibited by Article 319(3) of the Japanese Penal Code.[12]

Notes

1. N.S. Haynes, "Delinquency Areas in the Puget Sound Area," *American Journal of Sociology* 39 (November 1933): 314–28.

2. Edwin H. Sutherland and Donald R. Cressey, *Criminology*, 8th ed. (New York: J.B. Lippincott, 1970), chap. 5.

3. Donald Taft, *Criminology* (New York: Macmillan, 1956) chap. 2.

4. "Role of Citizens Police," *Mainichi Daily News* (Tokyo), July 29, 1984, p. B2.

5. *Japan Echo* 16, 2 (Summer 1989): 71.

6. Takie Sugiyama Lebra, *Japanese Patterns of Behavior* (Honolulu, HI: University of Hawaii Press, 1972), p. 72.

7. "Task Persistence of Young Children in Japan and the United States." Paper presented at the Western Conference of the Association for Asian Studies, University of Washington, Seattle, WA, October 22, 1988.

8. Richard H. Mitchell, *Thought Control in Prewar Japan* (Ithaca, NY: Cornell University Press, 1976).

9. Nobuyoshi Araki, "The Flow of Criminal Cases in the Japanese Criminal Justice System," *Crime and Delinquency* 4 (October 1985): 601. For further readings on factors behind Japan's low crime rate see generally *Crime Prevention in the United States and Japan*, V. Kusuda-Smick, ed. (Dobbs Ferry, NY: Transnational Juris Publications, 1990); Akio Kasai, "Some Causes of the Decrease of Crime in Japan," United Nations Asia Far East Institute for the Prevention of Crime (UN-AFEI), Report for 1972, Resource Material Series No. 6, Fuchu, Tokyo, Japan.

10. See R.Y. Thornton, "Training Lawyers and Judges in New Japan," *Judicature* 58, 3 (October 1974): 128–33.

11. Oregon Laws 1989, chap. 1067.

12. *Encyclopedia of Japan* (Tokyo: Kodansha International, 1983).

5

The Police

The Role of the Police in Salem

Operating under the supervision and direction of the mayor, the city council, and the city manager, Salem's police department is responsible for law enforcement within the city boundaries. Territory outside the city boundaries is handled jointly by the Marion County Sheriff and the Oregon State Police. Salem police maintain a close but unofficial liaison with both the sheriff and the state police, but there is no chain-of-command relationship. Salem police are unionized and by state law have the right of collective bargaining as to wages, hours, and working conditions.

Crime Prevention Unit

Salem's crime prevention unit is part of the community services section, under the prevention and investigation division. Presently it consists of two uniformed officers, a civilian administrator, and five citizen volunteers. The primary focus of the crime prevention unit is the neighborhood crime watch program. Its secondary focus is the city watch program, which is comprised of radio-equipped garbage trucks operated by a private concern franchised to collect garbage within the city. The unit makes frequent detailed informational presentations to the public and distributes pamphlets to neighborhood groups, usually at meetings, on crime prevention topics including home security, burglary prevention, and rape and molestation prevention. It also erects crime prevention displays in shopping centers and at such public functions as the annual state fair.

Home security lectures regularly stress actions citizens can take, including:

• Engrave identifying numbers on valuable household items with an electric engraving tool, which may be borrowed from the crime prevention unit.
  • Use deadbolt locks and reinforced strike plates on all doors.
  • Place a wooden dowel or a pinning device on all glass patio doors.
  • Use timers for house lights and a radio when absent from the home.
  • Join the neighborhood crime watch program.

Another innovative tool is the "bookmark" project, which consists of a simple bookmark-size piece of heavy paper with a variety of different crime prevention tips printed on it. Some are targeted for children, while some are aimed at adults and even senior citizens. An example is the following list of "Play It Safe Rules":

1. Lock up, coming and going from home.
2. Don't open your door to strangers.
3. Don't go anywhere with strangers.
4. Walk with a friend to and from school.
5. If a stranger bothers you, go into the nearest business and ask someone to call the police.
6. If you feel "funny" about someone touching you, say NO! and tell someone you trust.

Police hand out these bookmarks at bicycle rallies, youth track meets, Boy Scout jamborees, in shopping malls, at the state fair, and at other large gatherings. The unit has published a special pamphlet with crime prevention tips specifically for senior citizens. It also conducts tours of the police station for various groups, reviews applications for relief from penalties levied for false alarms by private burglary alarms, and has researched measures to counter the cruising problem, explained in Chapter 6.

Neighborhood Crime Watch

By far the greatest amount of time spent on crime prevention by police officers is devoted to the neighborhood crime watch program. The two officers assigned to this program estimate that half of their time goes into organizing, instructing, and servicing these neighborhood programs, with 25 percent of their time spent on public presentations and 15 percent on displays. Maintenance of crime watches is also the responsibility of coordinators in each neighborhood.

Among the ten citizen volunteers in the crime prevention unit, two retirees keep track of burglary statistics and maintain the roster of the neighborhood watch participants. Three retirees work on crime watch liaison and recruit crime watch participants and other volunteers.

When a neighborhood crime problem requires special attention—for example, the vice activity on Portland Road—uniformed crime prevention officers call in person on the businesses on the street, advising them on special crime prevention measures to enhance their security and the safety of their employees.

Cadets, Reserves, and Volunteers

Some other innovative programs undertaken by the Salem police department include the police cadets, police reserves, and police volunteers.

- Cadets are youths between the ages of fifteen and twenty-one who are interested in police work. They are uniformed but unarmed, and assist the regular police in such duties as directing traffic at public events. They also perform contract work (e.g., traffic control at fairs, sports events) for private organizations; the hourly fees charged go into a special fund used for operations and training expenses.
- Reserves are sworn uniformed police officers who have received 304 hours of accredited police training at Chemeketa Community College. They are unpaid, but the city provides uniforms and equipment. On August 10, 1988, the Oregon Court of Appeals ruled that the city was required to bargain collectively with the Salem police employees union, which had opposed the program, before it could be implemented.
- Police volunteers are some forty private citizens who donate their services on a part-time basis to perform a variety of needed clerical tasks in and around police headquarters. Most work as bookkeepers and recordkeepers, including three who regularly assist in keeping burglary records in the crime prevention unit.

Other Programs

Among other Salem police programs, *City Watch,* the crime watch liaison with the radio-equipped garbage truck drivers who cover the entire city, has been a successful program. Drivers involved in City Watch are fully schooled in how to report suspicious activity in the neighborhoods they serve. (We might mention here that the Japanese police have a similar cooperative arrangement with taxi drivers who inform the police about any law violations that they may know about.)

Two state-of-the-art high-tech systems recently acquired by the Salem police department deserve special mention. The first is *Land Trac,* a computer program that logs all criminal incidents in a computer bank that can be called up and projected on a large electronic screen. Thus, a detailed, citywide crime picture can be displayed by location, time, and criminal demographics of a neighborhood. An unusual feature is the enlargement capability, which can pinpoint a single home, showing crime specifics at that site. Thus, police can easily determine not only where crimes are being committed in Salem, but the nature of the crime and the time of day that the crime is committed. Neighborhood crime watch groups as well as the Salem police-neighborhood liaison committee are given monthly reports of crimes in each area to alert them to the current situation in their neighborhoods. The base computerized map for the project was created under the GLAD computer mapping system. It is now being expanded to include an optical scanner that can "read" the officer's crime report and automatically transcribe its contents into the computer bank. The scanner reads 1,500 reports (both sides at once) per hour.

The second system is *vehicle tracking,* which uses the LORAN principle and was developed by a Salem electronics firm. Vehicle tracking can follow the movements of all police patrol vehicles, enabling headquarters instantly to locate any police cruiser on patrol anywhere in the city. It also operates as a secondary communications system for the on-patrol officer, allowing location and status reporting without use of the police radio network, which can be extremely important in certain kinds of emergencies, or when the police radio network is overloaded or out of commission.

One of the most troublesome problems facing the limited resources of police departments everywhere in the United States is how to cope with the huge numbers of telephone calls demanding police service. In the course of a detailed study of the problem, the Salem police department discovered that more than 85 percent of the calls they received resulted in an officer being sent to the scene. As a result of the study, the Salem police adopted an innovative procedure that was already being used successfully in several eastern U.S. cities. The system, Differential Police Response (DPR), whose basic purpose is to permit overloaded police departments to respond to calls for police service on a priority basis according to the urgency of the request, is capable of enabling a police department to manage incoming calls for police service effectively; to reduce patrol force workload; to improve collection of incoming information for the proper handling of calls; and to preserve as much as 35 percent of patrol officers' time for proactive policing.

In Salem, as in most U.S. cities, most patrolling is done by motor vehicle, although foot patrolling has also been used for short periods in special situations. It has been estimated that in the United States, 87 percent of patrol officers' time is spent responding to citizens' requests for help or reports of victimization; this is characterized as reactive patrolling. Although no precise figure has been calculated in Salem, it is estimated that the national figure probably held true there until 1987. When Salem became the first city in Oregon to implement DPR, the Salem police department found that the system allowed for increased proactive, or preventive, police patrolling.

Bicycle Patrols

In recent years, the police departments in Seattle, Washington, and Portland, Oregon, have established special police bicycle patrols in high-crime areas. Both departments report that results have been excellent in terms of discouraging street crimes, as well as in public approval and appreciation of police anticrime efforts.

Not to be outdone by Seattle and Portland, in November 1989 the Salem police added two bicycle patrols to their existing street crimes unit. The bike-mounted officers patrol the downtown area at irregular intervals, concentrating on such crimes as drug dealing, panhandling, purse snatching, drinking in public, as well as skateboarding or bicycling on sidewalks. The bike officers carry radios on their belts, and the bicycles are equipped with saddlebags for citation books, arrest reports, receipts for any articles impounded, gloves, and other articles needed on patrol.

The bike patrols have won high praise from Salem's downtown merchants for their effectiveness. Says Morris Saffron, co-owner of Saffron Supply Company, "They move in quickly and quietly and much more efficiently than a patrol car can." Saffron says the bike patrols have helped clear out the drug dealers who congregated behind the Union Gospel Mission and under the bridges that cross the Willamette river, and adds, "I believe the bike patrols are here to stay."

Apparently, no other cities in Oregon have regular bike patrols. In the neighboring state of Washington, in addition to Seattle, Spokane started a bike patrol in the summer of 1989. "We wanted to establish a little closer contact with the people," says Spokane Patrol Captain John Sullivan. "We felt like we were losing some of the personal contacts we feel are important to keep officers close to the community."

The city of Boise, Idaho, which (like Portland, Oregon) has a horse patrol, plans to experiment with bicycles in summer, 1990. Officers in that city will focus on the parks.

Salem Special Street Crimes Unit

In October 1987, a new street crimes unit was created in Salem to target street crimes in the downtown areas. Included as target crimes are narcotics trafficking and other drug-related offenses, traffic crimes, and to a lesser extent prostitution. Comprised of six officers, the unit has succeeded beyond all expectations, according to Chief of Police Riley. Between October 1, 1987 and March 31, 1988, the unit reported a total of 697 arrests, 180 for drug-related offenses, 11 for prostitution, and 9 escaped prisoners or parole violators. Most arrests were made in three problem neighborhoods that had been the focus of alot of citizen complaints. The unit also issued 849 traffic citations and warnings for offenses ranging from driving without a license to reckless driving. The unit has now accounted for a total of nearly 4,000 arrests since it was created, according to its current commander Sergeant Jerry Moore in a presentation to the monthly meeting of the South Salem Neighborhood Association, November 29, 1990. "Having visible police protection—that's the key to crime reduction in the downtown [area]," according to Casey Campbell, owner of Casey's Hot Dogs located in the core area of the city near the problem areas where several drug arrests were made.

The Role of the Police in Kawagoe

As might be expected, there are a number of differences between the police systems of Salem and Kawagoe, perhaps the most significant of which is that city police departments in Japan are part of a national police system, although they are administered from the prefectural level.[1]

Crime prevention officers in Japan perform a wide variety of activities, ranging from showing films on residential security and molestation prevention to installing pick-proof locks sold at cost by neighborhood crime prevention associations.

The Kōban System

The *kōban system*, officially called *hashutsusho,* is used by Kawagoe police, as it is by all police departments in Japan. Believed to have originated in Germany more than a century ago, and borrowed along with the German criminal code and police and military systems by Japan's leaders shortly after the Meiji restoration in 1867, the kōban system is best described as a network of police substations, each of which serves as an official police contact point for any citizen to report a crime or to seek police assistance and advice with minor problems ranging from directions to a friend's house to complaints about a neighbor's barking dog or noisy motorcycle.

Operating on a three-shift system, duty assignments of police officers are rotated from "full-day" (8:30 A.M. to 8:30 A.M. the next day), to "off-duty" the second day, to "day duty" (8:30 A.M. to 5:15 P.M.) the third day. Within the Kawagoe city limits are seventeen kōban, seven of which are classed as *chuzaisho*, which are mostly located in rural or semirural areas and are usually occupied by one police family, the spouse taking calls when the officer is on patrol or investigating crimes.

Police officers assigned to the kōban perform a variety of services, such as visiting all homes and businesses in their districts at least once a year, and keeping a record of everyone who lives or works there. This practice provides a liaison and two-way communication with residents, including a channel for disseminating crime prevention advice and listening to grievances. In addition, officers make it a practice to visit the homes of the aged, physically handicapped, and persons living alone, giving advice regarding crime prevention and how to contact the police in emergencies.

In Japan, the police and even the courts frequently exercise moral as well as legal authority. For example, the police sometimes enforce such societal norms as proper behavior of school-age children, parental responsibilities, manners in public, respect for parents and the elderly, and even the obligations of friendship—all matters that would be studiously avoided by most American police agencies.

Only 1.5 percent of Japan's police officers are women, and these were not recruited until 1946. Women police are generally assigned to such tasks as traffic regulation, juvenile protection, plain-clothes surveillance of pickpockets and shoplifters, and internal administration. Female police officers are not assigned to general patrol duties.[2]

Most kōban publish a newsletter known as the *Kōban Shimbun* that carries a variety of news items such as neighborhood traffic accidents, burglary reports, lost and found articles, crime prevention tips, etc. And, just as some American police departments conduct athletic programs for inner-city youth as a crime prevention activity, many police stations have a *dōjō*, or small gym, at or near their installation. The dōjō is not only for the police to maintain their own physical fitness, it is also used to teach self-defense (*jūdō*), Japanese fencing (*kendō*), and even calligraphy (*shōdō*) to neighborhood residents, mainly young people. Officers also often participate in a variety of community meetings as a means of fostering favorable police-community relations.

The patrol activities of kōban officers nationally result in about 65 percent of all arrests for penal code offenses. (Salem police, in contrast, keep no statistics on this specific point, but estimate their arrests by patrolling officers at just 5 to 10 percent.)

Perhaps the most important feature of the Kawagoe system is the fact that police officers assigned to duties in a kōban know their neighborhoods. They are required to survey all dwellings and their occupants at least once a year, so they are generally aware of who belongs in their neighborhood and who does not.

My wife and I can personally verify their expertise. The day after we moved into an apartment in a residential area in South Kawagoe to research this project, I went to the neighborhood kōban to introduce myself and to ask about the location of a bank. To my great surprise, the policeman in charge already knew that we were there. A similar experience was reported by a former Salem-area couple who speak Japanese and are long-time residents of Tokyo. In 1984, when they moved to a different section of that city of 8 million people, a knock came at their front door in only a matter of days. It was a Tokyo police officer, an *"omawarisan"* (translated literally as "Mr. Walk Around") who introduced himself saying, "I am from your nearby kōban. I stopped to become acquainted and to let you know that if you should have any problem, your neighborhood kōban will be happy to be of assistance." One last example: Japanese patrolmen are noted for keeping a sharp eye out for cars with body or fender damage. If they observe such damage, they routinely stop the vehicle and inquire how, when, and where the damage was sustained. These anecdotes illustrate the lengths to which the Japanese police go to foster good public relations, and may account for the fact that the Japanese police seem to enjoy a higher degree of public cooperation and support than their American counterparts. One indication of the importance the average citizen attaches to his neighborhood kōban is found in a public opinion poll conducted for the Prime Minister's office in 1972 that found that 56 percent of the citizens who requested police help during the previous year did so by going to the kōban rather than by calling the "110" telephone number or other means.

Police Visibility

In Japan, police officers are highly visible in urban areas, both at the kōban and patrolling the neighborhood on foot (*gaikin keisatsu*), by bicycle, or by motor vehicle. There appears to be a higher sense of police presence and visibility in Japan than in the average U.S. city.

To capture the essence of all Japanese policing in one simple sentence: *Police presence at all times, places, and incidents is the key to crime prevention.*

In Kawagoe, the crime prevention police have an even longer list of extracurricular assignments than their Salem counterparts. On the list is investigation of violations of what are classed as special criminal laws (narcotics, illegal possession of guns, pornography, prostitution, and hunting violations), as well as licensing of firearms, licensing and regulation of business affecting public morals (*fūzoku eigyō*), such as pachinko halls (vertical pinball machines), mah-jongg parlors, bars, nightclubs, turkish baths (sometimes used for clandestine prostitution), porno theaters, strip shows, and motels. (Although prostitution has been outlawed since 1958, so-called "love motels" are routinely still used as assignation sites.)[3] The juvenile unit is part of the crime prevention section, which is also responsible for enforcement of antipollution laws—an increasingly heavy responsibility, considering Japan's recent widespread industrialization and the consequent damage to the environment.

Japanese police also enforce the election laws, which are both complex and strict. There are occasions, however, when the Japanese police choose to be inconspicuous. I recall a summer public celebration to welcome home the souls of departed relatives (*obon*) in Kanazawa, when police were present but remained in the shadows across the street from the festivities. In contrast, several members of the uniformed citizen volunteer crime prevention groups (*bōhan-in*) stationed themselves at the entrance of the schoolgrounds where the festivities were taking place. When I asked the reason for their presence, I was informed that they were there to see that no gangsters (*yakuza*) came on the premises.

Public Relations

Japanese police are unhesitating in stating matter-of-factly that they could not begin to provide the present high level of public safety throughout the nation of some 121 million without the whole-hearted support of the vast majority of Japanese citizens. Their professionalism and readiness to serve the community before self, their tact and diplomacy in dealing with the public, and their willingness to accept advice and even criticism are all factors that make the police generally popular and respected. It would not be an exaggeration to say that the citizenry are the eyes and ears of the Japanese police.

The ability of the police to collect intelligence from the public is of the utmost importance in crime prevention strategies, and the intelligence network must be efficient. Prior knowledge of what is likely to occur is vital to effective crime prevention. This ties in with on-the-spot street interrogation, which is widely practiced in Japan.

As an important part of the ongoing program to secure and maintain widespread public support, it is standard operating procedure for the police to give appropriate public recognition to citizens who have performed meritorious acts in assisting the police in prevention, control, suppression, or investigation of crime, as well as in saving human life. Recognitions range from letters of commendation from the local police chief or the chief of the prefectural police to medals presented at formal public ceremonies by the commissioner general (*Keisatsu Chō*

Chōkan) of the National Police Agency. In a society that holds its public officers in highest esteem, such recognition carries great prestige for recipients.

By no means the least of publicity media for promoting good public relations are the police marching bands (*Keisatsu Ongakutai*) located at the various metropolitan and prefectural police headquarters and at the imperial guards police headquarters. Not only do these bands play at regular police crime prevention functions, they perform at a seemingly endless series of public events sponsored by the prefectures, cities, and towns. In addition, they present an estimated 4,000 public concerts heard by 20 million persons each year. Musicians practice during off-duty hours.

Japanese police undergo a longer period of training than do American police. Their turnover rate is significantly lower. Many take the entrance examination, but only a few are chosen. Police officers are not allowed to smoke in public or eat in public establishments while on duty or in uniform. And police regulations prohibit any form of outside employment. They have a high degree of esprit de corps and consider themselves the spiritual descendants of the legendary Samurai of old Japan, famed for their high professional moral code (*bushidō*).

Comparisons between Salem and Kawagoe

Kawagoe police were unable to estimate the percentage of time spent in reactive patrolling. However, as detailed in Chapter 3, their calls for police service for 1986 were only 10,773, compared to 55,649 in Salem. And in Japan, the police employ a saturation technique in high-crime areas and in districts experiencing a high rate of juvenile delinquency.

It is interesting to note that Salem employs more patrol motor vehicles than does Kawagoe: fifty-nine for Salem compared with only ten for Kawagoe. Kawagoe, however, uses forty-one motorcycles, and Salem has just seven; and Kawagoe uses ninety-one bicycles, while Salem reported none in use in 1986, although two were added to the force in 1989.

Mention should be made of the element of danger in police work, the comparative danger faced by police officers in Salem and in Kawagoe, and how the danger factor influences the behavior of the police. According to a study by Professor Randolph D. Hicks of Laredo State University in Texas, on a per-capita basis, fifteen times more police are killed in the United States each year than in Japan.[4] It is probable that the comparative rate of assault on U.S. police is much higher.

Over the past five years, there were an average of twenty-two physical assaults on police in Salem per year, and in 75 percent of the cases, there was some degree of physical injury. By contrast, in Kawagoe there were no physical attacks or assaults on police officers whatsoever during the same period.

In summary, although the hours of work are longer and more irregular, police work in Japan appears to be much less stressful and vastly less dangerous.

Deployment

It is interesting to compare the deployment of police manpower in Japan and the United States. According to the National Police Agency of Japan, approximately 40 percent of total manpower is devoted to patrolling, 15 percent to criminal investigation, 13 percent to traffic enforcement, 11 percent to security, 6 percent to crime prevention, 5 percent to riot police work, and 2.4 percent to administration.

The Salem Police Department has never calculated its manpower deployment in this fashion; it estimates, however, that approximately 15 percent of total police manpower is devoted to patrolling, 30 percent to criminal investigation, 10 percent to traffic enforcement, 5 percent to security investigations, and 20 percent to administration, including preparation of reports, equipment maintenance, training, court appearances, etc.

Crime Prevention

We might also note that in Japan, crime prevention is assigned a much higher priority than it receives in most American police departments. One indication of this is the fact that in Japan, crime prevention has the same divisional status as patrol, criminal investigation, security, and traffic. In Tokyo, some 6 percent of the uniformed police serve in the crime prevention division.

There are indications that U.S. law enforcement agencies may now be giving more attention and emphasis to crime prevention than they did in the past. In a recent national poll conducted for the National Crime Prevention Council, it was reported that approximately nine out of ten U.S. police chiefs and sheriffs believe that "the primary goal of law enforcement agencies should be the prevention of crime."[5] Approximately three out of four said that they expect crime prevention programs to become more important in their departments within the next five years. The chiefs and sheriffs said that an average of 8 percent of their annual budgets currently goes to crime prevention. More than 90 percent of the officers responding to the poll held that effective crime prevention requires that selected officers be trained and deployed as crime prevention experts and that every officer should receive some training in the subject.

Firearms

One major difference between the two cities and the job faced by their respective police is the matter of private ownership of handguns. Under Oregon law, all dealers in pistols, revolvers, concealable weapons, or machine guns must be licensed, and they are required to keep an official record of all sales. The dealer must mail a copy of the record to the chief of police on the evening of each purchase. The law further provides for a fifteen-day waiting period before the weapon may be delivered to the purchaser.

No convicted felon, person under eighteen years of age, or anyone who possesses a sawed-off shotgun, switchblade knife, blackjack, brass knuckles, etc., may purchase such weapons. It is also a felony to possess ammunition capable of piercing soft body armor such as bullet-proof jackets. Sales or gifts of firearms or explosives to persons under fourteen years of age is likewise prohibited. County sheriffs may for good cause issue a license to carry a concealed weapon to any person of good moral character.

In a praiseworthy effort to place tighter controls on the purchase, sale, and possession of firearms, the 1989 Oregon legislature enacted a new statute (Oregon Laws 1989, ch. 839) that, among other provisions:

• Requires a detailed application and a fifteen-day waiting period for handgun purchases in order to permit background checks on prospective purchasers.

• Revises procedures for obtaining concealed weapons permits and punishes unlawful possession.

• Severely penalizes false statements on all applications required under the new law.

• Requires registration of purchases of all used firearms.

• Establishes mandatory sentences for certain crimes when a firearm has been used.

Japan, on the other hand, has a much stronger gun control law that is strictly enforced. No one but police officers, members of the self-defense forces, and international pistol team members licensed by the police may legally possess a handgun.[6] As an indication of the much greater personal risk faced by the American police officer, it was estimated in 1980 by one source that the number of handguns possessed by private individuals in the United States was twenty-four million.[7] The same source also estimates that the total is increasing nationally at the rate of 2.5 million a year.

According to the most recent available statistics, in 1979 only 171 crimes were committed with guns in Japan. In the United States, however, in order to persuade victims to hand over their money and valuables, robbers almost invariably threaten them with a handgun. In New York City in 1978, for example, according to press reports 23,000 robberies were committed with handguns and a total of 9,000 handguns were confiscated.

Table 5.1 compares the incidence of handgun murders in several countries; the number for the United States is striking. And, apart from these figures, in America, one child under the age of fourteen is accidentally killed by a handgun every day.

In Japan, only 16 police officers were killed between 1969 and 1973. In the United States, 127 police officers were killed in 1973 alone.[8] We asked Officer Sawada, the chief of Kawagoe's crime prevention unit, how often one of their officers is faced with a suspect armed with a loaded handgun. After a moment's thought, he replied that he could not recall a single instance when this had occurred!

Neither the Japanese man-in-the-street nor police officers we interviewed can understand the American obsession with gun possession. Some gun enthusiasts seem to believe that anyone is entitled to have a gun, regardless of the social cost. One high-ranking Japanese police official in the city of Kanazawa, who had visited several different police departments on the East Coast of the United States and had observed their operations at close range, offered an observation on the

Table 5.1

The Incidence of Handgun Murders during 1985

Canada	5
Australia	5
Great Britain	8
Switzerland	31
Japan	46
United States	8,092

Source: Handgun Control, Inc., Washington, DC.

prevalence of handguns in the United States, "Why, in New Jersey, even girls carry guns!"

Canadians, across the international border to the north, who have had gun control in one form or another for a hundred years and saw further tightening of laws in 1978, are equally puzzled by their American neighbors. When New York's Governor Mario Cuomo recently proposed a new law for a statewide ban on the sale of military-style assault weapons, more than 800 angry gun owners jammed a public meeting in Buffalo to protest. Commenting on the heated debate over the new proposal, the mayor of Grigsby, Ontario, a small Canadian community about thirty miles from Buffalo, said, "We [Canadians] have almost a complete lack of understanding about your resistance to strict gun control. It's perceived as one of your downsides. It's one of the things I hear continuously that your cities aren't as safe as up here."[9]

The type of organized political pressure exerted by opponents of gun control to intimidate elected officials may be best illustrated by a recent public confrontation in Oregon: after numerous public hearings, and over the highly vocal opposition of local pro-gun groups, in Portland, the Multnomah County board of commissioners adopted a relatively mild gun control ordinance by a one-vote margin. The measure restricts where people may carry guns in the unincorporated areas of the county and also prohibits semiautomatic assault weapons from public places and requires that such weapons be disassembled and locked in the trunk if carried in an automobile.

Undaunted, the opponents of gun control unlimbered the ultimate retaliatory weapon—a recall campaign against Commissioner Rick Bauman, the chief sponsor of the gun control measure. (Under Oregon's constitution, every public officer is subject to recall by the electors. If any pro-recall forces are successful in collecting 7,731 valid voter signatures from a commissioner's district, a special election must be held to decide if he or she should be removed from office.) In this case the necessary signatures were thereafter obtained and the recall election was subsequently held. Commissioner Bauman, however, won the election by a small margin and thus retained his position.[10]

Tables 5.2 and 5.3 present comparative data on other crimes.

Prioritization

As an important part of our comparative study, we asked the two police agencies what the enforcement priorities were for their respective departments. According to Salem Chief of Police Riley, the first priority in his department is crimes against persons, particularly crimes of violence such as homicide, rape, sexual assault, and sex abuse. Of second priority are property crimes, especially residential burglaries. In Japan, however, priorities are quite different. Of primary priority are attacks by terrorists, such as the notorious Red Army and similar extremist groups. Fortunately, there have not been any such attacks in Kawagoe, but attacks by other violence-prone groups have occurred at Narita International Airport in nearby Chiba Prefecture, keeping Kawagoe police constantly alert to the danger.[11] The second priority is robbery, followed by juvenile crimes and delinquency; fourth priority is consumer fraud, with traffic in dangerous drugs listed in fifth place, according to Yoshizo Sawada, Chief of the crime prevention unit.

Citizen Support Groups

Mention should be made of the popularity of citizen support groups (*Keisatsukan Tomonokai*), formed by citizens to express their backing of the police function on a broad scale. There is even a special citizen support organization, *Kidōtai Hagemasu Kai* (riot police encouragement association), dedicated to providing moral support for the highly skilled riot control police (*kidōtai*).[12]

Also to be noted is the Police Association (*Keisatsu Kyōkai*), a voluntary group that provides financial aid to police personnel or citizens injured in cooperating with the police in the performance of their duties. It may provide aid to the families, as well as conducting memorial

Table 5.2

Number of Homicide Cases Reported, Crime Rate, and Clearance Rate, by Countries (1960–1987)

Year/Item	USA	Japan
1960		
Homicide cases reported	9,110	2,784
Crime rate	5.2	3.0
Clearance rate	92.3	96.7
1965		
Homicide cases reported	9,960	2,390
Crime rate	5.1	2.4
Clearance rate	90.5	97.2
1970		
Homicide cases reported	16,000	2,028
Crime rate	7.9	2.0
Clearance rate	86.5	97.0
1975		
Homicide cases reported	20,510	2,140
Crime rate	9.6	1.9
Clearance rate	78.3	96.0
1980		
Homicide cases reported	23,040	1,729
Crime rate	10.2	1.5
Clearance rate	72.3	97.3
1985		
Homicide cases reported	18,980	1,847
Crime rate	7.9	1.5
Clearance rate	72.0	96.1
1987		
Homicide cases reported	20,100	1,645
Crime rate	8.3	1.3
Clearance rate	70.0	97.6

Notes:
1. Based on the following sources:
   United States   Crime in the United States
   Japan   Statistics of the National Police Agency
2. The number of reported homicide cases in the respective countries are based on the following criteria:
   United States   Murder and manslaughter (negligent manslaughter and attempted cases are not included).
   Japan   Murder and manslaughter (robbery causing death is included).
3. "Crime rate" means the number of reported offences per 100,000 population.

Table 5.3

Number of Larceny Cases Reported, Crime Rate, and Clearance Rate, by Countries (1960–1987)

Year/Item	USA	Japan
1960		
Larceny cases reported	3,095,700	1,038,418
Crime rate	1,726	1,112
Clearance rate	—	50.1
1965		
Larcency cases reported	4,352,000	1,027,473
Crime rate	2,249	1,046
Clearance rate	—	50.1
1970		
Larceny cases reported	7,359,200	1,039,118
Crime rate	3,621	1,002
Clearance rate	18.4	47.5
1975		
Larceny cases reported	10,252,600	1,037,942
Crime rate	4,811	927
Clearance rate	18.5	51.6
1980		
Larceny cases reported	12,063,800	1,165,609
Crime rate	5,353	996
Cleaance rate	16.5	55.0
1985		
Larceny cases reported	11,102,600	1,381,237
Crime rate	4,651	1,141
Clearance rate	17.8	59.9
1987		
Larceny cases reported	12,024,800	1,364,796
Crime rate	4,940	1,116
Clearance rate	17.7	60.2

Notes:
1. Based on the following sources:
    United States   Crime in the United States
    Japan   Statistics of the National Police Agency
2. The number of reported larceny cases in the respective countries are based on the following criteria:
    United States   Larceny-theft, motor vehicle theft and burglary (Until 1973, motor vehicle theft had been called "Auto theft".)
    Japan   All kinds of theft
3. See the note 3 of Table 5.2.

services, an important custom in Japanese culture. It also compiles and publishes reference materials to help with the professional education and training of police officers, including some textbooks used at police professional training schools, and it provides assistance and awards to various police competitions and athletic meets.

To publicize police activities, the police association handles translation and publication of the accepted condensed version of the annual "White Paper on Police Operations," an informational pamphlet containing a concise summary of police operations during the past year.

Notes

1. R.D. Hicks, "Some Observations on Japanese and American Policing," *Journal of Police and Criminal Psychology* 1, 2 (October 1985): 68–78. For a more complete discussion of the relationship between the National Police Agency and the local police, see L. Craig Parker, Jr., *The Japanese Police System Today* (Tokyo: Kodansha International, 1984); Walter L. Ames, *Police and Community in Japan* (Berkeley: University of California Press, 1981); William Clifford, *Crime Control in Japan* (Lexington, MA: Lexington Books, 1976); and David H. Bayley, *Forces of Order* (Berkeley: University of California Press, 1976).

2. G.T. Kurian, *World Encyclopedia of Police Forces and Penal Systems* (New York: Facts on File, Inc., 1989), p. 312.

3. "Japan's Love Hotels Keep Trysts a Secret," *Oregonian* (Portland, OR), September 9, 1990, p. A16.

4. R.D. Hicks, "Some Observations on Japanese and American Policing," op. cit.

5. *Criminal Justice Newsletter* 20, 12 (June 15, 1989).

6. "Law Controlling Possession of Firearms and Swords, Article 4," *Law*, 6 (March 1958).

7. National Commission on the Causes and Prevention of Violence, "Firearms and Violence in American Life" (Washington, DC: Government Printing Office, 1970).

8. Ezra Vogel, *Japan as No. 1* (Tokyo: Tuttle, 1984), p. 205.

9. "Proud Canadians Say Theirs is a Kinder, Gentler Nation," *Oregonian* (Portland, OR), March 18, 1990, p. A13.

10. "Petitions Turned in to Recall Bauman," *Oregonian* (Portland, OR), March 29, 1990, p. A1.

11. For further background on Japan's Red Army terrorists see Dae Chang and Masami Yajima, "The Japanese *Sekigun* Terrorists: Red Army *Samurai* Warriors," *International Journal of Comparative and Applied Criminal Justice* 6, 2 (1989): 169.

12. For a description of Japan's riot control police, see R.Y. Thornton, "Kidōtai: Mobile Task Forces of Japan," *The Police Chief* 38, 7 (July 1971): 65.

6

Citizen Involvement

Salem

The participation of individual citizens in prevention of crime and delinquency is vital. Salem, Oregon, boasts an outstanding volunteer program, Neighborhood Crime Watch, in which entire neighborhoods are organized to watch each other's property as a mutual defense against burglary, prowlers, and vandals. Statistics indicate that the program is unquestionably effective in the neighborhoods where it is in operation. Unfortunately, only 25 percent of the neighborhoods in the city are involved. The others have simply failed to organize and participate.

Along the boundaries of each organized crime watch neighborhood are posted permanent signs that read:

WARNING
Neighborhood Watch Program in Force.
We immediately report all suspicious activities to our police department.

Police-Neighborhood Liaison

Establishment of police-neighborhood liaison is often stressed by advocates of increased community-oriented policing and increased police responsiveness to the community's needs. In Kawagoe, this has taken the form of a city-wide crime prevention liaison committee (*Bōhan Renraku Shō*) with representatives from each district in the city.

Strikingly similar is the Salem police-neighborhood liaison committee, whose bylaws state several purposes:

• To improve communications between the Salem police department and neighborhood associations. (There are eighteen in Salem.)
• To provide an opportunity for neighborhoods to bring their concerns to the police department.
• To provide neighborhood representatives and, through them, their neighborhood associations, with information about crime prevention efforts, crime trends in the city, and police department operations and organization.
• To assist the Salem police department in reaching its objectives related to crime prevention and providing police services in the city of Salem.

The Salem committee began in 1980 under the aegis of former Chief Roy Holladay. According to Lieutenant David Hunter, a senior officer since 1962, the innovative Holladay wanted to establish a committee of local representatives from each neighborhood to explain police operations to each neighborhood association and to answer questions raised by residents. Conversely, these representatives would serve as a conduit to bring neighborhood concerns to the attention of the department.

The committee was originally chaired by Hunter, who was chief of the special operations section. In due course, however, it was decided that the committee should be chaired by a private citizen elected by the committee itself. Officers of the committee are elected for a one-year term, but an officer may not serve in the same office for more than two consecutive terms.

Meetings are held monthly, on the first Wednesday, typically at noon. Copies of monthly crime statistics are distributed and reports are heard from the police department on specific law enforcement problems, neighborhood issues, and community concerns previously raised by members. Reports are then made by the neighborhoods concerning new complaints and concerns, ranging from suspected criminal activity and traffic problems to reports of vandalism and possible youth gang activity. From time to time the chairperson arranges for special presentations on matters of particular concern, such as vandalism in city parks or a proposed "drug house" abatement ordinance. The meetings usually last only one hour.

Richard Montag, committee chairman and retired U.S. Navy Captain, explains:

> The police neighborhood committee program has worked because we have a good police representation at the meetings. In addition to the chief of police, who usually attends our meetings, the captain in charge of operations, the captain of detectives, and the sergeant in charge of police school liaison are always in attendance.
>
> The principal item on the agenda is neighborhood and community concerns. Most importantly, we have feedback from the police department regarding questions previously raised by the committee and presentation to the police department of new problems as they arise.

Special Citizen-Police Committee on the Use of Force

A related example of community-oriented policing involves securing citizen involvement and input in setting police policy on the use of force by officers, and emerged after an incident in 1985 in Portland triggered intense interest in the subject. A citizen who was being subdued with a carotid artery hold by a police officer suddenly collapsed at the scene, and efforts to revive him failed. The so-called "sleeper" hold, which had been a common police restraining method throughout the country, immediately became the object of heated controversy. Both public confidence in the police, and officers' confidence in their ability to counter force used against them, were seriously threatened.

To assess these developments and to reevaluate Salem's policies, training, and tactics for the use of force, Chief Brian Riley appointed a committee of citizens and officers. As a result of its review of the entire matter, the committee produced a detailed eighty-page report, including the following, among many recommendations:

• Drastic revision of the department's policy on the use of force, restricting deadly force to what is generally called the "defense-of-life principle." (The chief of police implemented this recommendation in August 1985.)

• Modification in training in the use of a nonlethal chemical agent, mace, and emphasis on appropriate and inappropriate circumstances of use in order that it may be used more properly and effectively.

• Equipping police officers with batons—not the "billy club"—to fill the gap between mace and firearms with a simple, effective nonlethal weapon. The police baton now in use in Salem is a longer instrument than the "billy club" and is designed for striking the resisting offender below the waist rather than on the head.

• A significant revision in training in the use of the carotid hold to emphasize its lethal potential and the subsequent moral and legal obligations. (The chief of police implemented this recommendation immediately. The hold may still be used but its use is reduced to severely limited circumstances.)

• Training of all patrol officers in the use of the shotgun, hitherto restricted to sergeants only.

• All patrol cars to be equipped with shotguns because of their versatility and effectiveness in emergency circumstances.

Japanese police, in comparison, rely almost exclusively on jūdō in hand-to-hand combat or even in disarming a suspect with a knife or a sword. A Japanese martial art that may be described as a refined form of jūjitsu, jūdō uses special applications of principles of movement, balance, and leverage in which the opponent's own weight is used to subdue him. Before a police trainee graduates from the police academy, he must attain "black belt" status in jūdō or its equivalent in bamboo sword fencing (kendō). All officers are required to practice regularly what is called "the art of arrest," which combines the techniques of jūdō and kendō and keeps the line officer in excellent physical shape. In my travels in Japan, I cannot recall ever having seen an overweight line police officer.

Other Citizen Involvement Programs

One promising innovative school program called "Kids' Watch" was started in December 1981, as a pilot program at Schirle School. It enlisted and trained school-age youngsters in grades one through six to watch out for suspicious activities in their neighborhoods. Charts showing how the program functioned were displayed at the Oregon state fair that summer, and a set of slides was developed to illustrate active watching, listening, and reporting to show how kids could be a part of crime watch. The full-scale program was launched during the 1982–83 school year.

For a variety of reasons, including some concern expressed by both law enforcement officials and the educational community, erosion set in and unfortunately this program, which showed such promise, was abandoned the following year.

The Block Home program, organized under the auspices of the Salem-Keizer school district, successfully provides approved safe homes throughout the city where schoolchildren may seek shelter in an emergency, such as when someone tries to accost or molest them on their way to or from school. The block homes program is now found nationwide. It is believed to have originated in Salem. (In contrast, all Kawagoe elementary schoolchildren go to and from school in small organized groups under the leadership of an older pupil. Again, we see that the Japanese emphasize the importance of group cooperation, along with the duty of looking out for one another.)

Like most other American cities, one response of the citizenry to the high rate of burglaries in both businesses and residences in Salem has been the widespread installation of high-tech burglary alarm systems. A permit must be obtained from the Salem police department before any installation is made, whether or not the alarm system is tied electronically with the police switchboard. Alarm systems are usually quite effective in discouraging break-ins, particularly when warning signs are also posted on the premises. There are currently more than 2,100 burglar alarm systems licensed by the Salem city police.

Along the same lines, a number of firms and businesses in Salem contract with private security guards at their plants, factories, and businesses.[1] All security companies must by licensed by the city in order to conduct their business in Salem. The annual fee is $47.50, and there are currently twelve firms licensed to conduct a private security business operation in the city.

According to a local press report, there has recently been a boom in private security services in Salem, fueled in part by the rise of crime and corresponding drop in the capacity of the Salem police to respond to lesser problems.[2] A co-owner of the two largest security services says the business has grown at the rate of 30 percent a year for the past five years. Today the two services together employ about 100 security guards: "We are a preventive measure. We can keep something from happening, while police respond after it happens." Salem's city government supports the hiring of private security guards. According to Chief Riley, "The guards serve a valuable function—as long as they don't overstep their bounds." Security guards do not have the same powers as police, but they are allowed to carry a weapon—not concealed—and to make a citizen's arrest the same as a private citizen.[3]

Kawagoe

Crime Prevention Contact Point Program

Among several volunteer programs in the city of Kawagoe is the crime prevention contact point program (*Bōhan Renrakushō*), in which a contact person is selected by the local neighborhood association (*Chōnai kai*) to serve as the representative of a subdistrict comprised of about thirty homes. Thus, there are 2,380 crime prevention persons in Kawagoe, together constituting the *Bōhan Kyōkai*. Their jobs are:

• To keep the police (crime prevention unit) informed regarding all incidents, accidents, and any possible criminal violations in their respective neighborhoods.
• To transmit crime prevention information and pamphlets from the police to the residents.
• To transmit residents' requests and opinions regarding area crime prevention countermeasures to the police.

A neat metal sign is displayed on the house of the contact (*renrakushō*) so that citizens who need police assistance or who report possible violations will know where to find their contact person. Whenever the police have a crime prevention training program to conduct in the neighborhood, the contact person informs the residents of his area. Unlike the *bōhanin* in some Japanese communities, such as the city of Kanazawa, the *bōhan renrakushō* do not patrol the neighborhood on foot. Contact persons, who receive no compensation but are given handsome official scrolls at the end of each year, attend an annual general training conference conducted by the Kawagoe police headquarters.

Citizen crime prevention groups also include the crime prevention association (*Bōhan Kyōkai*), a committee comprised of the chairman of the self-governing association (*jichikai*) of each neighborhood, plus representatives from the Kawagoe Municipal Assembly, and certain others. The mayor is chairman, and the function of the association is to discuss and oversee most crime prevention activities. It is funded by an annual city appropriation of two million yen ($15,625). There are twenty-four members, and its office is in the crime prevention unit at police headquarters.

The *Bōhan Kyōkai* cosponsors national crime prevention campaigns with police, conducts "on-the-street" patrolling at peak times in high-crime areas, cosponsors meetings to promote the popularization of crime prevention, and distributes pamphlets.

Liaison Councils and Other Auxiliary Groups

In order to control and prevent such crimes as insurance fraud, bank robbery, sale of stolen goods, and loitering by juveniles in unsuitable locations, many police agencies have established special liaison councils with a variety of appropriate business groups such as insurance companies, financial institutions, pawn shops, second-hand goods merchants, and gambling and pachinko establishments. These councils provide liaison, guidance, and two-way communication and coordination to help prevent crimes associated with these particular business and occupations.

The *Kawagoe Business and Industrial Crime Prevention Association (Sho-Kōgyō Bōhan Kyōkai)* is an organization of commercial and industrial companies formed to prevent crimes against member companies. It is funded by annual dues of 350,000 yen ($2,734) from each member. Current membership is eighty-two, and their office is also in the crime prevention unit of police headquarters. Nationwide, police helped organize more than 12,000 crime prevention workshop groups, centered on businesses whose premises have been frequently victimized by crime.

The *Kawagoe Financial Institution Crime Prevention Association (Ginko Bōhan Kyōkai)* was organized to prevent crimes against financial institutions. It is funded by annual dues of 450,000 yen ($3,516) from each member. Current membership is ninety. Their office is in the crime prevention unit of police headquarters.

Membership in the *Kawagoe Firearms Safety and Crime Prevention Association (Jūhō Anzen Bōhan Kyōkai)* is open to all who have registered long guns. Organized to prevent accidents and thefts involving guns, this association has an annual budget of 910,000 yen ($7,109) funded by membership dues. Current membership is 546 persons. Their office is at the Ohara Gun Store.

The *Kawagoe Business Crime Prevention Association* (*Shōten Bōhan Kyōkai*), an organization of major store owners, was formed to control and prevent crime against businesses, especially shoplifting. Current membership is twenty-eight. Their office is also at the crime prevention unit of Kawagoe police headquarters.

Other associations include the *Kawagoe Youth Guidance Committee* (*Shōnen Annai Bōhan Hodōin*), with a current membership of twenty-three, and the *Kawagoe School-Police Liaison Association* (*Gakko-Keisatsu Renraku Kyōkai*), which is funded by the Kawagoe schools. The budget is 192,000 yen ($1,500), and their office is in the crime prevention unit of police headquarters.

Bicycle Registration

The prefectural police have established a bicycle registration system to prevent bicycle thefts and to expedite the recovery of stolen bicycles. A registration seal is attached to every bicycle, and a corresponding individual file card is kept by the police to permit speedy identification of stolen bicycles. All bicycles must be registered at the time of purchase. The Kawagoe Bicycle Crime Prevention Association (*Jitensha Bōhan Kyokai*) is an organization of bicycle shop owners. Its budget is 380,000 yen ($2,969), the current membership is ninety-seven, and the office is at the chairperson's residence.

Big Brothers and Big Sisters

The big brothers and sisters movement was started in Kyoto in 1947, following the end of World War II, when there was an increase in juvenile delinquency. In a move to help solve this problem, a small circle of civic-minded young students in Kyoto formed a group under the slogan: "Guidance for the young by the hands of the young."

The movement spread rapidly into other prefectures, and in 1950 it was named the BBS (Big Brother-Big Sister) movement. In 1952 a national federation of big brothers and sisters associations was established. Although started by students, many young working people joined to help befriend delinquents and predelinquents both in person-to-person activity and in a type of group work activity. Because of the nature of the BBS's work, group members range in age from eighteen to thirty at the time of admission. Any person between the ages of seventeen and thirty may join, regardless of educational or occupational background. Applications are screened by the prefectural federation of BBS associations.

Every local BBS association is affiliated with one of the fifty prefectural associations, each corresponding to the location of a probation office. They in turn form eight regional federations that are amalgamated into the national federation. Recently, BBS has encountered increasing difficulty in recruiting enough young volunteers who are willing to devote the time necessary to provide probation and parole supervision for youthful offenders and predelinquents. Cases are referred to the BBS by probation offices, family courts, child guidance centers, police, schools, or other public agencies.

In Salem, in contrast, the BBS program does not receive referrals from the family court or law enforcement agencies. The program serves girls as well as boys, but its primary emphasis is to provide guidance from a young adult volunteer for boys under the age of fourteen who have no suitable male figure in their lives.

The Sunflower Girls

One of the most effective methods of bringing crime prevention to neighborhoods that we observed in Japan was the sparkling presentation by the "sunflower girls" (*Himawari Musume*), three personable, specially trained, uniformed policewomen from prefectural police headquarters in Urawa. Each of the young women gave a well-prepared and cleverly presented talk—an extemporaneous one—on one aspect of crime prevention, such as fastening windows and doors with a specially designed latch. Another nattily uniformed female officer gave a similarly impressive lecture on how to deal with a spurious door-to-door salesperson. All three "sunflower girls" were active in displaying pertinent exhibits, charts, and pictures to illustrate the points made by the speaker. The presentation was carried out with enthusiasm and professionalism. It was almost like watching the famed "Rockettes of Japan" (*Takarazuka Musume*).

One of the charts, demonstrating common methods of unlawful entry by burglars, read:

• In 45 percent of the cases, the door or window of the house was unlocked!

- In 37 percent, entry was gained by breaking a window.
- In 6 percent, entry was gained by "slipping" the lock with a plastic card or metal plate.
- In 12 percent, entry was gained by miscellaneous other means.

The sunflower girls also presented a skit on how to carry a purse in order to avoid having it snatched. An unusual feature of the skit was a demonstration of a tiny commercial alarm inserted in a woman's purse with a pullstring pinned to the owner's clothing. When the purse was snatched, the alarm let off with a piercing screech.

This talented team travels from neighborhood to neighborhood throughout the entire prefecture, putting on similar demonstrations before such groups as neighborhood associations, senior citizen organizations, and homemakers' groups.

An important part of the show is the sunflowermobile, an unusually large, custom-built van equipped as a mobile showroom with myriad crime prevention locks, bolts, chains, and anticrime devices. It appeared to be a very expensive vehicle, resembling the Bookmobiles operated by large public libraries in the United States. We asked if the car was ever taken to Kawagoe schools to educate the children in crime prevention. The answer was no. Later we were told that "The students are too busy with school work."

Youth Hotline

Consultation corner (*sōdan konner*) and telephone corner (*denwa konner*) both function as a clearinghouse (*madoguchi*) for citizens to consult with a police officer on routine but possibly embarrassing matters such as home problems, friends, juvenile troubles, drugs, sex, school, and organized crime. These consulting services are similar to so-called "hot lines" maintained in Salem by several volunteer social service agencies and organizations.

Drug Prevention Associations

Drug prevention associations are volunteer groups that help the police in educating the citizenry, especially the youth, about the harmful effects of drugs. The associations also help the government in rehabilitating drug-dependent individuals.

Citizen Patrols

On-the-street juvenile guidance personnel (*hōdoin*) operate two successful programs: one is organized by the youth guidance center of the city government; the other is under the auspices of the police department. Hōdoin are citizens appointed to patrol inner-city areas where young people congregate at night and to offer guidance and advice to youth who appear to be in moral danger. The 52,000 hōdoin throughout the country receive a small amount of compensation for their services.

Environmental Purification

One of the most unusual programs carried out by the police is what is termed "environmental purification," aimed at assuring a more wholesome environment for the youth of the area. For example, the police encourage vending machine operators to eliminate machines that sell pornographic magazines in localities frequented by young people. They also advise merchants on how to make merchandise displays less tempting targets for shoplifting (*monbiki*) and encourage the installation of mirrors and surveillance cameras.

The police may also ask vendors of paint thinners and toluene (often sniffed by delinquent youth in Japan), as well as pornographic books and magazines, to refrain from selling to youths by pointing out cases of delinquency possibly triggered by such items.

Locks, Bolts, and Burglar Alarms

The National Police Agency establishes national standards for crime prevention devices such as locks, bolts, chains, and so on, to prevent burglary, and issues certificates for devices of superior quality that meet these standards.

High-tech electronic home security systems are already on the market in Japan. Their features include sensors and other electronic technology that automatically detect such disturbances as fires, gas leaks, and intruders. They are designed to summon security officers from a control center. Systems have been installed in very few homes, however, because of their cost: a standard system now on the market for a four-bedroom apartment requires an initial outlay of $500 for installation, a lease deposit, and a monthly maintenance charge of $36 to $42. Nearly 75 percent of the respondents to a market survey said that they would install a home security system if the initial cost were reduced to $83.

Other Measures

Other special crime prevention measures undertaken by the police include identifying "blind spots" (*shikaku kūkan*). Special attention has been devoted to developing a cooperative relationship with neighborhood volunteers for better surveillance of so-called blind spot spaces in newly constructed skyscrapers and underground streets and shopping centers where crime may develop.

Another focus has been the designation by city police of neighborhoods with an unusually high number of burglaries as "priority areas for the prevention of larceny through housebreaking." In this way, the area can be targeted with special crime prevention countermeasures such as special patrols by both police and citizen volunteers.

Notes

1. Clifford Shearing and Philip Stenning, "Modern Private Security: Its Growth and Implications," in *Crime and Justice: An Annual Review of Research*, ed. Norval Morris and Michael Tonry (Chicago: University of Chicago Press, 1981).

2. "Many Salem Businesses Turn to Private Guards to Keep Peace," *Statesman Journal* (Salem, OR), March 19, 1990, p. 1, 2A.

3. Oregon Revised Statutes 133.225, *Arrest by a Private Person*, provides: (1)"A private citizen may arrest another person for any crime committed in the presence of the private person if the private person has probable cause to believe the arrested person committed the crime. A private person making such an arrest shall, without unnecessary delay, take the arrested person before a magistrate or deliver the arrested person to a peace officer." (2)"In order to make the arrest, a private person may use physical force as is justifiable under ORS 161.255." Incidentally, Japanese law (Penal Code, Article 212, 213) contains a similar provision authorizing a citizen to arrest a "flagrant offender."

7

Educational Systems

Preschool Education

Salem

Whereas 70 percent of the kindergartens in Kawagoe, Japan, are privately owned and operated, in Salem the majority of kindergartens have been operated for the past three years by the Salem-Keizer school district under a recently passed Oregon state law. Pupils must be five years old by September 1, when the school year begins. There are currently 2,050 children attending public "k" classes in Salem. Schools for children between the ages of three and five are termed "preschools."

Private kindergartens are allowed. Unlike Japan, however, private preschools and kindergartens are not required to register with any governmental agency. Registration with the state department of education is purely voluntary, and the majority of such schools are unregistered. If the school operates for more than four hours a day, however, it is considered a childcare facility and must conform to childcare facilities regulations of the children's services division, which is part of the state's department of human resources.

The public kindergarten is best described as a developmental program with a social studies curriculum. It is structured to tie in with the social studies curriculum in the elementary school grades one to six. There are forty-four teachers in Salem's kindergartens, each of whom must be certified by the state department of education. One teacher and one instructional aide are provided for every twenty-five children, with two-and-a-half hours of program provided per day for a total of 175 days a year. A major part of the program is the two half-hour conferences a year with parents. The kindergarten curriculum plan revealed several references to topics related to crime prevention, within the "kindergarten skills check list objectives" under "social interaction":

I.   Sensitive to feelings of others

     Shares
     Takes turns
     Cooperative
     Can be a good leader and follower

II. Citizenship

     Respects the rights of others
     Respects the property of others
     Is able to follow school rules

III. Guidance Scope and Sequence

The student will develop skills in self-understanding. The student will identify feelings about self. The student will accept responsibility for his/her actions. The student will interact cooperatively with others. The student will learn the importance of taking turns, talking, and listening.

The only other references to crime prevention-related topics are found in the *HBJ Social Studies Teacher's Handbook* in a section on "friends," under the heading "government and citizenship"[1]:

> Families, schools and communities have rules.
> Rules help people get along together and stay safe.
> We can be helpful and kind in many ways.

Both the state and the U.S. departments of education set certain standards and guidelines for all schools from kindergartens through the twelfth grade. Not infrequently, federal grants for local education programs are conditioned upon compliance with federal standards and guidelines.

Kawagoe

Preschools in Kawagoe include nursery schools (*yōchien*) and day care (*hoikuen*). According to the Ministry of Education, in 1979, 65 percent of five-year-olds, 50 percent of four-year-olds and 7.5 percent of three-year-olds were enrolled in either nursery schools or kindergartens. Although most are private institutions, all are required to conform to Ministry of Education standards and guidelines, including:

- Pupils must be between the ages of three and five.
- Schools must have an administrator and at least one teacher for every forty children.
- Schools must provide four hours of programs a day for at least 200 days a year.
- Schools must meet prescribed standards for room and playground size and equipment, both indoors and outdoors.

Guidelines for instruction established by the ministry include:

- To foster the sound development of body and mind.
- To foster the fundamental patterns of behavior in our daily life and appropriate social attitudes; to build up emotional harmony, and thus to cultivate the germ of moral sentiments.
- To arouse an interest in nature and social affairs, and thus to cultivate the ability to think.
- To provide guidance in accordance with the special needs of individual localities, by improving the living environment of the kindergarten.
- To provide guidance in accordance with the characteristics of kindergarten education, which is different from elementary education.
- To make close contacts between home and school, and thus to raise the efficiency of kindergarten education in cooperation with education at home.

In Kawagoe, as elsewhere in Japan, private kindergartens are often conducted at Buddhist temples, where teaching includes a certain amount of religious instruction as well as fundamental precepts of centuries-old Confucian philosophy. Confucius, the renowned Chinese philosopher, taught the practice and cultivation of the cardinal virtues of filial piety, kindness, righteousness, propriety, intelligence, and faithfulness. As with character education in the regular school curriculum, the content and emphasis in preschool and kindergartens have been the subject of considerable controversy. There has been pressure from parents demanding more academic content in order to enable their children to enter a better elementary school and thus be launched on the road to a better academic and occupational future. This view is opposed by some kindergarten teachers and some citizen advisory bodies, who argue that the purpose of kindergartens is to help children develop, acquire good habits, and learn to share and play with other children. There is also a move to lower the compulsory primary school entrance age to five or even four years.

Crime Prevention Instruction in Salem

In Oregon, instruction in good citizenship, even instruction in ethics and morality, is specifically mandated by a state law enacted in 1929. It now appears in the Oregon Revised Statutes as section 336.067 and provides in part:

> • In public schools, special emphasis shall be given to instruction in: honesty, morality, courtesy, obedience to law, respect for the national flag, the Constitution of the United States, and the Constitution of the State of Oregon, respect for parents and the home, the dignity and necessity for honest labor, and other lessons which tend to promote and develop an upright and desirable citizenry. [...]
> • The superintendent of public instruction shall prepare an outline with suggestions which will accomplish the purpose of this section, and shall incorporate the outline in the course of study for all public schools.

Striking similarities become apparent between Japanese moral education (*Dotoku Kyōiku*) and the provisions of these Oregon statutes. The similarities, however, end here, with the statutes. As far as can be determined, the Oregon statute has not been enforced at either the state or local level since at least the late 1970s, perhaps earlier.

We were informed by the curriculum department of the Salem-

Keizer school district that although there is no specific course offering covering the requirements of the statute, many of the topics are touched upon in other courses. According to Ed Dotson, school district curriculum director, neither is "crime prevention" a separate course or curriculum. The subject may, however, be touched upon or receive some attention in several other courses, including "guidance" in elementary and junior high schools and "social studies" in senior high, including "U.S. history," "sociology," "American government," "home economics," and "health."

In the spring semester of 1988, South Salem High began offering an eighteen-week course entitled "youth and the law," also referred to as "street law." Topics covered include criminal law, juvenile justice, family law, individual rights, the criminal justice system, and personal law.

Crime prevention education in Salem begins at the elementary level, with the elementary counseling program. At Candalaria Elementary School, for example, under the direction of a school counselor who leads a form of cooperative learning, students work together in teams toward common goals once a week for two hours. The object is to arrive at a group consensus, the teacher taking an approach aimed at building positive concepts, including a sense of values and self-worth in each student. Topics include:

- Latch key children
- Alcohol and you
- Shoplifting
- Vandalism, stealing, lying, hurting people
- Child abuse: a kid's guide
- Self-protection
- Drugs and you
- Resisting peer pressure; refusal skills

Third-graders are introduced to the problem of child abuse by the police liaison officer, and other outside speakers with special expertise inform the students about drugs and alcohol. Special attention is given to early recognition and treatment of children at risk, and where necessary, such children are referred for professional counseling. If a possible criminal violation is involved, the child may be referred to the nearest youth services team.

A similar counseling program is continued to some extent in junior high. On request of school authorities at the junior and senior high level, the police liaison officer assigned to each school presents lectures on drug abuse, alcohol, child abuse, and rape awareness. It is at this level that the role of youth services teams begins; the number of referrals, however, is relatively low in junior high.

In senior high, crime prevention education seems to get crowded out of the curriculum, or at least it receives little attention. Coincidentally, this is the level at which the incidence of behavior and delinquency problems begins to increase. (A similar phenomenon was pointed out in Japan.) Asked the reason for this phenomenon, Larry McMurrie, assistant to school district superintendent Homer H. Kearns, explained:

> Elementary school is a nurturing environment. The relationship between teacher and pupil is a nurturing one. As the pupil enters junior and senior high, the schoolwork becomes progressively more difficult, placing more pressure on the student. As this is occurring, the student's earlier troubles and failure patterns surface and cause more serious behavior problems.
>
> Contributing further to the problem are the hormonal changes of adolescence and [use of] the so-called platoon system [students moving from classroom to classroom for different subjects]. In addition, we find that in some cases there is a breakdown of supporting family structures.
>
> By the time the student finishes seventh, eighth, and ninth grades, the dropout process has already begun. When you finally reach the 10th grade, chances are you've lost most of your potential dropouts.

According to one administrator, the biggest and most alarming trend in the area of school discipline problems is the apparent increase in student drug use: "There are more thefts. Most thefts by youth are in some way related to drug use. In some cases the parents may also be abusing drugs."

School authorities are countering this development by adding drug abuse education to the school curriculum, and urging strict law enforcement for driving under the influence of alcohol and drugs. According to Principal Ed Johnson of South Salem High School: "We must provide more opportunity for youth who do not adjust to school, who lack a sense of purpose. Experience shows us that dropouts often drift into crime." Johnson believes there is a need for special classes to help academically deficient freshmen, to keep them in school, as well as to expand peer counseling and establish more alternative education programs.

Officer Steve Smith, police liaison officer at South Salem High School, Candalaria Elementary School, and Leslie Junior High School, reported:

> Fifty percent of our time is spent in resolving reports of antisocial behavior problems of students. The other fifty percent is spent in classroom presentations, mainly on child abuse problems, dangerous drugs, and driver education.
>
> We are seeing more drug and alcohol related problems of juveniles. Police liaison officers have developed a good rapport with students we deal with.

Smith feels that this rapport is the reason why PLOs, as they are called, are nearly always able to communicate with and relate to the students with whom they work. He also sees a positive result from the special drug-free youth task force and "drug awareness week," a citywide program staged annually in March.

Bonnie Peters, a school counselor at South Salem High, whose duties include dealing with students with behavior problems, explained:

> I try to build self-esteem in my students. Students who feel better about themselves will not engage in crime. Insecure students often try for an escape into crime or drug abuse.

Parenting Education

Causes of juvenile delinquency and crime pinpointed in both our Salem and Kawagoe interviews were family failure, family breakdown, and inadequate parenting. A number of experts in child development and crime research in the United States agree with the conclusions expressed by some of those we interviewed in Japan and Oregon. According to Rolf Loeber, University of Pittsburgh psychologist and former Oregonian:

> Researchers ... have found that parents of delinquent children often lack involvement with their children, provide poor supervision, and administer inadequate or erratic discipline. Some parents of delinquent youngsters are themselves not law abiding, thus providing examples of

deviant behavior and values that their offspring may imitate.

There is substantial evidence that children raised in adversity are disproportionately likely to become delinquent.

Increasingly ... childrearing experts are focusing their attention on early rather than later child problem behavior. A primary reason is that most children learn deviant and approved behavior in the family home long before they are exposed to deviant peers.[2]

To address this problem, four out of five Salem senior high schools offer an elective course in the Home Economics department entitled "Parenting," with topics including:

- Development: physical, social, emotional and intellectual.
- Wholesome environment.
- Children's needs, behavior, guidance, discipline.
- In-school preschool lab experience.
- Activities, environment, and special parenting situations, including prevention of child abuse and neglect, single parenting, blended families, and support groups for parents and children.

Twice a week, students work directly with preschool children ages three to five, to accomplish such course objectives as:

I. Discipline

- Understanding discipline as an ongoing process that is based on parental modeling.
- Modeling positive methods of controlling behavior of young children.
- Realizing advantages and disadvantages of each of several disciplinary methods, particularly for immediate application to the setting; demonstrating understanding of basic tenets of behavior modification as a tool for changing behavior.

II. Needs

- Recognizing that human needs are unique in the combination within each individual but are changing, not static, within the child's power to define and important to deal with in order to define priorities, values, and consequent decisions.

III. Feelings

• Learning and practicing some "how to's" in dealing with difficult emotions in children; learning constructive methods of rechanneling potentially "negative" expressions of emotions in children.

IV. Self

• Learning the tie between self-concept and views of other people; understanding defense mechanisms.
• Checking one's own self-acceptance and contract to change behaviors considered unacceptable to one's own value system.
• Recognizing the difference between constructive and destructive self-disclosure and the value of self-disclosing in communication.

V. Constructive Communication

• Becoming aware of self-expression, verbally and nonverbally; becoming aware of the role of selective perception in communication; learning the transactional analysis model for effective communication and how to detect personal "games" and "rackets" that may interfere with constructive communication.
• Becoming aware of how to listen with special attention to nonverbal messages; learning and demonstrating the skills of "mirroring," "I messages," and "no lost problem solving" as models for coping effectively with conflict.

VI. Values Clarification

• Learning to recognize that decisions actively or passively made are an ongoing reality and that prethought and integrated decisions can make the difference in one's ability to achieve "happiness" and therefore successful selfhood and parenthood.

VII. Constructive Changes

• Learning a process of constructive decision making; to experience the application of this method to personal examples.

A related elective course offered in Salem entitled "human relationships" covers such topics as:

- Communication.
- Why people do what they do.
- Boy-girl relationships.
- Dating.
- Critical decision making.
- Sexually transmitted diseases.
- The birthing process.
- Child development and guidance.
- Child care.
- Families and family problems.
- Single parenting.
- Teenage parenting and its impact.
- Divorce and separation.
- Suicide.
- Adulthood, old age, and death.

Unlike the award-winning Medford parenting education course, which is required of every student—male and female—in Salem, the course is an elective and draws almost exclusively girls. Despite the valuable content, very few boys sign up. At Sprague High School in Salem, for example, twenty-seven students are enrolled—twenty-six girls and one boy. Kathy Sansone, who has taught the course for eight years, commented:

> To be a parent is probably the most important job anyone will ever have, and yet it is a job that very few people have training for. Parenting training is like career training. This class gives the students a look at what the responsibilities of parenting really are. It is very serious stuff . . . but we have fun learning it.

The importance of parenting in the crime and delinquency equation was addressed by Emil Brandaw, superintendent of the 850-member Oregon State Police:

> It all starts with the family. The importance of proper parenting and family background is difficult to overemphasize. We see it in the inter-

nal administration of this department. Officers who come to our department from good solid family backgrounds and upbringing never have difficulty in adjusting to the guidelines for our personnel.

Special Services for Special Children

The Salem-Keizer school district provides special services for handicapped and severely emotionally disturbed students with deviant behavior problems, even to the extent of furnishing alternative schooling. There are two emotional growth centers at the school district headquarters—one for middle school students and one for high school students—with about twenty in each. There is also an ongoing effort by a special task force to reduce the number of dropouts. Among the options available is referral of the elementary or secondary level at-risk student to a student services team made up of special educators in each school building: a counselor, a learning disability teacher, and an educational resource teacher. For the middle or high school child at risk, there is the mentor program, in which a classroom teacher is assigned to provide special assistance as a mentor. "Mentor" is a term Salem educators learned and borrowed from local private businesses in the course of setting up and operating a series of on-the-job learning partnerships with local firms. Other school programs for the emotionally disturbed child include "poyama land," a day treatment program with a strong parent-education component.

Health Department Assistance

The Marion County Health Department is involved in several ways in drug abuse education in the Salem school system. A health department drug-alcohol specialist serves on each youth services team to provide input on how best to deal with students experiencing drug and alcohol problems. In addition, the specialist presents classroom lectures on alcohol and drug issues and counsels with at-risk students and their families.

Jo Stuckart, a drug-alcohol specialist, reported that "Approximately two percent of the at-risk students are alcohol abusers. The balance are polyabusers, primarily marijuana." Stuckart, whose other responsibilities include sobriety groups, awareness groups, and monitoring drug abusers by urinalysis, added: "We're planting seeds with kids. The results may not show immediately."

Student Representation

One especially noteworthy aspect of the student discipline process is student representation and participation, in the following two methods:

• The attendance appeals board, which handles appeals by students who are being subjected to possible discipline for nonattendance. The board consists of one school administrator, one teacher, and one student.

• The disciplinary advisory committee, which handles the setting of policy on school discipline rules, tardy policy, and so on. The board consists of one administrator, two teachers, two parents, and two students.

PTA and Community Input

Parent-teacher associations perform valuable services in providing parent and community input and are permanent fixtures in the environment of the schools. Each school in Salem has a local school advisory council (LSAC), whose function is to provide input through review of program changes and to bring community concerns to the school administration. The South Salem High School LSAC has recently become involved in community efforts to control drug and alcohol use among students.

Youth Services Teams

One of the most successful crime prevention programs operating in Salem is the youth services team program (YST), whose main elements are:

• Early identification, control, and prevention of crime and delinquency problems involving students attending junior high and high schools.

• Creation of interagency youth service teams at each high school and junior high school made up of representatives of the school administration, county juvenile department, family court, county mental health department, school counselors, state children's services division, and the school-police liaison officer.

The purpose of the program is to conduct preventive programs to head off student problems before they lead to suspension from school, arrest, or juvenile court involvement. The program is targeted at youths between the ages of twelve and eighteen. Children not in school are also eligible for counseling. Referrals are received through schools, police departments, team members, the communities, families, or the youth needing help. Typical activities consist of intervention in cases involving sexual or physical abuse of students, first-time misdemeanors, minor traffic offenses, runaways, school problems, parental divorce, status offenses, drug or alcohol abuse, serious family/emotional problems, and depression/suicidal ideation.

In addition, YSTs cooperate with other public agencies, such as family juvenile court, children's services division, mental health, etc., to which a student may have been referred. After referral, a team member is assigned to meet with the youth and with his or her family to assess the situation, make recommendations, and refer the youth to an appropriate team member or other agency. By the team approach, several members can be involved with a youth at the same time to provide coordinated services. The services provided may include individual counseling, family counseling and consultation, group counseling, referral to other community agencies, and setting of consequences for crimes in lieu of court trial.

Other specific services include crisis intervention and counseling; short-term counseling for youth and families; consultation services for parents, schools, and families; training in parenting skills; information referral services to the community; and listing of local jobs for youth.

School-Police Liaison Program

Another police program that has been very well received in the Salem community is the school-police liaison program, whose basic element is assignment of a specially trained police officer to each school. Because of budgetary constraints, the officer is usually assigned to cover several schools—elementary, junior high and senior high—simultaneously.

The police liaison officer performs several important functions, including serving as the police department representative in all law enforcement matters involving the schools; acting as the liaison between the community, the schools, and the police department; serving as the police member of the interagency youth services team at junior and senior high schools; conducting investigations of any school-related criminal incidents, including reports of child abuse; and making classroom presentations on a variety of appropriate topics. Police liaison officers do not patrol school hallways or schoolgrounds, but do occasionally patrol the neighborhoods adjacent to schoolgrounds.

One of the most important benefits of the program, according to Police Chief Riley, has been the development of a much more positive relationship between the Salem Police Department and the youth of the community:

> The police liaison program has had a very good reaction from both the students and the educators. It is a respected program enabling students to get to know the police officer in an informal setting as a person, rather than simply an aloof and impersonal authority figure.

Resolving Student Disputes

Rose Marie Marsh, principal of McKinley Elementary School in Salem, and her counselor Bonnie Ross have devised what might be called the "round table method" for resolving playground altercations. Possibly borrowing from the success of the dispute-resolution technique developed by Willamette University Law School's dispute resolution unit, Marsh invites the two students involved in the altercation to join in an informal meeting at her office round table. She begins by stating: "I understand there is a problem. Anthony, it is your turn first." When Anthony finishes, she turns to the other youth and says: "Gary, now it's your turn." Principal Marsh explained:

> Often in listening to Anthony, Gary will realize that he now understands the other's point of view for the first time. Nine times out of ten the child in the wrong will admit error and apologize. But I never ask a person to say "I'm sorry." Not only does the "round table" approach work, the students actually enjoy being invited to the principal's office to air their disputes. . . . We have seen a dramatic turnaround at McKinley school.

Principal Marsh reports that during the past school year, disciplinary expulsions of students from McKinley school have been reduced by 50 percent from the previous year as a result of her "round table" program, but she is careful to point out that she does not hesitate to call the police liaison officer to investigate if it appears that a crime—such as shoplifting—is involved, especially since, as March explained, "Shoplifting has a cumulative effect and must be dealt with immediately." In addition to encouraging regular parent-teacher conferences, she believes in bringing in the parents of the children whenever appropriate. She described one incident involving a child who was not handing in his homework. Upon contacting the parents, she learned that the child had informed the parents that he was not permitted to bring his books home! That, of course, was not the case; contacting the parents brought out the full story behind the problem.

Youth Employment

Deserving of special mention is the innovative approach to preventing juvenile delinquency by providing after-school employment for high school–age youth at Corvallis High School. The youth employment service (YES) program is the highly successful brainchild of Mrs. May Carlson. Believing in the old adage, "The devil finds work for idle hands," Mrs. Carlson, then a civic-minded private citizen, conceived the idea of having high school students themselves set up an employment service to provide after-school jobs for interested youth. She later became a teacher-student counselor at the high school.

The YES office was set up in a spare room at Corvallis High School, equipped with furnishings, office supplies, and a telephone from funds donated by various Corvallis civic organizations. An adult advisory board met once a week, and the program was launched with a barrage of publicity carried by local news media, led by the Corvallis *Gazette Times.*

The idea caught on almost immediately. Interested youth began registering for instruction in babysitting, ironing, cleaning, pruning, window washing, painting, etc. Homeowners and business firms started calling YES, asking for students to mow lawns, wash windows, take refuse to the dump, rake leaves, prune trees and shrubbery, do housework, babysit, and an almost endless variety of jobs and chores, ranging from store clerking to manual labor. Rates of pay were set by mutual agreement between students and the advisory board. From a summer program, YES quickly grew to year-round viability.

A key feature is that employers were required to rate students as to their performance, and one of its many benefits is that a number of students went on to perform extended employment with their part-time employers.

The Educational System in Kawagoe

Following World War II, the American and allied occupation of Japan began. One of the first items on the agenda was how to effect major changes in the educational system. The occupation authorities started with the premise that education would be the backbone of political and social reform in the war-torn country. Initially, the American educational system was adopted as the model for Japan. This provided for decentralizing the entire setup and wiping out the dominant role of the formerly all-powerful Ministry of Education (*Mombushō*). Instead, local school boards were to be elected as in the United States and a parent-teacher association would be created for each school, along with a national teachers union (*Nikkyōsō*).

The elected school board plan soon ran into all kinds of political difficulty, and a lively battle ensued between the conservative political leadership who backed the proposal and dominated the school boards and the Japan teachers union, which opposed the idea. After a period of pulling and hauling, the elected school board idea was shelved. Slowly but surely, the Ministry of Education regained many of its former powers. In due course, Japan ended up with a unified national education system similar to what it had before the war, but with a measure of decentralized local administration and local control.

Differences between the United States and Japan

Prior to 1979, in Salem, Oregon, the educational system was divided into the same academic divisions used in Japan—six years elementary school, three years junior high, and three years senior high (6–3–3). In 1979, however, Salem changed its division to 6–2–4. In Japan, where schools are part of a national education system, all under the general supervision of the Ministry of Education, and private schools are also subject to Ministry of Education guidelines, school attendance is compulsory only through the ninth grade; in Oregon, children must attend until they reach sixteen years of age.

All Japanese students who wish to enter senior high school must apply for admission and pass a rigorous entrance examination. Only the top students are admitted to the first-ranked public high schools. Others go to private high schools or enter the work force essentially as unskilled labor. No such examination is required to enter a public high school in Oregon, or anywhere else in the United States. Approximately 91.5 percent of those in Japan who finish junior high school, which is compulsory, do go on to senior high school, leaving approximately 7 percent who either enter technical vocational training or the work force or become temporarily unemployed. Most, if not all, Japanese senior high schools formerly operated on a two-track system: academic (college preparatory) and vocational. In other words, all students were enrolled in either a college preparatory program or a vocational program. However, this system is no longer followed. All students are combined into one track, even though some may be enrolled in more vocational education subjects.

Likewise, Salem schools do not divide students into college-bound and vocation-bound groups. Although the Salem-Keizer school district offers a range of so-called "vocational clusters," including courses in construction, welding, wood shop, electricity, business, public service, etc., it is not designated a two-track system. According to Wes Ediger, supervisor of secondary education, approximately 60 percent of Salem High School graduates go on to college or university. About 40 percent enter business, public service, one of the various trades or vocations, or become temporarily unemployed.

In Japan, 94 percent of students entering senior high school actually graduate; in Salem, in 1987, the corresponding proportion was 88 percent. Statewide in Oregon, however, the rate is approximately 77 percent.

The school day in Kawagoe's elementary schools generally runs from 8:30 A.M. to 3:50 P.M. Many, if not most, middle school students also attend a private late afternoon school to prepare for university entrance examinations. The Japanese system of rigorous entrance examinations has in all likelihood been influenced by, if not patterned after, a similar system that existed in ancient China.

Japanese middle and high schools place considerable emphasis on school clubs, which usually meet in the late afternoon after regular classes and are devoted to a wide range of academic interests such as foreign languages and cultures, computer science, or sports. In addition to specific subjects, these club meetings foster the development of group consciousness and mutual cooperation so highly valued in Japanese society. As a result, a Japanese student may not return to his home until six in the evening. Clubs also serve as an antidote to delinquency, according to Kawagoe educators, who encourage student participation.

The Japanese school year commences in April following an annual spring vacation of two weeks. There is a forty-two-day summer vacation in August and a two-week vacation beginning at the end of the calendar year and extending through the national New Year holidays.

In Salem, the school year begins in September, with a one-week holiday during Christmas and New Year's and a one-week spring vacation. The major difference is summer, when Salem students enjoy a three-month vacation. Historians tell us that the tradition of this lengthy summer vacation goes back to the days when American agriculture required a great deal of hand labor and school children were needed to help cultivate and harvest the crops.

The effect of longer school hours and shorter aggregate vacation time is that by the time the Kawagoe student has graduated from senior high school, he or she has spent a full year longer in elementary and secondary education than his or her Salem counterpart.

The assigned homework appears to be greater in Kawagoe schools than in Salem. In Japan, class size is limited by statute to forty-nine students. In Salem, the school board policy limits class size to twenty-five students at the elementary level and thirty-three at the secondary level, except in special circumstances. School lunch arrangements are also different. In Kawagoe, food is prepared in a central kitchen, as in Salem, but student monitors from each room (even first-graders) don white masks and caps and cart the hot food from the kitchen to their regular classrooms, where teacher and students eat together. The monitors serve each child an individual lunch on a tray.

It should be mentioned that the average Japanese family, particularly the mother, is much more heavily involved with the education of their children than is the average American family. It is not uncommon for a Japanese mother (nicknamed *"Kyōiku Mama"* or "Education Mama") to work through a child's elementary and secondary education virtually as a fellow student. The school expects parents and teachers to have frequent conferences concerning the students' progress. Also, Japanese schoolchildren will usually have their own special desk and study area in the home.

Another unique feature is the home visitation program, where elementary teachers visit the homes of students (*katei hōmon*) at least once a year. Visits, usually in the spring, are an occasion for parents and teachers to discuss the student's behavior at school and at home, as well as any problems. Parents and teachers both feel that these visits help prevent juvenile delinquency problems at the outset.

According to Barry Duel, a former Oregonian now living and teaching in Kawagoe, the PTAs of Japan have become more powerful and more active in their transplanted form than their U.S. counterparts (see the discussion of PTAs in Salem earlier in this chapter). Parents in Japan, for example, have asked for deemphasis of Japan's notorious entrance examinations, particularly those required for entering senior high school. Many parents have called for the elimination of expensive after-school cram schools (*juku*) and controlling the practice of bullying (*ijime*).

In addition, the PTAs of several Kawagoe schools have on occasion become action groups. In at least one instance, a PTA banded together and moved against what it considered to be an immoral business enterprise operating in the school area. In another case, after reports of young girls being accosted in a public park in a school area, the men of the PTA formed a group that patrolled the park at night, armed with flashlights, until there were no more such problems.

Corporal punishment of students is prohibited by statute in Japan (article 11, School Education Law of Japan). Nevertheless, teachers frequently use physical punishment to keep wayward students in line, even in Kawagoe. Some cases of life-threatening punishment have been reported in the Japanese press. Under Oregon law (ORS 339.250), a teacher may use reasonable physical force to enforce discipline if necessary. However, the 1989 Oregon legislature passed a new law prohibiting "corporal punishment" of school pupils. For a discussion of disciplinary procedures in Salem schools, see the section on student discipline below.

Character Education

Another unusual and noteworthy feature of Japanese education is the compulsory teaching of what is often translated as "moral education" (*dōtoku kyōiku*); a better translation would be "character education," with self-discipline instruction (*shūshin*) starting in the first grade and continuing through senior high school. In addition to the "three Rs," teachers are expected to teach moral values, character, and respect for others. The teaching of religion is prohibited in both the American and Japanese public school systems.

With ethics and moral training, it becomes apparent that Japanese schools are considered an extension of the family. Twenty-eight different items or categories are taught throughout the school years. Unlike the prewar moral education course, which was decidedly nationalistic and pro-emperor, the present course contains no such emphasis. The directive of the Ministry of Education states that the new morals course is to teach:

> Basic patterns of daily life, moral sensibility and judgment, development of individuality and [a] creative attitude toward life [as well as a] moral attitude as a member of both national and local communities.

The morals course contains a collection of stories from Japan and around the world teaching everything from good manners to brotherly love. One Japanese educational leader stated that about 70 percent of the content was based on the new postwar democratic ideals and that 30 percent was drawn from traditional Japanese values, including respect for and obedience to one's parents and other authority figures.

Stories of George Washington, Benjamin Franklin, and Abraham Lincoln, along with famous heroes from Japan's past appear in both the old and new versions of the morals course, as do such world-renowned figures as Mahatma Gandhi and Helen Keller, all of whom are figures who presumably illustrate traditional qualities that the ideal Japanese should possess. A directive states:

> The aim of morals education is to cultivate morality so that (1) the child will grow up applying the spirit of respect for humanity in the home, school, and society, (2) he will help develop a democratic society and state with a creative culture, and (3) he will be able to contribute to the realization of a peaceful international society.

Some of the required moral virtues are:

> • To respect human life [one's own and others'], promote health, and try to secure safety.

• To be careful of one's dress, language, and behavior, and be courteous.

• To keep one's belongings in order, and the immediate surroundings clean and neat.

• To use things carefully, and spend money wisely and efficiently.

• To be sincere and act honestly.

• To love justice and hate injustice, and to act courageously [against injustice].

• To persevere to the last for the realization of right aims.

• To be kind to animals and plants with a tender heart.

• To respect the beautiful and sublime with purity of mind and heart.

• To be aware of one's own personal characteristics and try to develop one's strong points.

• Always to be hopeful and try to realize one's highest aims.

• To think rationally, never losing the spirit of inquiry.

• To try to be original and creative.

• To be kind to everyone, treating the weak and unfortunate with tender care.

• To respect and be thankful to the people who have done service to you and society.

• To understand the spirit of rules and regulations and observe them willingly. If the case necessitates amendment, try to amend the rules or make new rules [by legal means].

• To insist upon your proper rights but to discharge your duties without fail.

• To respect labor and work for others.

• To be public minded, observe public morality, and not trouble others.

• To love and respect the other members of your family, and try to make a better home.

• To love and respect everybody at school, and to try to develop a better tradition for the school.

• To love your country and to try to contribute to its development with self-consciousness as a Japanese.

• To try to understand all peoples in the world with proper affection, and to try to become a person who will help humanity.

In junior high, a number of concepts are added:

• Lead a steady life with self-control.
• Try to enrich the community life.
• Contribute to the betterment of the community.

- Try to understand the spirit of law so that you can discipline yourself.
- Honor the rules of groups.
- Value the attitude of respect for law; try to carry your responsibilities to the letter as well as to assert your rights.
- Make a clear distinction between public and private affairs and try to develop the morality necessary as a member of a democratic society.
- Love your country as a Japanese and aim to be a man who can contribute to the welfare of his fellow men as well as our country.

The focus in senior high school is on moral ethics. According to Professor Y. Kawashima of Tokyo International University, this is similar to the elementary ethics course taught in American colleges but reflecting traditional Japanese values and norms.

No textbooks are used, and the teacher has considerable discretion in deciding how the topics should be taught. Most follow the practice of illustrating each point with a variety of stories, anecdotes, homilies, and incidents from the lives of familiar historical and contemporary figures. A young college-educated businessman offered the opinion, with which a number of his peers agreed, that he derived more benefit from the occasions when these points were presented as part of other courses and subjects rather than in the narrow confines of the moral education course. In fact, he frankly discounted the value of the formal moral education when it was presented as a separate subject.

Recently, as might well be expected, the Japanese educational system has found itself caught up in the continuing clash between tradition and a fast-changing society. The moral education course in particular has been the subject of the sharpest controversy. It is at the center of the generation gap debate in Japanese households. On one side are the parents and the older generation who have expressed widespread dissatisfaction with what they see as their children's lack of discipline, their departure from traditional moral values, and their lack of the "Japanese spirit" (*seishin*). On the other side of this lively dispute is the younger generation itself, who express their disdain for morals education and other "old fogey" approaches to today's problems. Solidly aligned with the young people is the left-leaning wing of the Japan teacher's union, which opposes much of the moral training currently being taught and counsels that students should be taught political doctrine, democratic principles, and even Marxist-Leninist and Maoist ideologies.

A 1987 report from the U.S. Study of Education in Japan has this to say about moral education:

> Although occupying only one class hour per week, moral education has a fundamental role in Japanese education. It is a distinct area of instruction at every level of compulsory education, and attitudes, habits and behaviors which are consistent with the Japanese value system are infused throughout the curriculum.
>
> The Japanese concept of moral education is far from vague or formless. Twenty-eight themes in six categories are covered at the elementary level, among them: Importance of order, regularity, cooperation and thoughtfulness, participation, manners, and respect for public property; endurance, hard work and high aspirations; freedom, justice, fairness, rights, duties, trust, and conviction; the individual's place in groups such as the family, school, nation and world; harmony with nature and its appreciation; need for rational and scientific attitudes toward human life.[3]

School Housekeeping Chores

A most unusual facet of school life in Japan beginning in the first grade is the requirement that students spend the last twenty minutes of their lunch hour sweeping and cleaning their classrooms and the adjoining hallways and stairways. They also cover the school playground and adjoining areas, picking up scraps of paper and other refuse. This activity is believed to teach group responsibility, mutual cooperation, and respect for government property, among other things. There is, however, one typically Japanese exception. For one or two months after first-graders enter school, the fifth- and sixth-graders clean the first-graders' rooms, desks, and chairs. This is to teach the first-graders how to do the work. As a result, first-graders learn to respect senior pupils and both learn a lesson in mutual help and fellowship. To see these busy little people tidying up their school is truly a sight to remember. A similar practice has reportedly been followed since ancient times in Chinese schools. (Students are, of course, required to remove their street shoes at the school entrance and wear slippers while in the school building. Anyone who has visited a Japanese home will immediately recognize this custom.) It is readily apparent that this housekeeping aspect of school discipline has a salutary effect on the physical appearance of the school facilities. It also discourages students from injuring or defacing school property; we saw no graffiti on the campus of any school property that we visited!

Student Discipline

Attending classes of all sorts and doing assigned homework occupy the main portion of a Kawagoe high school student's time. Compared to the life of an American student, life is generally much more closely supervised and circumscribed, with little time to become involved in deviant behavior. It should not be assumed, however, that a Japanese boy or girl has no leisure time. The average Japanese student spends an estimated two hours a day watching TV and reading magazines, comic books, newspapers, and the like, plus about one hour in sports.

School rules and regulations are severe by U.S. standards, and are strictly enforced. They usually cover the student's conduct both in school and after school hours. Rules cover details from hair length, width of pants cuffs, and the number of buttons and tucks in pants and skirts down to the number of eyelets in shoes. Virtually all middle and high schools require their students to wear the prescribed school uniform consisting of a high-collared navy or black jacket and matching trousers with a military-style cap for boys and navy middie blouse and skirt for girls. A school insignia is usually worn on the collar, making the student's school easily identifiable as he or she goes to and from school. Conduct reflecting adversely on one's school is often severely dealt with by school authorities. This operates as an informal social control of students' off-campus behavior, since every Japanese student wants to avoid being guilty of conduct reflecting adversely on his or her group, including the individual's school, and thus shunned.

The most commonly encountered infractions include:

- Smoking.
- Entering an adult game center.
- Playing an adult game.
- Associating with known juvenile delinquents.
- Using drugs.
- Wasting money.

Regulations may prohibit frequenting pachinko parlors and coffee-houses, where older youth congregate, or a student may be detained by the police for cigarette smoking, which is prohibited for youth. It is not at all uncommon for a school official as well as the parents to be asked to come to the station to take part in "police guidance" (*keisatsu shidō*).

The school's response to police reports of delinquent behavior is sometimes more severe than that of the parents. In general, however— and we base this assertion purely on casual observation—it would appear that Japanese society tends to be more tolerant of adolescent deviant behavior than does U.S. society.

A Japanese youth is not eligible to drive an automobile until eighteen years of age (the minimum age in the United States is sixteen). A Japanese youth may be licensed to operate a motorbike when he is sixteen, but most high schools prohibit their use. Car ownership and operation by high school students is practically unknown, thus avoiding the kinds of problems that U.S. school administrators encounter as a result of high school students driving during school hours.

In Salem, internal school discipline at the senior high level is handled by two assistant principals. It is based on the seriousness of the infraction and on the theory of escalating consequences for repeated violations. It is best described as a continuum ranging from self-discipline to referral to the youth services team. A school discipline matter might later become a police liaison officer referral or a YST referral. The YST might, for example, refer the matter to a specialist member to deal with the student's family. Another option might be to refer the student to a drug counselor or another member of the YST.

As to punishments, the longest suspension in Salem would be for five days of community service, a frequently imposed punishment for serious violations of school rules and regulations.

Classroom discipline is seldom a problem in a Japanese school, according to Michio Okayasu, an assistant school superintendent. A student who causes a disturbance or discipline problem or does not immediately follow a teacher's order is sent to the principal's office for further direction. Should these steps prove unsuccessful in correcting the problem, the student may be sent to the counseling center, which is a branch of the prefectural counseling service. According to Okayasu, schools do not have special counselors. This is considered a part of a teacher's normal responsibilities.

No police officers are assigned to Japanese schools on a regular basis. Moreover, it is very rare for a police officer to enter a school building. In the event a crime is committed by a student, the police are notified.

Each school has a representative on the citywide school-police liaison committee (*gakkō-keisatsu renraku kyogikai*), which meets two or three times a year and keeps the police advised of any possible law-enforcement-related problems in the school system. Police officials never give crime prevention lectures in the schools. Traffic police, however, do give lectures on traffic safety to primary students from time to time. Okayasu informed us that vandalism and defacement of school property were a minor problem in Kawagoe schools four or five years ago but have not been a problem in recent years.

Officials indicated that some instances of physical attacks upon teachers by students had occurred in some Japanese middle schools in the past, but there had been none in either elementary or senior high schools in Kawagoe. From a nationwide perspective, the statistical incidence of physical attacks on teachers is very small, although such incidents that do occur receive a great deal of attention in the media, which may give the problem a disproportionate prominence.

Asked about school expulsion, the assistant superintendent of education said that a school principal is empowered to expel a disruptive student but that such action is rarely taken. A student may appeal his or her expulsion to the city superintendent of education. Like its Salem counterpart, the Kawagoe school system conducts special classes for potential dropouts but Kawagoe's antidropout program did not appear to be as extensive as that currently underway in Salem.

According to officials, no drug problems have been reported in Kawagoe schools. Occasionally some students have been caught sniffing glue or paint thinner, but there have been no indications of students using amphetamines, barbiturates, marijuana, cocaine, or like substances.

Asked to express an opinion on the underlying causes of crime and delinquency, Assistant Superintendent Michio Okayasu said:

> One of the leading causes is family breakdown and family failure. Also one must attribute a large share of the problem to economic factors. Poverty is responsible for a substantial amount of crime and delinquency.

Mr. Okayasu indicated that in the final analysis, parental pressure on students to study intensely day and night in order to pass the all-important high school entrance examinations is a big part of the delinquency problem. It should be noted, however, that some Japanese educators, as well as Americans, who have studied the Japanese educational system have expressed a contrary opinion on this issue. Rather than blaming the parents, these critics place the blame squarely on the educational system itself and the unrelenting pressure it places on Japanese schoolchildren to pass the rigorous entrance examinations in order to enter a top-grade senior high school and a ranking college or university, which will control the student's entire future.

A similar view was recently expressed by Toshiko Miyagawa, director of the Institute of Japanese Composition Education. In an article reported in *Asahi Shimbun* on May 29, 1989, Miyagawa faulted the Japanese educational system for a major share of current juvenile delinquency problems:

> The current educational process does not provide a caring and protective environment for still-maturing juveniles to grow. Rather, it shifts the responsibility to the policing authorities. I would like to propose that the juvenile delinquency problem is rooted in the less responsive educational environment.

Similar criticism has also been directed at the teacher evaluation scheme presently used in Japan. According to reports, teachers are evaluated, at least in part, on the basis of how many of their students pass the entrance examination to top-rated colleges and universities. According to the critics, this leads inevitably to teachers spending a disproportionate amount of their time and effort with the best students, leaving the "late bloomers" and the lesser achievers in the lurch; the forgotten students of Japanese education today, these children sit in the rear of the classrooms unable to follow the instruction, becoming what might be termed "in-school dropouts." Frequently they become full-fledged dropouts (*ochikobore*). Some such as Toshiko Miyagawa see this as one of the indirect causes of the recent (since 1982) "third wave" of Japanese juvenile delinquency.

Finally, we asked Mr. Okayasu about the security of student lockers. He told us that student lockers are not locked, either in elementary or in middle school.

Student Bullying

The one area of student misbehavior where Japanese schools may have nearly as much of a problem as do some inner-city schools in the

United States—though not Salem—is bullying (*ijime*). One difference seems to be that in Japan the practice is historically much older and is not limited to inner-city schools. In American's inner-city schools, the practice tends usually to involve youth gangs.

Ijime is the practice, usually by groups or gangs of students, of beating or tormenting a fellow student who is in some way different from his peers. As with physical attacks on teachers by students in Japan and the rare and occasional student suicide, *ijime* incidents are given wide publicity in the Japanese media. According to a recent estimate, 25 to 33 percent of youth suicides in Japan are the result of systematic and protracted harassment by school bullies.[4] The parents of one thirteen-year-old Tokyo boy who hanged himself after experiencing extreme bullying sued the Tokyo metropolitan government and the parents of the two alleged perpetrators for twenty-two million yen (approximately $175,000).

The *Harvard Education Letter* reported that the parents of Japanese school-age children have begun an antibullying campaign that the government has now joined. This marks an abrupt departure from the previous "hands-off" policies of Japanese school and police authorities. As a result, antibullying messages are now being carried in all of Japan's mass media. The constant message of the media campaign is that *ijime* is "inconsistent with traditional Japanese norms of courtesy and kindness." It does not end, however, with mere polite admonishments appealing for kinder and gentler behavior. In Tokyo the message was backed up by a so-called "bully buster" force that reportedly arrested more than 900 young bullies during the first half of 1985.

One cross-cultural study conducted in an American and a Japanese junior high school received mention in the *Wall Street Journal* (November 12, 1985). This study reported that 58 percent of American junior high students had been beaten or otherwise bullied by fellow students, compared with only 40 percent of Japanese students at a junior high school. Most of the cases involved the use of physical force.

In the United States, bullying usually involves a single, strong, and domineering youth, male or female, who picks on a smaller or weaker student. In Japan, on the other hand, bullying is typically a group affair, with a number of students ganging up on the hapless victim.

Another difference involves the reaction of bystanders and teachers. In the United States, other students and teachers tended to intervene. In

Japan, other students simply observed, rarely intervening. Some teachers did not intervene, fearing that they might themselves be attacked if they stepped in. The lack of intervention may indicate that *ijime* is somehow seen as permissible behavior in Japanese schools. Of the total number of incidents reported in both countries, one-third were perpetrated by female students, which may be surprising to some readers.

Some observers of the Japanese scene, domestic and foreign, see *ijime* as the precursor of more serious juvenile crime and delinquency. For example, published reports have described how some youth gangs have set up juvenile "protection rackets" in which student victims must pay a regular fee to youthful gangsters to avoid being bullied. Students who do not pay are physically injured. In his book, *Gaijin! Gaijin!*[5] Kenneth Fenter, a schoolteacher in Springfield, Oregon, describes his experience when he, with his wife and their twelve-year-old son and nine-year-old daughter, went to Isahaya, Japan, to teach school for two years. Both children were subjected to severe and prolonged bullying by their Japanese schoolmates and the bullying did not taper off until the daughter started fighting back. It finally ended after she hit one of her tormentors with a well-thrown rock.

Although there have been a few reports of bullying in Salem junior high schools, the incidents reported seem to be confined to the "hazing" variety, with upper-class members "hazing" freshmen. No physical injuries have ever been reported. Wes Ediger, superintendent of the junior and senior high schools, said:

> While there have been isolated instances of physical encounters between students at Salem secondary schools, I am not aware of any systematic bullying or hazing of students as you describe. Should there be such physical attacks on any student, it would be regarded as an assault—a criminal violation—and a complaint would be lodged with law enforcement authorities.

Meeting the Dropout Problem—
East and West

A problem of considerable concern in both Salem and Kawagoe is the increasing number of school dropouts. School administrators are well aware of the widely demonstrated correlation between poor school performance and delinquency as well as of the frequency with which dropouts drift into crime.

In Japan, as elsewhere, youthful deviant behavior most often occurs among youth who are school dropouts, or who had poor records in school. Peer groups comprised of these types of youth frequently soon drift into gang activities and crime. Delinquent youth become more attached to their delinquent peers than to their families, schools, work groups, etc.

Priscilla Blinco's study on task persistence led her to believe that this same factor has a direct bearing on Japan's significantly lower school dropout rate.[6] According to Blinco, Japan's national dropout rate is only 2 percent, compared with 30 percent in the United States. Blinco comments:

> There is a relative lack of persistence and a tendency to "give up" when performing tasks by American children. Thirty percent of U.S. children "give up" and drop out of high school in contrast to less than two percent in Japan. The result is a large number of U.S. students not properly prepared for the modern work world. This lack of persistence has important implications in an age of rapid technological progress.

If Blinco's conclusions are valid, they would also be applicable to the various antidropout programs currently carried on in Oregon and elsewhere. Interestingly, her conclusions were echoed in a frank comment by a member of a group of Japanese teachers who spent six weeks in Oregon in the fall of 1988. Said a high school mathematics teacher in his candid written evaluation: "Here [Oregon] the students give up more easily than in Japan."

If part of a subsequent dropout problem takes root even before the child enters elementary school, should we not be instilling task persistence in our children at a much earlier age? Japanese juvenile probation officers report that delinquency generally is peaking younger, and the number of offenses committed by junior or senior high school students increases every year. Typically, delinquents are youths who have failed in a series of entrance examinations and other academic or financial hurdles, who have given up hope of ever attaining a higher socioeconomic status. Poor school performance can be very alienating because in Japan today, as in the United States, the number of unskilled jobs is steadily shrinking.

The Salem school district has long carried on a variety of remedial programs to help youth who do not adjust to school and are at risk of becoming dropouts. At South Salem High, which in 1988 won a national award from the U.S. Department of Education for the excellence of its academic programs, the antidropout program starts with freshmen who are having difficulty keeping up with the regular academic program. Special teachers are assigned to help them catch up and keep up. Another approach is peer counseling, where student volunteers give academic help to students having difficulty. The mentor program is also used particularly in middle schools, where a teacher volunteer trained to develop a close working relationship with at-risk youth gives academic help and emotional support.

In addition to the YWCA-school district teen parent program and the juvenile court alternative school program (discussed below), several other alternative school programs are worth mention. One such program is the Chemeketa Community College alternative classes. In 1982, the Salem-Keizer school district and Chemeketa Community College (CCC) developed a joint alternative school program for students in the sixteen-to-twenty-one age bracket who are unsuccessful in the public schools and are at risk of dropping out. Courses that emphasize basic thinking skills and those required for graduation are held at the college. The goal is to enable the student to reenter the public schools by changing unsuccessful academic attitudes. The program is jointly funded by the district and the college, and students are referred by their respective high schools.

The youth assistance program is a year-round program inaugurated in 1981, serving students who have previously dropped out of school. Participants are sixteen to twenty-one years old and are referred primarily by high school staff and outside agencies such as the state children's services division, juvenile court system, and Chemeketa Community College. The program is operated and funded jointly by the Mid-Willamette Jobs Council and the Salem-Keizer school district. Students are encouraged to obtain a GED (general educational development) certificate or to complete the requirements for a high school diploma, and heavy emphasis is placed on job training and the development of occupational skills through placement of students in community businesses.

Community Outreach

The Salem-Keizer school district is in the process of reaching out with a novel program to enlist the cooperation of the business community in keeping school-age youth in school. Employers are being asked to be on the lookout for youth wandering about in the downtown shopping areas during school hours and to ask them why they are not in school. They are also being asked to refrain from hiring youth who are not in school or are not drug-free. In recognition of the importance of strengthening family structures, some employers have already agreed to support noontime parenting education classes for their workers to be held at business sites.

In Kawagoe, the antidropout program is not as structured as it is in Salem. Formerly, the troubled student was not given much individualized or remedial instruction in school. Parents of children needing extra help were obliged to send their offspring to private after-hours schools (*juku*). This is still the rule rather than the exception, although there has been some degree of change in recent years. Some individualized help outside of class time is now given by teachers to help students keep up with the demanding school curriculum. In addition, special classes for dropouts have been established. In some cases, the teacher may initiate instruction, as in Salem, for the student who is at risk of becoming a dropout.

New Antidropout Initiatives

During the 1986–87 school year, the Salem-Keizer school district redoubled its efforts to attack the dropout problem by sponsoring a series of events and activities. More than 500 parents, youth, citizens, and professionals representing more than fifty businesses and public agencies participated in putting together an expanded, comprehensive antidropout program. Measures include:

• Establishing a new district alcohol and drug program under a special teacher coordinator.
• Developing an expanded career vocational education program to teach basic, analytical, and interpersonal skills required for entry-level jobs.
• Establishing staff development training programs to focus on at-risk youth and effective intervention.
• Requiring each school to develop and implement a plan for early identification and intervention for at-risk youth at all grade levels, especially in elementary school.

• Creating a district-wide committee to establish guidelines and to evaluate programs for at-risk youth in elementary, middle, and high schools.

State Antidropout Help in Oregon

A discussion of antidropout programs currently operating in Salem would not be complete without mention of Governor Neil Goldschmidt's school retention initiative, designed to help school districts and local communities start programs to help youth at risk of dropping out of school. Pointing to a statewide high school dropout rate of 25 percent, the initiative provides technical assistance, information about model programs, strategies for developing adequate local funding, and seed money to help start such programs. The governor and the 1987 legislature agreed to set aside nearly $8.1 million for the initiative during the 1988–89 budget period, with $4.6 million for competitive grants to local communities. The overall goal is to increase the number of high school students who graduate from approximately 75 percent to 90 percent by 1992.

Teacher Support

In America

One thing that tends adversely to affect the Oregon public's otherwise positive image of its teachers is the financial support structure for public education. Except for a contribution by state government of about 29 percent of the overall cost, Oregon public schools are supported by local property taxes, which are subject to the so-called "6 percent limitation" provision of the state constitution. This limits any increase in budget levies to 6 percent of the previous year's levy, and not infrequently, a school district is faced with the necessity of increasing its budget by more than 6 percent. When that happens, the district must go to the voters to increase its tax levy, which sometimes makes schools and even teachers the target of verbal and media-carried attacks by irate taxpayers. A favorite avenue is the "letters-to-the-editor" column of newspapers.

Schoolteachers in Oregon, unlike those in Japan, by state law have the right to collective bargaining. That is true of most, if not all, public employees, including police and firefighters. In recent years, there have been several teacher strikes in Oregon for higher wages and other benefits, with teachers picketing the school premises. Minor altercations between picketers and would-be strikebreakers have occurred, initially producing some adverse public reaction against teachers. At the same time, however, students and their parents have voiced a good deal of support for granting pay increases to striking teachers.

On balance, Oregon teachers retain a large measure of public support for the vital and difficult role they perform. As a group, teachers are satisfied with their pay and working conditions. Many augment their incomes by working at short-term jobs during their annual three-month summer vacation.

There have been no recent public opinion surveys on the occupational prestige status of Salem and Oregon schoolteachers, but earlier national surveys have shown that teachers, at least until very recently, have enjoyed a high level of professional or occupational prestige when compared with other professions and occupations. In a nationwide Gallup poll taken in November 1981[7] on how various professional and occupational groups are rated in terms of "perceived general good to society," schoolteachers rated third highest, behind clergymen and medical doctors, and ahead of judges, funeral directors, bankers, and lawyers.

On the related question of "perceived status and prestige," however, schoolteachers were far down the list, well behind clergymen, medical doctors, bankers, judges, lawyers, public school principals, and business executives, but ahead of funeral directors, local political officeholders, advertising personnel, and real estate representatives.

A 1987 opinion poll found that 49 percent of the public gave teachers in local public schools a grade of "A" or "B," as they had in previous polls. Public school parents rated teachers even higher; nearly two-thirds gave them grades of "A" or "B." The ratings of administrators, however, lagged behind those given teachers (43 percent received either an "A" or a "B"). School personnel in elementary schools were rated higher than those in high schools.[8]

In a 1988 poll, the rating was on a slightly different question; the schools were graded, instead of the teachers. Forty percent of respondents rated the schools "A" or "B," while 45 percent rated them "C," "D," or "F." People living in communities of 50,000 or more residents tended to rate their schools lower than those living in smaller communities.[9]

Finally, in a similar nationwide poll taken in 1988 by the same polling organization on the question of "perceived honesty and ethical standards," *college* teachers rated second, behind pharmacists and ahead of clergy, medical doctors, dentists, engineers, police officers, funeral directors, bankers, journalists, television commentators, building contractors, senators, and lawyers.[10]

As in Japan, Oregon teachers are members of a professional union, the Oregon Education Association, which is a formidable political force in state and local politics. They give sizable financial contributions to federal, state, and local political campaigns, and are a force to be reckoned with when the state legislature meets in biennial or special sessions. Usually, a few teachers and former teachers are elected as members of that body at each biennial statewide election.

Because schoolteachers have been held by the courts to be state employees, they were formerly prohibited from becoming state legislators. In 1958, however, educators and their affiliated organizations mounted a successful campaign to amend the Oregon constitution to allow them to become legislators. All other state employees are still prohibited from serving in the Oregon legislature.

In Japan

The schoolteacher enjoys high status in Japanese society, a reflection of the public's conception of the function and the person's competence in performing it. Teachers are fairly well compensated, compared to other government employees as well as those in private industry. After observing and studying Japanese society for some thirty years, including a stint as guest professor in one Japanese university and guest lecturer in others, I have gained the definite impression that Japanese teachers still enjoy higher status and esteem among students, parents, and the public, and wield more "clout" than their American counterparts. If this is true, it is undoubtedly because of the paramount importance the Japanese attach to the educational development of their youth, which has been true for at least the past century and is still true today.

Although we were unable to find any more recent public opinion polls or surveys comparing the public esteem of the teaching profession to other professions and occupations in Japan, out of eighty-two occupations listed in a 1975 survey, elementary principals and teachers ranked ninth and eighteenth, respectively, in public esteem. The prestige of principals ranked higher than that of department heads of major corporations. Elementary teachers ranked higher than civil engineers, mechanical engineers, white-collar employees in large private firms, and city government department heads.

It would be difficult to overstate the importance of education in the value scheme of Japanese society. We are not aware of any comparative studies on this point, but it is our impression that the proportion of family income devoted to education of children may well be greater in Japan than in any other developed country, including the United States. For the average Japanese family, no self-denial or financial sacrifice is too great if it will advance their child's opportunity for a better education and thus a successful future career.

Most teachers belong to the Japan Teachers Union (*Nikkyōso*), reportedly the largest labor organization in the country. Although the JTU has won many benefits for teachers, teachers do not have the right to collective bargaining, as they do in Oregon. Instead, the National Personnel Authority, a government agency, gives teachers periodic cost of living adjustment (COLA) protection and sees to it that their salaries are commensurate with private industry.

Among other differences, Japanese classroom teachers are tacitly considered responsible for their students' behavior off campus as well as on the school grounds, after school hours as well as during school. In fact, in Kawagoe, teachers are occasionally observed in the downtown areas determining whether any school-age children are engaged in antisocial activities or frequenting questionable establishments.

Notes

1. *HBJ Social Studies Teacher's Handbook* (Teacher's Edition), Government and Citizenship Strand (Orlando, FL: Harcourt Brace Jovanovich, 1985), p. T25.

2. See R. Loeber and T. Dishion, "Early Predictors of Male Delinquency: A Review," *Psychological Bulletin*, 94, 1 (July 1983): 68–69.

3. U.S. Department of Education, *Japanese Education Today* (Washington, DC: U.S. Government Printing Office, 1987), pp. 21, 31–32, 69.

4. "The Harvard Education Letter," (November 1989).

5. K. Fenter, *Gaijin! Gaijin!* (Springfield, OR: Interculture Press, 1984).

6. Priscilla Blinco, "Task Persistence of Young Children in Japan and the United States." Paper presented at the Western Conference of the Association for Asian Studies, University of Washington, Seattle, October 22, 1988.

7. "The Gallup Poll" (Wilmington, DE: Scholarly Resources, 1985), 254–55.

8. Gallup Report No. 264, Sept. 1987, Princeton, NJ, p. 11.

9. Gallup Report No. 276, Sept. 1988, Princeton, NJ, p. 43.

10. Gallup Report No. 279, Dec. 1988, Princeton, NJ, p. 3.

8

Juvenile Courts and Services

In this chapter we will cover two related topics—youth behavior problems and Juvenile Courts and Services in America and Japan.

In discussing youth behavior problems we will undertake to describe: the difficulties encountered by the authorities with relation to the operation of motor vehicles by young people, other types of youth offenses, and some of the underlying causes of juvenile misconduct and measures taken by the police to control the problems.

The segment dealing with the Juvenile Courts and Services will in the main be a straightforward description and comparison of the two systems.

Youth Behavior Problems

Dealing with the "love affair" between young people and the motor vehicle is a problem for both Japanese and American police. Salem's young "cruisers" do not appear to be part of any gang behavior, but until a short time ago, every Friday and Saturday evening they congregated in large numbers with their cars along a section of Portland Road, called "the gut." The procedure was to proceed at stop-and-go speeds, bumper to bumper, squealing tires, racing motors, and making as much noise as possible. They would circle the area repeatedly until late into the night.

An avalanche of complaints to the mayor and city council from neighborhood residents and business owners claimed that the activity constituted a public nuisance and a serious traffic hazard. Police began issuing between 200 and 250 citations each weekend, yet this did nothing to stem the flow of cruisers. The normal traffic in the area was roughly 200 cars an hour, but on Friday and Saturday nights it ballooned to 1,600 cars an hour. Police reported a huge influx of cruisers from communities up to fifty miles away, and estimated that three-quarters of the cruisers were from outside Salem.

After studying the problem, the city council passed an ordinance especially designed to halt cruising. Police posted warning signs on the streets designated by the ordinance as "traffic congested." When a vehicle had made three round trips past a point, a police officer issued a warning. On the vehicle's fourth trip, the officer issued a citation for cruising and gave written notice that if the violator passed through the area a fifth time in an eight-hour period, the vehicle would be towed away. The ordinance is similar to one adopted by the city of Portland that is believed to have been largely responsible for ending that city's cruising problem.

At last report, the new ordinance had apparently solved the "cruising" problem in "the gut," but it resurfaced several blocks away on Lancaster Drive, a busy four-lane shopping thoroughfare, part of which is outside the city limits. The county police (sheriff's office) are now moving to enforce a newly enacted county ordinance on their portion of Lancaster Drive. It is too early to predict the outcome of the latest confrontation between the cruisers and the two police agencies.

In Japan, large young gangs called "*bosozoku*" (hot rodders) operate automobiles, as well as motorcycles, in a reckless manner, speeding, disregarding traffic signals, and illegally overtaking and passing other vehicles. They are active mainly from Saturday night to dawn Sunday, driving recklessly and illegally in swarms, endangering other traffic and the general public. According to police, about 80 percent of the *bosozoku* are under twenty years of age, and about half are dropouts from senior high school. After the road traffic law was amended in 1978 to prohibit hazardous driving, the problem seemed to abate. It soon resumed, however, and law enforcement agencies have redoubled their efforts with some success. Nevertheless, the problem persists.

Mention should also be made of other delinquent youth street gangs called "*chinpira*." These kids, wearing bell-bottomed trousers and short jackets, are found mainly in major cities. Their fields of activity include shop and auto break-ins, car thefts, "rolling" drunks, and extorting money from other adolescents, including other *chinpira*.

Curfews

Under both state law and Salem's curfew ordinance, designed to control nighttime activities of youth, people under eighteen are required to be off the streets after midnight, unless accompanied by an adult. In Kawagoe, there is no legal curfew for youths. Most Japanese schools as well as Japanese families, however, habitually have what might be called a family curfew, depending upon the age of the child. Kawagoe police generally do not send a child home unless he or she is loitering or engaging in antisocial conduct. Schools sometimes recommend a specific curfew hour to parents.

The Third Wave

In sharp contrast to the statistics for adult crime, problems with juveniles in Japan have steadily increased. In 1982, police reported a so-called "third wave" of juvenile delinquency, with previous peaks occurring in 1951 and 1964. In 1981, the proportion of juveniles (ages fourteen to twenty) among the total arrested for penal-code-related crimes was 44 percent; in 1982 it was 50.8 percent; in 1983, it was 52 percent. According to the latest available figures, the percentage of juvenile cases cleared by the police is only 28.5 percent. The comparable figures for 1982 and 1983 would be 30 percent and 30.9 percent, respectively.

The age of juvenile delinquents has also declined in recent years. Before the 1960s, juvenile crime (excluding negligent homicide) was highest among eighteen- and nineteen-year-olds, and lowest among fourteen- and fifteen-year-olds. In 1961, fourteen- and fifteen-year-olds became the group with the highest rate, with sixteen- and seventeen-year-olds in second place, while the rate of eighteen- and nineteen-year-olds actually decreased. Even more startling, the rate for juveniles aged fourteen to nineteen for 1980 was five times the adult rate.[1]

Curiously, the increase has occurred in only two offenses, larceny and embezzlement, consisting largely of such nonviolent infractions as shoplifting, bicycle theft, and unauthorized use of bicycles. Under Japanese law, the latter infraction (sometimes referred to as "joyriding" in the United States when applied to autos), is classified as embezzlement.

According to a number of Japanese sociologists and criminal justice professionals, the problem has several different causes, all traceable to deep-rooted changes in society and behavior since World War II, including urbanization, population mobility, decline of the traditional three-generation households, less neighborhood social supervision of youth, decreased moral training in the school system, increased emphasis on preparing students for entrance examinations, and increased juvenile-directed police activity replacing the traditional informal controls of social culture.

The unlikelihood of expulsion for misbehavior by students in junior high school is often cited as a reason for more attacks on junior high teachers than senior high teachers, and it is believed by Japanese educators that the difference in rates of violence is simply a function of the certainty of punishment.

Controlling Juvenile Delinquency, Japanese Style

Japanese police believe that the most effective action to prevent juvenile delinquency is to "nip it in the bud" by making "protective arrests" and giving "police guidance" (*keisatsu shidō*). This, they reason, is the best way to block the formation of habitual delinquency patterns (*shokuho shonen*).

Often blamed for the upsurge in youth crime is the powerful pressure put on Japanese schoolchildren by their parents to pass rigorous entrance examinations. An account published in the American press[2] in July 1988 tells of a fourteen-year-old Tokyo schoolboy who killed his parents and grandmother, supposedly because of family pressure to study harder. According to newspaper accounts and the boy's confession to the police, on the night of the killing his mother scolded him for not studying enough. His father also admonished him and demanded that he "study harder." The boy said that he considered killing himself as well, because he felt that he would never get into college and thus had no future.

Japanese newspaper editors have taken note of the problem. The *Yomiuri Shimbun* editorialized:

> There is a trend in our society in which parents show extraordinary interest in the development of their children's intellectual ability, but little interest in their emotional development.[3]

As part of youth police guidance services, the police have established what are termed "windows" (*madoguchi*), where juveniles and their parents or guardians may be counseled by an officer. Police have also set up experimental delinquency prevention programs in 278 high-delinquency districts where special meetings and classes are conducted in cooperation with parents and schools to prevent youths from committing delinquent acts.

The public agency responsible for activities aimed at guiding youth and preventing delinquency is the youth section (*seishōnenka*) of the city welfare department (*fukushibu*). The youth section operates the youth guidance center. The council for its management (*Seishōnen o Sodateru Shimin Kaigi*) has fifteen members representing voluntary probation officers (*hogoshi* in Japanese),[4] the instructors association, the municipal schools association, the juvenile welfare division of the city government, the city police department, and so on. It sponsors sports competitions, essay contests, international exchanges, and various group activities to foster healthier development for young people. It also publishes in a city government newspaper informative articles on how to prevent juvenile delinquency. There are 1,600 youth development members in Kawagoe.

Other groups of volunteers who aid in providing guidance for young people include the children's center management committee, which supervises the operation of the children's center, also known as the "children's castle," counselors for youth (*seishōnen sōdan-in*), youth groups liaison council (*seishōnen dantai renraku kyōgikai*), council for healthy youth development, council for youth problems, and youth protection volunteers (*shōnen hodōin*). These are comprised of 160 volunteers who periodically patrol the downtown area to see that children do not loiter in adult amusement centers or attempt to play game machines. About 70 percent are women, usually over fifty years of age. If they observe a crime, they notify the police. They wear a badge and carry identification, but do not wear a uniform.[5]

Salem

In Salem, the juvenile court is officially the "Circuit Court for Marion County, Juvenile Department," but it is often referred to simply as "family court." It is a specialized court, dealing exclusively with domestic affairs and juvenile delinquency cases, but it is part of the state court system, rather than the national system as in Japan. The concept of a separate juvenile court is believed to have originated in the United States, the first established by statute in Cook County, Illinois, in 1899. The judge is elected, not appointed. Its area of jurisdiction is Marion County.

As part of the state judicial system, Oregon family court judges are elected for a term of six years, and are subject to the so-called "recall provision" of the Oregon constitution, which provides that whenever 15 percent of the voters of the district petition for a special election, an officer may be removed from office by a majority vote. This is a seldom used provision, and so far as we could determine, has never been successfully invoked against a judge.

The only similar provision in the Japanese constitution is the requirement that all justices of the supreme court must face a popular review by the voters at the first general election of members of the house of representatives (the Diet) after their original appointment. So far, no justice has been removed from office under this provision.

In Oregon, the family court has exclusive jurisdiction over all children under eighteen years of age, or those who have committed a violation of law, or are beyond parental control, or whose behavior is dangerous, or who have been abandoned or mistreated by parents. The judge is empowered to appoint an attorney for a juvenile whose parents are indigent. The law also spells out standards required for detention facilities that separate juveniles from adult offenders. The law limits punitive detention of twelve-year-olds to eight days and only after a hearing.

A child found to be within the court's jurisdiction may be remanded to adult court if he or she is fifteen years or older. However, a child under sixteen may not be remanded unless represented by counsel at the hearing and unless the offense is murder, manslaughter, assault, rape, sodomy, or robbery.

One of the most important features of juvenile court services is the counseling and administrative staff, who are under the supervision and direction of the judge (changed to supervision by the board of county commissioners by the 1987 Oregon legislature); this staff is collectively referred to as the "Marion County Juvenile Department," which offers a wide range of family-related services, including:

- Juvenile counseling; predivorce conciliation and mediation; detailed custody studies in divorce cases; supervision of child visitations; family and marriage counseling; and parenting training classes (court-ordered group sessions).
- Supervised home detention of juvenile offenders.
- An alternative school with seven classrooms and an average of sixty students in attendance a day. Attendees are youth of both sexes who are juvenile offenders who have proved themselves disruptive in public school. A basic instructional program with a curriculum starting in middle school and extending through high school is provided. This program is intended to help the child learn appropriate classroom behavior, to permit the child to continue his or her education, and eventually to return the child to the public school system.
- Community service programs, which may include wood cutting (providing free wood to low-income families); on-the-job vocational training; and remodeling and carpentry projects.
- Mentor programs.
- Foster homes, where a youth goes to school and works on a family farm.
- Group care homes.
- Juvenile training schools, forest camps, and city camps with daytime job placement.

The typical first offender for a minor offense such as shoplifting receives a sentence (called a disposition) requiring:

1. That the stolen article be returned;
2. That the child writes an apology;
3. That the offender performs a day of community service.

If the offense is more serious, such as burglary, the offender is required to be arraigned in court before the judge and must enter a plea—either admitting or denying the charge. Disposition of this type of case might include:

- Restitution;
- An apology;
- Community service of more than a day;
- Participation in a work program.

Youth in home detention are monitored by surveillance officers from the department, who visit as many as eight homes each afternoon and evening to make sure the youth is in compliance with the court's order.

The Salem juvenile court is a much larger operation than the Kawagoe family court, in terms of both personnel and scope. With an annual budget of $3,456,000, its staff consists of approximately 100 persons, including 24 probation officers; 10 alternative program workers; 8 school instructors; 5 marriage and family counselors; 11 secretaries; 3 surveillance monitors; 25 administration supervisors and miscellaneous specialized technical personnel.

The Oregon juvenile court law authorizes the court after due notice and hearing to expunge (remove and destroy) from the official records all entries pertaining to proceedings concerning any youth who may have been brought before that court. The youth services teams in each junior high school are also considered a quasi-arm of the juvenile court.

During 1986, 4,604 Marion County juveniles were referred by police to juvenile court for disposition. Of those, 2,439 (1,849 boys, 590 girls) were handled officially and 2,165 (1,485 boys, 680 girls) unofficially. Of those handled officially, formal petitions to make the child a ward of the court were filed in 2,479 cases (the larger number of formal petitions than "official" cases is because some "unofficial" cases later become "official" ones because of subsequent events, such as new evidence). Charges included:

• 52 offenses against the state and public justice, including escape, false information, and resisting arrest;
• 194 offenses against persons;
• 98 sex-related offenses;
• 1,112 offenses against property such as burglary, theft, criminal mischief, and trespass;
• 27 fraud;
• 102 offenses against public order such as harassment, disorderly conduct, use of weapons;
• 93 offenses involving controlled substances;
• 331 offenses involving alcohol;
• 89 traffic offenses;

- 370 status offenses including protective custody;*
- 11 miscellaneous.

Kawagoe

During 1986, a total of 7,738 Kawagoe juveniles were referred to Kawagoe's family court (*Katei Saibanshō*). Of that number, 7,675 were processed and disposed of by the court. (There is no category "handled unofficially" as in Salem; the informal procedures used by Japanese police to handle minor infractions by juveniles are discussed later in this chapter.)

The number of unfinished cases reported for 1986 totalled 1,501. Kawagoe's family court does not keep separate statistics, because it is a branch of the main family court in the prefectural capital, Urawa. That makes a detailed comparison of caseloads impossible. It was estimated by Judge Kobayashi of the Kawagoe family court that 17 to 18 percent of offenders are female, which is also the national average.

Like family court in the United States, the family court of Japan is a specialized court dealing with domestic affairs and cases of juvenile delinquency, but it is part of the national court system and operates under the supervision of the national Supreme Court. It is independent from, but equivalent to, the district court in each prefecture. Its judges are appointed by the prime minister's cabinet from a list of names prepared by the Supreme Court. Judges serve a ten-year term and are eligible for reappointment.

The first juvenile court statute in Japan to follow Western models was enacted in 1900. This law was amended in 1923 to incorporate more modern sociological principles, and further major revision was made in 1949 during the Allied occupation after World War II.

The family court of Japan has many similarities with family courts in the United States, including the one in Salem. However, it has jurisdiction over anyone fourteen to twenty years of age rather than up to eighteen years, as in Oregon. Further, the Japanese family court may deal with those over twenty in special cases, such as when an adult has

---

*"Status offense" is a legal term for offenses by juveniles such as running away, smoking, being beyond parental control and so on which are punishable simply because the accused is a minor.

injured a juvenile. Under the Juvenile Law passed in 1948 juveniles subject to the Family Court's jurisdiction are classified as follows: A "juvenile offender" is a young person between the ages of fourteen and twenty who has committed a criminal offense prohibited by the Penal Code or some other statute. A "lawbreaking child" is a juvenile under the age of fourteen who has committed a criminal offense. A "pre-offense juvenile" is a young person who is in danger of becoming involved in criminal behavior. This could include running away, being beyond parental control, or associating with known juvenile delinquents or adult offenders.

A minor may be prosecuted as an adult by reason of the serious nature of the violation only when the offender is sixteen or older. An average of 13 percent of all juvenile offenders are transferred to public prosecutors for criminal prosecution as an adult.[6] Children under fourteen are primarily handled by the child guidance center (an agency under the welfare ministry), even though they may have committed an act that would constitute a criminal violation if committed by an adult.

Differences from the American Court System

Despite some basic similarities, the family courts of the United States and Japan differ in other significant ways. Perhaps the most prominent difference is the wider use of lay persons in the Japanese judicial process, with the notable exception of the absence of a jury system. Americans may be surprised to learn that up to five members of the fifteen-person Supreme Court of Japan need not be jurists so long as they have some knowledge of law and have knowledge and practical experience in business or government.[7]

Lay persons are also employed as court conciliation commissioners, court counselors, judicial commissioners, and expert commissioners, which allows the judicial system to take advantage of broad knowledge and practical experience in the settlement of legal and domestic problems and in juvenile cases. These citizens, often retirees, former business executives, lawyers, teachers, court officials, and even Buddhist priests, are part-time government employees who are paid a small fee per case. All are appointed by the Supreme Court.

The court conciliation commissioners (*chōtei-in*) play a vital role in pretrial mediation and conciliation proceedings, particularly in divorce cases. Their function is to secure an amicable settlement of civil disputes of any kind, as well as of conflicts in domestic relations matters, by recommending mutual concessions and compromise or by persuading the parties to reconcile themselves to an appropriate plan of compromise worked out by a committee of one judge and two or more commissioners. Divorce by agreement of the parties (*kyōgi rikon*) is permissible in Japan.[8]

The family court counselors (*sanyo-in*) are part of the decision-making process. They assist the family court judge in arriving at his or her decision in cases involving domestic relations, declaration of incompetency, partition of estate, and so on. Both conciliation commissioners and court counselors are chosen from the public at large upon recommendation of local officials, bar associations, and other civic organizations. Appointment is for a two-year term and carries considerable prestige. Women are particularly sought as conciliation commissioners and comprise about 40 percent of the total number.

Judicial commissioners may also assist the judge of the summary court in effecting a compromise of the parties to a civil lawsuit, or may attend the civil trial for the purpose of expressing a recommendation to the judge. Three expert commissioners, who have special knowledge and experience regarding issues before the court, may be specially appointed to assist the judge by making recommendations, particularly in landlord and tenant proceedings.

In addition to the above described involvement of lay persons, the Japanese family court differs from its American counterpart in that the accused is not normally represented by an attorney at a juvenile hearing, nor is a prosecutor in attendance. This and other due-process steps are now being considered for adoption. Also, witnesses are not normally sworn in before testifying in juvenile proceedings, and hearings are not open to the public or the press. From our inspection tour of the Kawagoe Family Court and its facilities, plus the inquiries we made on the site, it appeared that the administrative structure and support staff attached to the Kawagoe court was significantly smaller in size than that provided in Marion County.

In the juvenile hearings we attended, the court atmosphere was very informal and anything but authoritarian, except as noted below. The judge, who does not wear a judicial robe when sitting as a family court judge, was careful to ask the parties in each case if they had any objection to our presence as observers. (Incidentally, when the judge entered the courtroom, all present were commanded by the clerk to rise, "*Kiritsu!*" and to bow, "*Rei!*" to the judge!)

An unusually large number of cases—70 percent—are dismissed after or without a hearing.

The three principal sanctions used by Kawagoe's family court are probation, juvenile training school (*Shōnen-in*), and foster home (*Kyogo-in*). In disposing of a juvenile case the family court may:

- Dismiss the case without or after hearing;
- Place a juvenile under probation supervision;
- Refer to a public prosecutor for prosecution;
- Refer to a juvenile training school.

The Juvenile Classification Home

The juvenile classification home in Japan was established as an institution in 1949. There are fifty-two such homes, one located wherever there is a family court, and they are administered by the Ministry of Justice. They conduct prehearing examinations, investigations, and classification for juveniles referred to them by the family court. A juvenile is detained for a period not to exceed four weeks; his or her behavior is observed using all modern methods of investigation, including physical examination, psychiatry, psychology, and sociology. The juvenile's home environment is also examined.

A juvenile is rarely committed to a training school before another form of community-based treatment is tried, such as probation, except where the offense is a felony such as homicide, rape, or arson. Family court judges go to great lengths to avoid stigmatizing the offender by sending him or her to training school. Sentences are imposed in less than one percent of the cases. No incarceration is imposed unless it is necessary for the juvenile's own protection or unless there is no appropriate disposition that will protect public safety.

Once sentenced to training school, the youth is given standard school instruction. In some instances, training school inmates may cultivate agricultural crops that are used to feed the institution's inmates, but there is no manufacturing of products for sale on the open market, as is the case of adult and young adult correctional institutions in Japan.

On the effectiveness of these training schools, Judge Akihiko Kobayashi of the Kawagoe family court, observed:

Even if these sanctions are called protective measures, they are very effective in getting the young offender's attention and cooperation. In addition, they have a salutary effect as an example to other delinquents and potential delinquents.

It is interesting to note that Japanese judges apparently do not use one of the penalties most frequently used by American judges—requiring the performance of community service.

Virtually all probation and parole supervision in Japan, both adult and juvenile, is performed by volunteers, who are carefully selected men and women appointed by the Ministry of Justice in Tokyo and supervised by the professional staff. Unlike the Salem system, the family court in Japan does not operate an alternative school for confined juveniles. It does, however, operate a traffic school for juvenile motor vehicle law violators. Offenders are required by court order to attend a three-hour class one day each week for a month. A parent or legal guardian of the youthful offender must also attend each session. There were between fifty and sixty youth and parents in attendance at the school on one of the days we visited. Instruction typically begins with a traffic safety film, followed by lectures from a traffic police officer, a juvenile probation officer, and finally by a judge. According to Judge Kobayashi, the most frequent juvenile traffic offense is operating a vehicle without an operator's license. If the first-time violator completes the required course, the traffic charge is usually dismissed.

When Judge Kobayashi was asked about some of the underlying causes of juvenile delinquency seen in his court, he listed these:

• Family breakdown and family failure; disputes between parents; divorce; and the increasing number of single-parent families.
• School dropouts.
• Peer pressure.
• Substance abuse—glue or paint-thinner sniffing, but almost never amphetamines, barbiturates, or marijuana.

Finally, we asked Judge Kobayashi's probation officer about recent developments in juvenile delinquency. He offered the following comments:

- The age of delinquents has gone down. In other words, juvenile delinquents are getting younger.
- Classroom violence has increased in the past fifteen years, particularly in middle school.
- Female delinquency has increased—in fact, doubled—between 1975 and 1985.
- The number of major offenses—homicide, rape, robbery, etc.— has not increased, but lesser offenses such as shoplifting and petty theft have increased.

Having taken law courses at University of Notre Dame Law School in South Bend, Indiana, Judge Kobayashi was knowledgeable concerning current crime and delinquency problems in the United States. When asked what crime prevention steps he might recommend for U.S. consideration, he mentioned tighter gun control legislation, and proper nurture of children of divorced parents.

A Young American's Adventure

A strong testimonial to the effectiveness of the sanctions mentioned by Judge Kobayashi comes from a totally unexpected source—a young American businessman, whom we shall call James Green, who as a teenager ran afoul of the Japanese police.

When Green was seventeen years old, he was attending a prep school in Tokyo before he planned to take the entrance examinations in hopes of being accepted into a prestigious Japanese university. His bizarre experience with the Japanese criminal justice system began shortly after he formed a casual acquaintance with two other young men, one a Japanese and the other a Caucasian artist. Green's new friends were definitely on the wild side, as later events would soon reveal.

In due course, all three came to the attention of the authorities and were held for investigation for possible involvement in the smuggling of marijuana into Japan. Although Green, also a Caucasian, maintains that he was not involved in any illegal acts and was not a drug user, abuser, or trafficker, he was subjected to an intensive search and investigation by the Tokyo police. They searched his person, as well as his personal effects and tiny living quarters, but failed to find any contraband. Nevertheless, he was taken into custody, handcuffed, and transported to the police lockup, where, as a juvenile, he was placed in an individual cell away from adult detainees.

Within twenty-four hours, the American embassy was advised by the police of his detention, as was his American mother, who was working in Japan at the time. More investigation followed; his interrogators made extensive inquiries into his family background. They were particularly interested in how he managed to become involved with his questionable companions. He was held for two weeks while the police continued their unrelenting questioning and was then charged with "being a minor in need of guidance" because of his association with antisocial companions. (All interrogations were carried on in Japanese which Green spoke fluently.) At length he was taken to the Tokyo prosecutor's office, where he and many other defendants waited to be interviewed.

The prosecutor questioned him briefly, then informed him that he would be taken before the family court judge. According to Green, a competent lawyer was appointed to represent him at the expense of the Japanese government. (He had been advised by American friends that hiring a private attorney to represent him would not help his situation.) The youthful American then embarked on what might be called the second stage of his ordeal. He was sentenced by the family court judge to be confined in the juvenile "repentance" center at Nerima (*Nerima Kanbetsu Sho*), located in Tokyo. There he was confined for four more weeks, along with about 1,800 other inmates.

The "guidance" (*shidō*) regimen at Nerima was anything but easy. In fact, according to Green, it was both strict and rigorous, but humane. Breakfast, consisting of boiled barley, miso soup, *kamaboko* (fish sausage), and occasionally cooked whale meat, was served at 5:00 A.M. Then came a battery of written psychological tests in English to determine his mental condition. Four times a week he underwent a ninety-minute "guidance" session with a psychologist/counselor, for the purpose of encouraging him to "repent" and become a better person.

Green was given a daily writing assignment on topics such as why antisocial behavior is harmful not only to society but to the individual as well. He was also required to take part daily in ninety minutes of calisthenics and to study Japanese textbooks on Japanese and world history, classical literature, science, and mathematics.

He was weighed once a week by his guards. Contrary to his expectations, he gained weight on this spartan diet. This pleased the guards, who said, "If you gain weight, it shows that you have repented!"

After two weeks at Nerima, Green was brought back before the family court judge and informed that he had two possibilities for his future: first, the charge could be dismissed and he would be deported and never allowed to return to Japan, or he could submit himself to Japanese justice in the usual manner, including possible future probation. If he successfully completed the conditions of probation, the record of his arrest and confinement would be expunged.

He chose the second alternative, and there was never any trial as such. At this point, however, an unforeseen development occurred: a new group of juvenile offenders was booked into the Nerima center, including five or six belligerent, streetwise young Korean-Japanese offenders being held on serious charges. Although Green was, according to the rules of Japanese custom, the senior prisoner in the unit, some of the Koreans refused to recognize his seniority right, which consisted mainly of being seated at the head of the table at mealtimes. One complained, "No round-eyed guy is going to be over us!" Green refused to give ground, and an altercation ensued that required intervention of the guards before it could finally be quelled. As a result, both participants in the encounter were placed in solitary confinement for two weeks.

At the end of his four-week confinement at Nerima, Green was released and placed on probation for one year. He was required to report to his probation officer once a month, to give an account of his conduct and satisfy the probation officer that he was conducting himself in a proper manner and was not involved in any law violations.

None the worse for his experience, Green successfully completed his period of probation without further incident and is now a respected businessman living in the United States. Surprisingly, he expresses not the slightest animosity or resentment for the rigorous program he underwent at the hands of the Japanese authorities (Green says he was innocent; that he was never charged with possession or trafficking):

> It was strict and rigorous, but it was fair and humane. Very frankly, the confinement and counseling were probably what I needed at that stage of my life. It probably kept me from becoming involved in any serious antisocial behavior the remainder of my young life.

Reflecting on his experience, the older and wiser Green says that most of all he was impressed with the fact that all juvenile justice personnel attached to the center were working together with one objective—to achieve a complete understanding of the family background of young offenders. He was also impressed by the sensitivity of the police detectives, counselors, guards, and court personnel to the feelings of the family. According to Green, an enormous amount of staff time, certainly by U.S. standards, was spent in ascertaining all pertinent facts of his family from his mother and himself. Likewise, all officials stressed his need for repentance, reeducation, and resocialization, and took pains to inculcate in him a sense of self-discipline: "Everyone took part in the process of trying to turn me around."

As a result of this incident and continued study, we are convinced that American juvenile and corrections officials and counselors can profit from careful study of the behavior modification techniques used by the Japanese in successfully turning around significant numbers of juvenile and adult offenders. In short, the Japanese system can work!

Comparisons between
Japan and America

Japan and America take fundamentally different approaches to the question of how best to control and prevent juvenile delinquency. The Japanese have tacitly adopted a policy of "nipping juvenile delinquency in the bud" by giving the young first offender a brief jolt with a foretaste of the juvenile justice system. Sometimes the Japanese come down hard on the youths, at least by American standards. But, as Judge Kobayashi pointed out, if first offenders get a bit of a jolt at the outset—albeit a mild sanction—they are less likely to embark on further delinquent behavior. A psychologist might term this policy an "aversion technique."

On the other hand, the prevailing American approach is vastly different. The policy of most Oregon police and juvenile justice agencies is to issue a warning to the juvenile who commits a nonserious first offense, particularly a status offense such as running away, curfew violation, smoking, and so on. In addition, the child's parents or guardian are frequently called to pick up their child at police headquarters, instead of at juvenile hall after detention and processing.

The Oregon police officer at the scene is given a fair amount of discretion in these kinds of preliminary decisions. For a subsequent offense, the police and the juvenile justice system generally follow a policy that could be described as escalating consequences for repeated violations. As previously pointed out, in Salem in 1986, 26.5 percent of all criminal violation arrests were juveniles, while in Kawagoe 68 percent were juveniles! Does this mean that Kawagoe young people are twice as inclined to engage in antisocial behavior as Salem's youth, or on the other hand, are Salem police more tolerant of juvenile infractions? Or is it simply a matter of there being more rules for young people to violate in Kawagoe than in Salem?

Perhaps the most plausible explanation of this sizable disparity is the wide difference in police policies and practices in relation to juveniles. Typically, a detained youth is brought to the neighborhood kōban or sometimes to a police station, the parents are notified, and all are given "police guidance" (*keisatsu shidō*) on their future conduct. Although in some cases the youth's school may be notified, the offender is usually not remanded to family court except for a serious offense. School punishments are frequently more severe than either police reprimand or family court dispositions.

A drastic new proposal suggested by some American sociologists and criminologists is at the opposite end of the spectrum from the Japanese approach. After studying prevailing U.S. delinquency patterns in considerable detail, their view is that current American methods have had little effectiveness in preventing delinquency or rehabilitating youth. They have put forward the idea that minimal intervention or even leaving delinquent youth alone, wherever possible, may be the better policy.[9]

In the final analysis, government leaders and criminal and juvenile justice policy makers must decide crucial questions: What is the best approach in the long run for controlling and preventing delinquency and crime? What combinations of or alternatives to the Japanese or the American approaches are applicable?[10]

Notes

1. Government of Japan, Ministry of Justice, Research and Training Institute, "Summary of White Paper[s] on Crime" for 1982, 1983 and 1989, Tokyo, Japan.

2. "Family Pressure May Have Led to Murders," *Oregonian* (Portland, OR), July 22, 1988, p. A11.

3. As quoted in the *Oregonian*, op. cit.

4. Japan's voluntary probation and parole officer system (VPO) is discussed in Chapter 10.

5. Richard Terrill, *World Criminal Justice Systems* (Cincinnati, OH: Anderson Publishing Co., 1984), p. 288.

6. "Guide to the Family Court of Japan," Supreme Court of Japan, Tokyo (1987); "Thirty-two Years of the Family Courts of Japan," Supreme Court of Japan, Tokyo (1982); Richard Terrill, *World Criminal Justice Systems* (Cincinnati, OH: Anderson Publishing Co., 1984), p. 288.

7. "Justice in Japan," an official pamphlet issued by the Supreme Court of Japan, Tokyo (1987); R.Y. Thornton, "Training Lawyers and Judges in New Japan," *Judicature* 58, 3, pp. 128–33.

8. For a general discussion of dispute resolution in contemporary Japan see Takeo Kawashima, "Dispute Settlement in Japan," in "The Social Organization of Law," D. Black and M. Mileski, eds. (New York: Academic Press, 1973).

9. See Edwin M. Schur, *Radical Nonintervention: Rethinking the Delinquency Problem* (Englewood Cliffs, NJ: Prentice-Hall, 1973); Don C. Gibbons, *Delinquent Behavior* (Englewood Cliffs, NJ: Prentice-Hall, 1981).

10. For further readings on both juvenile delinquency control and the justice system in Japan see M. Yokoyama, "Delinquency Control Programs in the Community in Japan," *International Journal of Comparative and Applied Criminal Justice* 6, 2 (1981): 169; Haruo Noshima, "Individual Prediction Tables for Further Delinquency Used by Japanese/Juvenile Police," *International Criminal Police Review* 37 (1979): 118; T. Fujiwara, "Juvenile Delinquency and Its Environment in Japan," United Nations Asia Far East Institute for the Prevention of Crime (UNAFEI), Report for 1978, Resource Material Series No. 14, Fuchu, Tokyo, Japan; H. Tanaka, ed., *The Japanese Legal System* (Tokyo: University of Tokyo Press, 1977); H. Haraguchi, "New Aspects of Juvenile Delinquency in Tokyo and the Role of the Public," United Nations Asia Far East Institute for the Prevention of Crime (UNAFEI), Report for 1971, Resource Material Series No. 3, Fuchu, Tokyo, Japan; John M. Maki, *Court and Constitution in Japan* (Seattle, WA: University of Washington Press, 1964); A. Didrick Castberg, *Japanese Criminal Justice* (New York: Praeger Publishers, 1990); M. Shikita and S. Tsuchiya, "The Juvenile Justice System in Japan. Juvenile Justice: An International Survey," Publication No. 12 (Rome), United Nations Social Defense Research Institute, 1976, p. 55.

9

Auxiliary Crime Prevention Services

Salem

Many private and governmental agencies provide high-caliber auxiliary crime prevention services in Salem. Some of the more salient of these are discussed below.

Operation Head Start is a federally financed program designed to eradicate the cycle of poverty in low-income families by providing nurturing aid in a homelike environment to children three to five years old. Head Start also provides parenting education by teaching new parents, many of whom are single, parenting skills. Topics covered include: children's needs, the importance of a drug- and alcohol-free environment, behavior management, positive discipline techniques, prevention of child abuse and neglect, single parenting, support groups for parents and children, special parenting situations (including blended families), preventive health, nutrition, life skills for parents including financial planning and money management. A year-long commitment is required for participation, and the activities offered range from creative playing with the child to sessions with professional staff to talk about issues such as child abuse and drug or alcohol addiction.

The value of this program in giving children a better start in school has been demonstrated in several studies, including the Perry Preschool Project described in Chapter 1, which also showed that subject children were less prone to delinquent behavior. Another benefit indicated by the Perry research is a significant increase in child-family bonding.

The Gleaning Project, related to Head Start, offers a nutrition program presently serving 254 children from low-income families in Marion and adjoining Polk county. The program includes teaching parenting skills.

The Breakthrough Foundation, an interesting nonprofit organization formed in 1980 in the San Francisco Bay area, uses the concept of community intervention into the problems of high-risk youth to produce not only a "breakthrough" in their lives, but also to create new possibilities for community response to the entire phenomenon of youth at risk. Among its endeavors is the *Youth at Risk* program, which extends over two years and includes three primary components:

1. A start-up period during which volunteers are trained to organize, raise funds, and produce the program.
2. A ten-day program, which includes physical exercise to build self-esteem and trust for youth and youth agency staff.
3. A one-year follow-through program.

In 1984, the Breakthrough Foundation engaged the Center for Applied Social Research of the graduate school of Claremont College to evaluate the effectiveness of the Youth at Risk program. The study found that youth completing the program engaged in less criminal activity, accomplished more in school, got along better with their parents, and increased their employment chances and work habits. The Foundation is presently working with law enforcement groups and state and county agencies in several cities across the country.

Perhaps the most unique of all volunteer crime prevention organizations operating in Salem is the *Victim-Offender Reconciliation Project* (VORP). According to Dr. Hugh Dierker, a kindly, unassuming retired physician who is the volunteer coordinator of the project, VORP is designed to get the victim and the offender to work out their feelings through mediation, conciliation, and restitution.

Cases, most of which involve property offenses, are generally referred to VORP by a court or a probation officer. A coordinator assigns each case to one of fifteen local mediators, and at first the parties are approached separately. The objective, however, is to get them together. Then, when agreement has been reached, a contract is drawn up and signed by both parties. The parents of a young offender are allowed to be present at the session, but may not participate in discussions or decisions. The mediator never compels a solution or forces a settlement. Dr. Dierker said that approximately 80 to 85 percent of the contracts are fulfilled. The program is financed in part by small grants from the Mennonite and Lutheran churches and by the county juvenile services commission.[1]

One of the most extensive programs for youth recreation and physical development in Salem is operated by the city parks and recreation department under Ed Jochim, superintendent of recreation. The department organizes teams and events, as well as furnishing playing areas for baseball, soccer, football, track, and basketball.

A similar recreation program is operated as a community school program by the Salem-Keizer school district. Activities are on schoolgrounds, after school hours, and during school vacations, especially during the long summer vacation. In addition, the community school program provides after-school childcare to meet the needs of so-called "latch key" children—children whose parents both work and who have no after-school supervision. The district provides six coordinators in the neighborhoods who assist local volunteers in organizing and carrying on all programs. (The agencies mentioned below that are marked with an asterisk (*) are funded in part by United Way of the Mid-Willamette Valley, formerly Community Chest.)

Northwest Human Services* operates seven programs, including court-mandated counseling for controlling family violence, crime prevention counseling, a twenty-four-hour parents anonymous hotline, and an employment service for ex-offenders.

The Family Resource Council is concerned with child abuse in all its forms; FRC sponsors "parents anonymous" groups, a switchboard for help, crisis intervention, and runaway youth project. The program received 9,000 calls last year.

The Marion-Polk-Yamhill Council on Alcoholism renders expert assistance to persons suffering from alcohol abuse. It also operates an ex-offender employment service.

Also providing valuable crime prevention programs are the Salem Boys and Girls Club,* YMCA,* YWCA,* Campfire,* Girl Scouts,* and Boy Scouts of America.*

The Salem Boys and Girls Club (formerly the Salem Boys Club), now has a membership that is 35 percent female. Targeting at-risk and high-risk youngsters, it presently serves 1,500 children in the Salem area and an average of more than 300 a day on a drop-in basis. Its major athletic programs are basketball and football, and some 400 citizen volunteers are engaged as instructors and aides in its numerous programs. According to Lloyd Tolle, executive director, 75 percent of the youth belonging to the club do not belong to any other organization. The membership fee is only five dollars a year.

The Salem YMCA operates a wide range of family and youth recreational programs, childcare, day care for infants and preschool children, and parenting training classes. It also operates the only big brother-big sister program (BBS) in the area. The BBS has a lengthy waiting list and is presently suffering from a serious lack of volunteer big brothers and big sisters. (In Japan, BBS is one of the major voluntary organizations in the treatment of juvenile offenders. Its alumni are a prolific source of volunteer probation officers serving adult offenders.) Other programs of the YMCA include aquatics, camping, childcare and development, family life, handball, racquetball, youth programs, and youth sports. According to executive director John Mistkawi, the facilities and programs of the "Y" are available at minimal cost or no cost to families or youth unable to pay regular membership fees.

The Salem YWCA operates a similar range of outstanding crime-prevention-related programs primarily for girls and women, including the highly regarded YWCA-Salem-Keizer school district alternative school for teenage parents. The YWCA has also been active in helping Southeast Asian refugee families and their children adjust to new lives in Salem. In Salem, the YMCA and the YWCA are open to both men and women.

Campfire, Girl Scouts, and Boy Scouts of America are all well established, internationally known programs that are making special efforts to reach disadvantaged youth in the communities they serve. All provide scholarships to youth whose families would otherwise be financially unable to allow their children to become members and participate in their various programs.

The Mid-Valley Crisis Center* is a nonprofit corporation committed to preventing problems of domestic and sexual violence against women and children. It operates a twenty-four-hour hotline for victims of violence and provides battered and abused women and children with shelter, emergency transportation, food, clothing, counseling, support, advocacy, and children's programs.

Narcotics Anonymous (NA) is a praiseworthy nonprofit fellowship for recovering addicts who meet regularly to help each other stay drug-free. It has a religious but nonsectarian component. In 1987, the group had its second annual state convention in Salem. Portland was the site of the NA World Conference in September 1990. Alcoholics Anonymous (AA), a more familiar name to many, has long performed a similarly invaluable service to recovering alcoholics. Narcotics Anonymous employs many of the same successful techniques pioneered by AA, which is continuing to render its services in Salem with exemplary results.

Kidspace Collective is a parent-owned day care cooperative for preschool children. Parents contribute to the cooperative by performing odd jobs at the facility, ranging from assisting teachers to cleaning the premises. Marion-Polk Foster Parents* offers assistance to foster parents who are housing foster children with special needs. It also provides resources to improve foster children's lives. Poyama Services* provides counseling and treatment services for at-risk children and their families on an outpatient basis. Salem Area Family Counseling Service* provides counseling services on personal, marital, or family problems to persons of any age. Services include assessment and evaluation services, and long- and short-term psychotherapy, and crisis intervention.

Willamette Valley Youth Shelter* provides temporary shelter, emotional support, and related services to boys and girls ten to eighteen years (the average age is fourteen) on referral from Marion County family court or children's services division. All youths referred to the shelter are technically wards of the court and come from disrupted family situations.

The Salvation Army* provides a wide range of social services with a definite crime prevention component, including temporary family assistance (emergency food, overnight lodging, and financial assistance). Longer-term housing is also available, including service to ex-offenders to tie in with a supervised job search program. A Salvation Army chaplain is assigned to the prison system to work with persons in prison and after release. Toys for children of prisoners are provided at Christmas time. Persons in need of drug and alcohol counseling are referred for treatment to the Army's adult rehabilitation center in Portland, where two long-term, cost-free programs are provided. These are often beneficial even after years of problem drinking and drug abuse.

The Union Gospel Mission in Salem conducts similar worthwhile programs, also operating with an accompanying religious emphasis, stressing spiritual values in aid of their rehabilitation efforts.

An exceptionally effective specialized crime prevention organization is *Mothers Against Drunk Driving* (MADD). Organized nationwide, MADD is a group of mothers who became concerned over the number of people killed on the highways by drunk drivers, and by what they viewed as the failure of legislators, courts, and other public officers to pass and enforce laws to deal with the problem. Their activities in Oregon include:

• Legislative advocacy—MADD has been instrumental in the passage of new Oregon laws against drinking and driving. These include a mandatory one-year suspension of a driver's license for all juveniles convicted of any drug or alcohol offense and immediate ninety-day suspension of the driver's license of anyone who fails (or refuses to take) a breath test. The latter provision also contains a mandatory minimum penalty of either forty-eight hours in jail or eighty hours of community service upon conviction.

• Judicial monitoring—MADD observes court proceedings to ensure that the laws relating to "driving under the influence" are enforced.

• Public education—Members of MADD speak to groups of all sizes on the consequences of driving while under the influence of alcohol or drugs. The group also sponsors and supports numerous public awareness campaigns such as "project graduation," "No thanks, I'm driving," "red ribbon campaign," poster/essay contests, and an annual candlelight memorial for victims.

• Victims' assistance—MADD offers emotional support to victims by providing information and making referrals. The organization also successfully worked for the passage of Oregon's 1986 victims' bill of rights.

• Networking—MADD networks with other Oregon agencies to reduce drinking and driving, working with the state traffic safety commission, police departments, state mental health department, and community task forces.

Kawagoe

In Kawagoe, the unit of government that provides counseling services (*jidō sōdansho*) is a branch of the public welfare department (*kōsei sho*). As with the family court, the Kawagoe counseling center is a branch of the main center located at the prefectural capital. The center deals with youth under fourteen with behavioral problems in a bright, cheerful building in Kawagoe. Typical youth problems include fighting, stealing, running away, and refusing to accept parental control. The staff meets to discuss cases once a week, and it also dispenses advice to parents.

Children are usually referred by the police, parents, or occasionally, by teachers. If the child is beyond parental control, he may be sent to a foster home (*seto oya*) or to the juvenile home (*kyogo-in*), where the usual stay is a year to eighteen months and parental consent is required. Approximately 50 percent of the cases involve theft, and 80 percent of the referrals are boys. Family background is investigated first, then a psychological workup is done, along with examination of the youth's school background and behavior. In many cases, the youth is found to have two or three distinct behavior problems. Next, a caseworker visits the family.

About the trends in referrals, Minoru Hashimoto, director of the center, offered the following comments:

> We are seeing more school dropouts. Economic forces seem to be at work. In order to acquire a family home, both parents are in the work force. As a result, children are not receiving the necessary supervision. The high cost of housing is indirectly responsible for an increase in juvenile delinquency.
>
> Also with increasing frequency we are encountering a lack of cooperation from parents, particularly in keeping their appointments at the center.

Enumerating what he sees as the causes of juvenile delinquency, Mr. Hashimoto listed the following:

- Family breakdown and family failure.
- School failure: an increasing number of the youth we are dealing with today are dropouts. He is unemployed. Often he joins the gangster element, the so-called *boryokudan*. If he is attending school, there is no such problem.
- Influence of violence on TV and violent comic books, which are easily available from vending machines.

• Peer pressure from companions who are also dropouts and delin-quents.

• Affluence: parents are giving their children anything money can buy, creating unrealistic expectations in children.

Note

1. For a general discussion of dispute resolution in contemporary Japan, see Takeo Kawashima, ed., "Dispute Settlement in Japan," in *The Social Organization of Law*, D. Black and M. Mileski (New York: Academic Press, 1973).

10

Penal and Correctional Institutions

It is probably safe to say that the average American citizen considers the function of a penal institution to be to punish the offender for his or her criminal behavior, rather than to educate and rehabilitate, or to motivate the individual to refrain from future criminal acts. In other words, most people give scant consideration—if any—to the value and need of carrying on crime prevention education inside correctional institutions, as the Japanese do.

No doubt there are individuals in politics, government, and even the criminal justice system itself who take the same view; nevertheless, to exclude crime prevention as a function of penal institutions is both short-sighted and wrong. Incarceration and treatment can, in fact, be important components of crime prevention.

Why is this important? Quite simply, if a penal institution provides enlightened and practical treatment programs—including vocational training—that "turn around" or prevent even a small number of offenders from continuing to pursue a life of crime, it is clearly worth the cost to the taxpayers and to the prospective crime victims.

Salem

Of all Oregon penal institutions, Oregon State Correctional Institution (OSCI), located three miles east of Salem, most nearly resembles *Kawagoe Shōnen Keimusho*, Kawagoe's regional youth prison. Originally opened in 1959 as a medium- to maximum-security correctional institution for men under age twenty-six, OSCI has been hit in recent years with the same massive population explosion that has affected all correctional facilities in Oregon. As a result, it has been forced to "open the gates" to accommodate many more prisoners and to house older inmates as well. Although designed to accommodate 476 youth offenders, today a total of 1,025 inmates are confined there. The current age spread is seventeen to forty, with a few physically handicapped prisoners over forty. OSCI receives all physically handicapped offenders sentenced to the state correctional system.

A total of 140 correctional officers are assigned to OSCI, approximately ninety on day shift (8 A.M. to 4 P.M.), twenty-two on swing shift (4 P.M. to midnight), and fourteen on the so-called graveyard shift (midnight to 8 A.M.). Total staff of all types at OSCI numbers 247.

The Oregon constitution provides that "Laws for the punishment of crime shall be founded on principles of reformation, and not of vindictive justice" (Article I, Sec. 15). In keeping with this policy, the principal aim of Oregon's correctional institutions is to restore inmates to useful citizenship. Opportunities for self-improvement are available at OSCI, including development of steady work habits and completion of academic education and vocational skills. However, the extreme overcrowding hinders the attainment of individualized treatment, and some 250 inmates are reported to be without any form of work inside the institution. OSCI formerly operated a farm program with 440 head of beef cattle, but this program is now a part of the farm annex of the state penitentiary.

Prison Conditions

Prison security is exceptionally tight at OSCI, compared to correctional institutions nationwide. There have been only three escapes from inside OSCI in the past ten years. The recidivism rate, however, is another matter. Today, recidivism—defined as inmates who are returned to OSCI for various violations of parole or for new offenses—is presently 50 to 66 percent, according to John King, superintendent of vocational training at OSCI. King attributes part of this high reincarceration rate to the severe overcrowding: prisoners are often released early in order to make cells available for new arrivals. According to King, "Overcrowding has resulted not only in double-celling, but with the housing of many prisoners in former recreation rooms which have been converted into dormitories."

More than 90 percent of the average 700 men released from OSCI each year are under parole supervision until discharged. Inmates are transferred to a separate facility, the correctional division release center, for release programming, where they are allowed conditional passes for outside work, job search, and other personal business in order to prepare them economically as well as psychologically for reentry into the outside community.

Unlike OSCI itself, there is a surprisingly high escape rate from the release center, according to Robert Fleming, chief of release services, who says: "In an average month, eleven inmates will 'walk away,' eighteen will fail to return from temporary leave, and fifty-six will 'abscond.' The latter category are prerelease offenders on authorized leave status who suddenly 'become unavailable' for supervision by release center personnel." This adds up to a grand total of eighty-five "escapes" in an average month. According to Fleming, a career correctional administrator, this abnormally high rate of unauthorized departures is due to the absence of any penal sanction for such violations. This, in turn, is the result of an acute and widespread lack of jail space, not only in Salem but throughout Oregon.

Vocational Education

The vocational training program at OSCI is well equipped and probably the best in the entire Oregon correctional system, according to its director, John King. Training is provided in air conditioning, refrigeration, auto body and fender, automotive repair, baking, barbering, building maintenance, carpentry and cabinet making, food preparation, drafting, printing, small engine repair, welding, meat cutting, basic electricity, house wiring, and janitorial and custodial service (called orderly training).

The programs are all competency-based and are designed for progress on an individual basis, with program lengths varying from five to eighteen months. Fifteen slots are available to OSCI in an apprenticeship program for training in a wide variety of vocational pursuits. In addition, trainees in welding, drafting, printing, and small engine repair may obtain community college credit toward an associate degree in science or credit toward a one-year certificate in the various trades.

An average of 250 inmates are enrolled in vocational educational programs, and there is usually a waiting list of another 80 to 120. The dropout rate is approximately 20 to 25 percent. Vocational instructors are salaried employees and are scheduled for six student contact hours per day (8 A.M. to 11:20 A.M. and 1:20 P.M. to 4 P.M.).

Asked to express an opinion on some of the underlying reasons resulting in imprisonment of the scores of trainees he has known during twelve years with the vocational education program, John King said:

> Probably the biggest single contributing fact is drug abuse and drug dependency. Second, the subcultures previously frequented by the inmates accept imprisonment and incarceration without shame. Third, most if not all of these young men were immature—they wanted material things and they wanted them now. They were impulsive, taking whatever they wanted without any thought of the consequences of their behavior.
>
> All shared another characteristic—short-term goals, seldom thinking more than a couple of days ahead. They wanted immediate rewards.

When asked how he would correct this, King, a thoughtful professional probably in his forties, said:

> We need to mount a massive, intensive war against drug traffic. We must find ways to counter the prevailing materialistic, antiwork ethic of these offenders—that they can get things without having to work for them.
>
> We must teach our youth that they must work for what they get—like what the civilian conservation corps programs and the Works Progress Administration of the Great Depression [1930s] taught our young men of that era. These programs taught great numbers of our population a work ethic—that a decent living was not just going to be handed to them on a silver platter—that they had to work for what they received from society. We must once again reestablish and inculcate the work ethic in our society.
>
> So many of these young offenders that I have seen have never developed a work ethic. Unfortunately, many have not acquired a work ethic while they have been at OSCI. I think of one prisoner who said, "Why should I work at some trade when I can take in twenty thousand dollars a day dealing drugs?"
>
> Another offender, who had worked as a pimp and claimed to have had a dozen young prostitutes working for him, said, "I can take in five thousand dollars on an average Saturday night. Why should I spend my time working in a trade that you want me to learn?"

Both men regarded their imprisonment as only a temporary inconvenience and simply part of the cost of conducting their unlawful businesses.

Kawagoe

Foremost among the correctional facilities in the Kawagoe area is the regional youth prison (*Shōnen Keimusho*). As with all other prisons in Japan, it is part of the national correctional system operated by the Ministry of Justice. Established at its present site in 1969, it primarily serves youth up to the age of twenty-one. Since 1972, however, it has served a few offenders between the ages of twenty-one and twenty-six who have not been previously imprisoned. It currently houses a population of 1,371, and the average inmate stay is one year to eighteen months.

Prison Conditions

Unlike Oregon, there is presently no overcrowding problem in Japan, except in women's prisons, where the problem is due to an increase in female offenders sentenced to imprisonment.

In the early years following the Meiji Restoration (1867), the Japanese prison system adopted certain methods and techniques from other European prison systems, notably those of England and France. As with other borrowings of that period, Japan's leaders always made numerous changes to the systems they imported to reflect traditional Japanese values and culture patterns.[1]

The manner in which correctional services are administered in Japan's Ministry of Justice is particularly noteworthy. Institution operations are handled by the Corrections Bureau, while noninstitutional corrections matters are handled by the Rehabilitation Bureau. We were especially impressed that "rehabilitation" (*keimukan*) is deemed important enough to rate its own separate bureau equal in status to "operations" in the national justice ministry! The Rehabilitation Bureau is responsible for probation and parole (both adult and juvenile), community-based corrections, appointment of volunteer probation and parole officers, and after-care services (see the section on "Parole and Probation Volunteers" later in this chapter). It is also responsible for the ministry's crime prevention programs. Another agency within the Rehabilitation Bureau is the National Offenders Prevention and Rehabilitation Committee, which makes recommendations to the ministry regarding pardons, reduction or remission of sentences, and restoration of civil rights. It provides oversight for the work of eight district prevention and rehabilitation commissions. District commissions determine the granting of paroles, functioning in essentially the same way as parole boards in the United States.

A distinctive feature of Japanese corrections is the well-developed classification system and the absence of work release and conjugal visits programs. After prisoners have been psychologically evaluated and oriented to prison life, they are sent to a regional center, where they are classified according to background, criminal history, seriousness of offense, and type of treatment indicated. A treatment program is drawn up for each inmate, using classification categories for assignment and treatment. Classification is directly tied to the treatment process for each individual. However, the main emphasis is on maintenance of order within each institution. First offenders are kept from association with older and habitual offenders. Serious traffic offenders (e.g., vehicular homicide offenders, and drunk drivers) are confined in separate prisons. Prostitutes are not imprisoned but are sent to women's guidance homes for rehabilitation, including job training. A prisoner is usually assigned to a community cell and begins his term in the lowest or fourth grade. He may, with good behavior and change of attitude, progress to first grade (better quarters, maximum freedom, and privileges) as he works his way up to his time for release.

Even with all these exemplary programs and efficiencies, overall recidivism among incarcerated offenders in Japan may be in excess of 50 percent, depending on how the term is defined and the period covered in the computation.

Kawagoe prison warden Toyofumi Yoshinaga gave the following breakdown of offenses for which youths were incarcerated:

Theft: 30 percent
Drug-related: 30 percent
Robbery: 8 percent
Sex-related: 8 percent
Traffic: 5 percent
Homicides: 3 percent
Miscellaneous: 16 percent

Approximately 27 percent of released inmates are returned to the institution for various infractions such as parole violations or new offenses.

A number of outside groups as well as individuals come to the prison regularly to meet with inmates and assist in their rehabilitation. Foremost is the Women's Association for Rehabilitation Aid (*Kōsei Hogo Fujinkai*), a group of some twenty women who give birthday parties for the inmates, put on folk dancing (such as *Bōn*) exhibitions and festivals, and in general try to befriend prisoners. In addition, religious leaders and other individuals give counseling and teach. Interestingly, one of the most popular courses is *zazen,* a kind of religious meditation taught by a Zen Buddhist monk who comes to the institution on a regular basis.

Corridors were neat, clean, and very orderly, but the general conditions, while perhaps not harsh by some standards, would doubtless seem harsh to Oregon inmates. For example, the cells are usually not heated, although in some prisons inmates may earn transfer to heated cells by demonstrating satisfactory progress and adjustment to institution programs. Some institution rules, programs, and conditions such as unheated cells, restrictions on visitors, letters, beards, and long hair and reduction of calories in the violator's meals would doubtless be challenged in U.S. courts as a violation of both federal and state constitutional provisions against cruel and unusual punishment. No smoking or unnecessary talking is permitted during working hours or at meal times.

The atmosphere is militaristic—something like a U.S. Marine boot camp—with a good measure of military-style close order drill an important part of the regimen. Maintaining a safe, effective, therapeutic atmosphere and environment within the institution at all times is the paramount consideration. Prisoners are treated humanely but are required to follow strict rules and regulations. No radios or TVs are permitted in individual cells. Violence against inmates is strictly prohibited and is severely punished. Inmates are required to address guards in the most respectful form of speech, while guards address them only by their last names as superior to inferior. (In the Japanese language, different levels of politeness are customary depending on whether one is addressing a social equal, a superior, or an inferior.)

Correctional personnel are often university graduates and are, by Japanese standards, well paid, well-trained, and very professional.

They regularly give intense counseling and guidance to inmates throughout the course of confinement. The main impression a visitor might gain from touring a Japanese prison is that every inmate—except those in solitary confinement—is working. Unlike the situation in most U.S. prisons, we saw no idle inmates.

Under Article 59 of the Prison Law, a prisoner who offends against prison discipline is liable for punishment. Prison offenses include murder or violence against other inmates or prison staff, escape, fighting, destruction of property, possession of contraband, giving or receiving goods without authority, theft, gambling, negligence in work, self-inflicted injury, and so on. According to Americans who have been confined in Japanese prisons, discipline is strict but fair, and usually involves some withdrawal of privileges. The law prescribes twelve punishments:

- Reprimand.
- Suspension (up to three months) of good treatment previously awarded.
- Discontinuance of good treatment previously awarded.
- Prohibition of reading books and seeing movies up to three months.
- Suspension from work up to ten days.
- Suspension of using own clothing and bedding up to fifteen days.
- Suspension of self-supply of food up to fifteen days.
- Suspension of physical exercise for five days or less.
- Whole or partial deprivation of compensation for work in prison.
- Reduction of food up to seven days.
- Minor separate confinement for disciplinary punishment up to two months.
- Major separate confinement for disciplinary punishment up to seven days.

This last punishment has not been imposed since 1947 and is proposed to be abolished in an anticipated revision of the law, together with the reduction-in-diet provision.

Article nineteen of the Prison Law provides for the use of instruments of restraint in dealing with recalcitrant prisoners, including handcuffs, arresting rope, straitjacket, and gag. Except in cases of emergency, they can be used only on the order of the warden. The straitjacket is used only when an inmate is behaving violently or tries to commit suicide. Gagging is used for an inmate who continues to shout or yell, in defiance of an order to stop. The straitjacket cannot be used for more than twelve hours and the gag for not more than six hours. However, their use may be extended every three hours in special circumstances. The arresting rope or handcuffs are used on inmates who are violent, try to escape, or attempt to commit suicide during escort.

Classification of prisoners and individualization of treatment is a basic and important part of the corrections process in Japan. Under the present classification system, prisoners are grouped into allocation and treatment categories. Criteria for allocation categories rely on sex, nationality, type of sentence, age, term of sentence, degree of criminal tendency, and physical or mental disorder. For treatment, the norms of selection are the need for vocational training, academic training, social education, therapeutic treatment, special protective treatment, and similar therapy. Prisoners of a particular category are placed in a corresponding institution providing a specific treatment program. In each region, one prison is designated as a regional classification center with qualified specialists and all necessary supporting facilities.

Social casework, counseling, and psychotherapy are provided by properly trained subprofessionals under the supervision of a professional specialist. The offender is assisted in developing a better understanding of group living and the requirements of living in a free society. Group therapy, group counseling, and guided group interaction have been used widely and seem to be gaining ground in correctional treatment. Such methods are economical because they allow one leader to handle more than one client at a time. The use of peer groups appears to be even more helpful. Staff members ordinarily employed in clinical services are psychiatrists and clinical psychologists. Methods frequently involve psychoanalytic therapy, reality therapy, and psychodrama.

Particularly intriguing is a therapy often used in Japanese prisons, called *Naikan*, which has roots in the Buddhist faith, particularly Zen meditation, and means "concentrated self-reflection." With this method, the prisoner remains in his cell to reflect on the error of his ways. When he finally accepts responsibility for his past wrongful acts, which acceptance may include an apology, the therapy is considered successful. This approach is in direct contrast to that prevalent in some quarters in the United States, where the offender's criminality is seen as the result of environmental conditions beyond his control.[2]

Escapes in the Japanese prison system, unlike the United States, are extremely rare. Said Warden Yoshinaga: "There have been no escapes since I came here seven months ago. I understand, however, there was one about two years ago."

In the Japanese prison system in general, there were thirty-five escapes between 1978 and 1985, and the last recorded prison riot was thirty years ago. In the United States, there are an estimated 8,000 escapes a year, although Oregon State Correctional Institution has seen only three escapes in the past ten years.

In Japan's penal system, all wardens began their careers as guards and worked their way up through the ranks. Prison professionals lay great stress on the correctional aspects of their work in counseling, giving guidance, and teaching self-discipline. They are convinced of the effectiveness of their approach in "turning around" sizable numbers of inmates. As one former warden, Kiyoshi Taru, now retired, stated matter of factly: "With proper education, we can make even the worst offenders as calm as the others."[3]

Judges as well as prosecutors make a conscious effort to avoid sending an offender to prison, regarding prisons as "schools for crime." Judges and prosecutors favor—whenever appropriate—probation, suspended sentences and parole, post-prison halfway houses, and community corrections for aid and rehabilitation of prisoners.

Vocational and Other Training

In 1972, the Kawagoe youth facility was designated by the minister of justice as an institution specializing in vocational training. Also, since 1969, a separate minimum security prison for traffic offenders has been maintained at Ichihara in Chiba Prefecture. The youth prison offers thirteen different vocational courses for trainees elected and transferred from prisons throughout Japan. They include barbering, hairdressing, electrical work, plastering, laundering, welding, woodworking, making floor mats (tatami), boiler operation, gardening, carpentry, car maintenance, body and fender repair, and painting. Trainees who pass tests or examinations for a trade that requires an official license or certificate of competence may obtain such certification.

Inmates not enrolled in vocational guidance classes are employed full-time in a variety of prison factories and shops that produce quality goods sold regularly on the open market. Annual proceeds from these sales amount to about $250,000, which is automatically applied toward the cost of operating the institution. Inmates involved in prison industries or vocational training work forty-four hours per week, receiving compensation ranging from 2,000 to 10,000 yen per month (ten to fifty dollars). Some individual prison workshops are sponsored, funded, and fully equipped by private firms.

Group physical education, including jogging and calisthenics, is a large part of the prison program, and education plays an important role. Prisoners who have not completed nine years of compulsory education are given basic education in the Japanese language, mathematics, civics, and other courses common to the elementary school curriculum. Such education is particularly stressed for juvenile inmates. Prisoners are also encouraged to take correspondence courses such as bookkeeping, mimeograph operation, electrical work, architecture, shorthand, car maintenance, or English. Additional prison activities include audiovisual education, sports, living guidance, leisure time activities, and religious guidance. Of particular interest to foreign observers is the "living guidance" course, which is a form of social education that includes moral training in daily activities outside the institution. Its chief purpose is to assist in resocialization of the inmate, cultivating a proper attitude toward society and a "healthy mind."

Houses of Detention

The Corrections Bureau also supervises houses of detention, which are used only for short periods of post-arrest confinement prior to sentencing or release, usually from one to twenty-nine days.

Rehabilitation Aid Hostels

The usual length of stay in a rehabilitation aid hostel, or halfway house, is six months. Assignment to a hostel is made for a variety of offenders, including:

• Those who are discharged without parole at the expiration of their term of imprisonment.

- Those who receive a suspended sentence.
- Those whose parole period has expired.
- Those whose prosecution has been suspended.

Most hostel residents are employed in the private sector, in construction, manufacturing, and unskilled labor. If unemployed, they are referred to the public employment agency. Some hostels have their own sheltered workshops to create jobs for residents. Alcohol counseling, vocational guidance, and group and individual counseling are given in the evenings.

Approximately half the cost of operation of hostels is paid by the national government. Chronic problems are inadequate funding, insufficient staff, and local opposition because of misbehavior or new offenses by residents and absconding, since there is no law requiring the resident to remain at the hostel.

Aftercare

Japanese corrections researchers, as part of their recidivism studies,[4] have found that a prisoner is most at risk to commit another offense during the first year after release. To meet this problem, aftercare is available, but it is not automatic. The discharged offender who is in jeopardy must file an application with a local parole office. Aftercare may include provision of meals, clothing, medical care, recreation, travel fare, lodging, and referral to public employment and welfare agencies. The maximum period for aftercare is six months.

Women's Association for Rehabilitation Aid (WARA)

The antecedents of the Women's Association for Rehabilitation Aid were created before World War II in several cities, including Tokyo, Kyoto, and Takamatsu. The National Federation of WARA was organized in 1964, with purposes including:

- To convene meetings and conferences in order to study the crime problems, characteristics of offenders, and to strengthen group consciousness.
- To inform the public about the problems of offenders and their rehabilitation.

- To participate in crime prevention activities.
- To cooperate with volunteer probation officers for rehabilitation of offenders; for example, to present offenders with gifts in celebration of the successful termination of supervision.
- To assist rehabilitation aid hostels (halfway houses) by providing financial and other support.
- To assist big brothers and sisters associations, including financial support.
- To visit correctional institutions in order to encourage inmates.
- To participate in events of other concerned agencies and organizations.

Parole and Probation Volunteers

Like the other parts of the justice system, parole and probation is part of a national system operating under the Ministry of Justice. Direct parole and probation supervision is handled almost entirely by volunteer civilians (*hogoshi*), who are reimbursed barely enough to cover minimal expenses. The same volunteer parole officers handle adults as well as juveniles and females as well as males. The volunteer parole officers (VPOs) are appointed by the Ministry of Justice upon recommendation of local citizens after careful screening. Unlike the United States, the professional staff (*kansatsu kan*) supervise and coordinate the work of volunteers and are not involved in direct supervision of ex-offenders. As of January 1, 1981, an astounding 46,935 private citizens were reportedly serving in this capacity nationwide.

One of the great virtues of the VPO system is that it results in very close and intensive working relationships between the ex-offender and his or her parole officer. The caseload of the average parole and probation officer in Salem and throughout the State of Oregon is generally about seventy parolees and probationers, while the Japanese caseload is as low as one and no more than two or three parolees.

Volunteers are usually people of some stature in the community, often retired businessmen, teachers, and housewives whose children are grown and no longer living at home. The VPO's personal interest in the offender is legendary, although there is some criticism of a "generation gap" between VPOs and young offenders, as well as complaints that VPOs are too often much older than their assigned offenders. Nevertheless, according to a 1983 study reported by the Asia Far

East Institute for the Prevention of Crime and the Treatment of Offenders (UNAFEI) located in Fuchu, Tokyo, VPOs had compiled an 80.6 percent success rate in "turning around" the probationers and parolees assigned to them: the report showed that only 19.4 percent of ex-offenders had committed new crimes while under the VPO's supervision.[5]

Recently, difficulties have been encountered in recruiting VPOs because of a growing spirit of materialism and the reality of a demanding and burdensome task. According to L. Craig Parker, noted psychologist and author, the volunteer probation officer system offers an inexpensive but viable approach to reform the U.S. system, where the recidivism rate is often reported to be as high as 60 percent:

> The VPO program appears to be very worthwhile in offender rehabilitation. If the volunteers were offered more income, it might attract even greater numbers of younger volunteers, and yet still operate within its present structure. Given the poor record the United States has in rehabilitating criminals, it should carefully consider a program of this type. It is successful and relatively inexpensive to operate.[6]

Group Work in Probationary Supervision

Since 1974, group probationary supervision has been used, based on the assumption that a group worker makes greater use of the interaction among group members. The advantages of such a system are that:

- Many offenders can be treated at the same time.
- It is economical, especially in terms of manpower.
- Members can easily reveal their true identities in a group situation.
- The use of group pressure is effective to influence individuals.

Group pressure has been found to be particularly effective in dealing with young offenders and traffic offenders. The group treatment program for traffic offenders includes group discussions and activities; lectures on road safety and civic consciousness; and films on safe driving and the technical aspects of motor cars. The group treatment program for probationers who indulge in glue sniffing includes group counseling by professional probation officers; education films showing the physical dangers of glue sniffing; and a session with the offender's parents.

Helping Hands across the Pacific

An unusual benefit of our study of crime prevention strategies and the penal and correctional systems of the United States and Japan has been the establishment in 1989 of a sister correctional institution relationship between OSCI and the Kawagoe regional youth prison. The objective of the formal agreement is "to exchange information on correctional methods, techniques, and experiences so that both institutions can offer their staffs, inmates, and thereby the communities at large, the benefits of foreign efforts and experience toward the same goals in inmate correction and protection of the public."[7]

According to both Sister Cities International and Japanese correctional officials, this sister institution relationship is the first of its kind to be formed anywhere. As a result of the agreement, the Salem-Kawagoe Sister Cities Association obtained a grant from the Japan-U.S. Friendship Commission to send Carl Zenon, superintendent of the Oregon institution, on a two-week trip to Japan in the fall of 1989 to study the Japanese correctional system. A detailed report of his findings and conclusions is expected to be published soon in a national corrections journal.

While Zenon found much to be admired and borrowed from his study of the Japanese prison system, Japanese correctional officials were equally interested in learning from the American correctional experience. According to Zenon, the Japanese asked many pointed questions and expressed a keen interest in areas including inmate recreation programs and the American system of "work release"; i.e., allowing selected inmates to work outside the institution on a daily basis when feasible. Such programs are not currently used in Japan.

Japanese officials asked how America is coping with the widespread overcrowding of its penal institutions, and expressed interest in establishing regular exchanges of information on all aspects of prison administration, exchange of videotapes showing how American and Japanese correctional institutions operate, and exchange of correctional personnel to further the sharing of practical information. A total of three Japanese prison officials have already visited Oregon correctional institutions since the sister relationship was inaugurated. One

Kawagoe prison official, Takehiko Terasaki, a 32-year-old prison psychologist, after inspecting Oregon State Correctional Institution as well as the Oregon State Prison and the MacLaren School (a boys' training school) was surprisingly frank in his comments, citing idleness, lack of work and training for Oregon inmates. Declared Terasaki:

> In a Japanese prison, they would not be standing around. They would be working eight hours a day, six days a week, or they would be in counseling or academic programs.

Terasaki's criticism was thereafter the subject of a strongly worded editorial in Salem's daily newspaper. The editorial was captioned "Valid criticism from a visitor." The thrust of the editorial: "Oregon prisoners are idle because we give them nothing to do, no work to perform, no skills to learn, no discipline to develop and little counseling and schooling."[8]

Notes

1. *Encyclopedia of Japan*, Vol. 6 (Tokyo: Kodansha International, 1983), pp. 171–72; John L. Gillin, *Taming the Criminal* (New York: Macmillan, 1931), p. 6. See also Robert Wicks and H.H.A. Cooper, "Corrections in Japan," *International Corrections* (Lexington, MA: Lexington Books, 1979).

2. K.T. Favreau, "Japanese Offender Rehabilitation—A Viable Alternative?" *New England Journal on Criminal and Civil Confinement* (Summer 1988): 331.

3. J. Webb, "What We can Learn from Japanese Prisons," *Parade Magazine*, January 15, 1984.

4. Government of Japan, Ministry of Justice, Research and Training Institute,"Summary of the White Paper on Crime" (Tokyo: 1988), p. 22–47.

5. For a discussion of the VPO system and public participation in Japanese rehabilitation services, see "Criminal Justice in Asia," United Nations Asia Far East Institute for the Prevention of Crime (UNAFEI), Tokyo, Japan, p. 328.

6. L. Craig Parker, *The Japanese Police System Today* (New York: Kodansha International, 1984).

7. Excerpted from the official Sister Correctional Institution Agreement signed at Kawagoe, Saitama, Japan by the two wardens on November 6, 1989.

8. *Statesmen Journal* (Salem, OR), November 25, 1990, p. C1; *Statesman Journal* (Salem, OR), December 4, 1990, p. A8.

For further readings on Japan's correctional system, see Elmer Johnson and Hisashi Hasegawa, "Prison Administration in Contemporary Japan: Six Issues," *Journal of Criminal Justice* 15 (Jan.–Feb. 1987): 65; Atsushi Nagashima, "Corrections in Japan," Proceedings of the American Corrections Association (College Park, MD, 1980), p. 95.

11

Recidivism

Japan

In Japan any conviction within five years of discharge is counted for purposes of determining if the ex-convict should be tabulated as a repeat offender. The latest available statistics on recidivism come from the 1988 "Summary of the White Paper on Crime,"[1] which explains that:

> Every year some sixty-five percent of convicts in the first instance court have previous conviction records, and sixty percent of newly admitted prisoners have experiences of previous imprisonment. To make matters worse, the percentages of those offenders with previous convictions and imprisonments have been increasing in recent years.

As delineated in the chapter on prisons, Japan has exceptionally strong and comprehensive counseling, guidance, job training, and aftercare programs for its prison inmates. Further, by all accounts only serious offenders are sentenced to prison. Why, then, this surprisingly high recidivism rate, when compared with Japan's low crime rate, which is lowest by far among all industrialized countries?

One obvious explanation of this anomaly would be the longer statistical period—five years, compared to three in the United States—covered by the Japanese definition of a recidivist. Plainly, the longer the follow-up period, the greater the likelihood of more repeaters.

Another reason for the high rate might be the strong public policy of Japanese courts to avoid sentencing offenders to incarceration if at all possible. First offenders rarely enter the prison system. Judges prefer to sanction an offender with a fine or a minimum term. One result of this could be that a larger proportion of Japanese prison inmates are hard-core habitual offenders, notoriously resistant to any type of reformation.

The 1988 "White Paper" also provides significant input regarding the nature of Japan's repeat offenders. Japanese criminal justice researchers have gone to extraordinary lengths to analyze the underlying causes of recidivism and how it may be prevented. To accomplish this, the Research and Training Institute of the Ministry of Justice began a ten-year recidivism study in 1978, making full use of the computerized crime records for the period. Completed in 1988, some of the findings are worth summarizing:

I. *In General*

• In spite of the changing number of the total convicted population, a constant proportion of recidivism exists (20–30 percent).
• The number of prisoners who have been convicted six times or more has shown a steady increase since 1975.
• The proportion of dangerous recidivists (assaultive crimes) has decreased in recent years.
• The number of young recidivists has declined significantly in the last ten years.
• Recidivists tend to repeat the same crime over and over.

II. *Personal Profiles*

• Most repeat offenders were poorly educated; 85.6 percent were junior high level or below. The majority were either "mentally retarded" or had an IQ of sixty-nine or less (100 to 110 is generally considered the average), especially those who committed arson, rape, indecent assault, and murder.
• Most recidivists lived alone; 60.1 had no fixed address, especially those who committed arson, larceny, fraud, and robbery. Of the total, 51.9 percent were unmarried, 68.7 percent divorced or widowed. The unmarried predominated among those who committed arson, robbery, and larceny.
• A high proportion of "dangerous" recidivists were either "mentally disturbed" or suspected of being "disturbed."

• Larceny and fraud recidivists were predominantly from deprived and dysfunctional family backgrounds.

III. *Types of Offenses*

• Of those admitted to prison ten or more times, 59.7 percent had been convicted for larceny, 13.5 percent for fraud, 9.4 percent for a drug offense, and 2.9 percent for robbery.
• Earlier larceny offenders favored such methods as sneak theft in private houses or sneak theft at night. More recently, they have chosen picking pockets, theft from offices, shoplifting, and stealing from vehicles.
• Fraud offenders started out swindling by pretending to borrow, or larceny by trick; for repeat offenses the most popular has recently been jumping a restaurant bill.
• Drug offenders tend to repeat the same offense.
• Those with records of repeated violent crimes tend to repeat those offenses.
• Those who have been convicted of repeated property offenses may eventually commit heinous offenses.
• The more often the offenders repeat their crimes, the more difficult it is to apprehend them since they become more skillful in avoiding detection.

IV. *Youth Offenders*

• Young offenders form the core of the crime cancer. Most recidivists started their deviant careers as juveniles.
• The majority of recidivists received their first postjuvenile sentence early in their lives; 15.7 percent were under twenty and 61.3 percent were between twenty and twenty-four, for an aggregate of 77 percent under twenty-five. Accordingly, greater efforts must be made, say the Japanese, to determine how best to intervene with youthful potential and actual offenders before the pattern of antisocial behavior becomes firmly established.

V. *Suggested Remedies*

• The policy of lenient sentencing of young offenders, even after they have committed repeated offenses, should be examined.

• The provisions of the penal code allowing aggravated and augmented punishments for habitual offenders should be employed more often.

• Agencies charged with responsibility for community-based correctional programs should provide more effective supervision and assistance to the ex-offender.

• Rehabilitation aid hostels (halfway houses) should be expanded.

• The period of parole supervision of recidivists is not long enough to carry out effective supervision and resocialization.

• More effective policing and better investigation constitute one method of deterring recidivism.

• Measures should be instituted at every stage of treatment to keep gangsters (*bōryōkudan*) from returning to their former underworld associations, along with intensive suppression of gangster groups.

• More special treatment programs are needed for offenders who are or have been drug addicts, to eradicate their drug dependency.

• The keys to rehabilitation consist of: (1) properly coordinated overall policies including appropriate sentencing; (2) treatment based on the results of investigation as to an offender's personality and causes of crime; (3) obtaining the cooperation of governmental agencies other than the criminal justice administration.

America

The most extensive survey ever undertaken of U.S. recidivism rates was performed for a recent study by the U.S. Bureau of Justice Statistics.[2] The study was based on criminal records of more than 16,000 men and women released from prisons in California, Florida, Illinois, Michigan, Minnesota, New Jersey, New York, North Carolina, Ohio, Oregon, and Texas, and found that 62.5 percent of those released from prisons in these eleven states in 1983 were rearrested for a felony or serious misdemeanor within three years of discharge. About 41 percent of the U.S. sample were sent back to prison or jail. The survey covered both state and federal correctional data.

Although the American research does not appear to be directly comparable to the Japanese study, the Bureau of Justice Statistics of the U.S. Department of Justice has over the years conducted several detailed recidivism studies.[3] Not surprisingly, in a number of instances the conclusions drawn in the American research often closely parallel those reached in Japan. The study entitled "Profile of State Prison Inmates, 1986"[4] issued in January 1988, just mentioned above, found the following:

• Despite heavy increases in American prison populations, the composition has remained stable. The demographic characteristics and offense distribution have changed little since 1979.
• More than 80 percent of state prison inmates were recidivists, previously sentenced to probation or incarceration as a juvenile or adult.
• Of all recidivists, 64.4 percent were violent offenders, 35.6 percent nonviolent.
• Two-thirds of all inmates in 1986 were serving a sentence for a violent crime, and 55 percent of all inmates had a current violent offense.
• Of all inmates, 35 percent were under the influence of a controlled substance at the time of their offense, and 43 percent said they were using drugs daily in the month before their offense.
• About 70 percent of inmates were employed at the time of their arrest.
• Based on age at first arrest and current age, most recidivists had been criminally active for more than a decade.

In May 1989, "Recidivism of Young Parolees" reported on a six-year study of young adults paroled in 1978 from prisons in twenty-two states, and concluded:

• Approximately 69 percent of parolees between seventeen and twenty-two were rearrested for a serious crime within six years of release from prison, 53 percent were convicted for a new offense, and 49 percent were returned to prison.
• Approximately 10 percent of those paroled accounted for 40 percent of the subsequent arrest offenses.
• Recidivism rates were highest in the first two years after an offender's release. Within two years, 47 percent of those paroled had been rearrested.
• Recidivism was highest (71 percent) among those who had not completed high school.
• The longer the parolee's prior arrest record, the higher the rate of

recidivism; more than 90 percent of the parolees with six or more previous adult arrests were rearrested, compared to 59 percent of the first-time offenders.

• Those paroled for property offenses had higher recidivism rates (74 percent) than those paroled for violent or drug offenses.

• Those paroled for violent offenses were less likely to be rearrested than property offenders.

• Paroled burglars were more often rearrested for the same offense than any other group.

• Recidivism rates were highest among parolees with the longest criminal records.

• The amount of time served in prison by parolees for previous offenses bore no relation to their chances of being rearrested.

Implications

"Recidivism statistics should always be viewed with an abundance of caution before acceptance," according to nationally recognized prison consultant Amos Reed, who served as a director of corrections in a number of states, including Oregon. Now retired, Reed detailed the reasoning behind his statement in a personal interview:

> In most cases this is because of definitional differences—how recidivism is defined by the compiler of the statistics. Recidivism does not always mean the same thing in different settings. For example, does it include offenders on probation? On parole? Juvenile offenders? What period of time is employed? Two years following release? Three years? Five years?

Another example the veteran warden gave was of a juvenile detention facility that reported a phenomenally low recidivism rate. Subsequent inquiries revealed that under the rules of that particular institution, if a juvenile inmate escaped, he was never allowed to return. Escapees were thus not considered or counted in computing the facility's recidivism rate! Reed concluded: "Finally, and most importantly, extreme caution should be the watchword when comparing recidivism statistics between different jurisdictions and between foreign countries to make certain that the statistics are actually comparable."

That said, the surprising and unexpected similarity of the recidivism rates in Japan and the United States leads to the conclusion that although Japan has less crime by far than the United States, it has just as many career criminals on a per-population basis. It appears that notwithstanding the historical, ethnic, and cultural differences between the two nations, people are people and human nature is basically the same the world over. In short, despite the best efforts of each society to reform and rehabilitate its offenders, each tends to have about the same percentage of chronic offenders, who—for whatever reason—are hardcore habitual criminals who successfully resist all correctional and rehabilitation efforts on their behalf.

Notes

1. Government of Japan, Ministry of Justice, Research and Training Institute, "Summary of White Paper on Crime" (Tokyo: 1988), p. 22–47.

2. "Profile of State Prison Inmates, 1986," Bureau of Justice Statistics Special Report (Washington, DC: Government Printing Office, 1986). Note: totals do not include offenders in jails and juvenile detention facilities.

3. "Recidivism of Young Parolees, May 1987," Special Report of Bureau of Justice Statistics, NCJ 104916 (Washington, DC: Government Printing Office, 1987), pp. 181–478.

4. "Profile of State Prison Inmates," LEAA National Prisoner Statistics Special Report, NCJ 58257 (August 1979); see also "Prison and Prisoners," *BJS Bulletin*, NCJ 80697 (January 1981); and "Examining Recidivism," *BJS Special Report*, NCJ 96501 (February 1985).

12

Organizing Crime Prevention in Japan

In Kawagoe, as in virtually all Japanese cities and towns, organizing for community action starts with the *chōnai kai,* which is similar to Salem's neighborhood associations, but is a much more developed and complex organization.

Kawagoe is divided into twenty districts, each of which contains ten *chōnai kai,* with a total of 258 in the city. Prior to World War II, the *chōnai kai* was actually a political subdivision and the basic unit of local government administration, but this is no longer the case. Residents living within the *chōnai kai* district pay a monthly membership fee to support a variety of activities including staging festivals and athletic meets; cleaning public areas; spraying for mosquitoes; providing recreation for both young and old; teaching flower arranging, Japanese style painting, bonsai, and similar subjects. Many *chōnai kai* have their own meeting houses or neighborhood recreation centers.

During our stay in Kawagoe, my wife attended several classes in *sumi-e*, a type of Japanese brush painting, at a *chōnai kai* meeting house. The *chōnai kai* is called upon to do such things as recommend various volunteer officers for appointment by the city government, and it may also organize sports clubs for children and sponsor other delinquency prevention activities. Functioning in this manner, it is called a crime prevention association (*Bōhan kumiai* or *Bōhan Kyōkai*).

Nationwide organization of crime prevention volunteers is easily understood. Neighborhood units are combined at the city level in a citywide crime prevention association, and various city associations are combined at the prefectural level. The prefectural associations are then combined at the national level in a national volunteer federation

that is headquartered in Tokyo. All are tied closely with each city
police station for purposes of regular liaison and informal two-way
communication. It should be mentioned that there are sometimes
lower-echelon town, village, and school district crime prevention committees also affiliated with each local city committee.

In Kawagoe, Mayor Kiichi Kauai is chairman of the governing body
of the neighborhood association (*Jichikai*). His principal function is to
cooperate and provide liaison with all city crime prevention activities.
The twenty-four members of the governing body are representatives of
the neighborhood crime prevention units, the municipal assembly (city
council), and certain other groups. The association's office is in the
crime prevention section of the Kawagoe police department. It also
maintains liaison with the citizens' affairs department of city hall. A
total of 2,380 individual homes are presently serving as neighborhood
crime prevention headquarters (*Bohan renrakusho*). The prefectural
(state) crime prevention association is a federation of all city crime
prevention associations in Saitama Prefecture. Representatives are selected by the chairman of each city crime prevention association, with
the concurrence of the police. Qualifications for selection include:

- Belief in crime prevention.
- Active past support of crime prevention activities.
- Demonstrated community leadership.
- Civic-mindedness and public spirit.

The term of office for committee members is two years, but reappointment is possible. Members are not entitled to any special privileges or compensation. Their duties are to act as liaison between the
police and citizens living in the district; to provide information, guidance, and "diagnosis" of crime prevention matters to and for the citizenry; and to receive and report to the police all citizen requests or
complaints.

In order to provide protection for volunteers against accidental injuries during crime prevention activities, some prefectural crime prevention associations insure members through private companies. Volunteers
receive 3,000 yen per day plus a gift payment of 2,000 yen per day if
hospitalized, and in case of death, the family receives 2,530,000 yen
(roughly $18,000).

The operating expenses of some local committees are paid by their neighborhood associations. In some instances, one or more municipalities pay the expenses of a local crime prevention association. The prefectural association's expenses are paid by the prefectural government.

National Federation

The National Federation of Crime Prevention Associations is a private, nongovernmental body that provides liaison and coordination for crime prevention activities of prefectural federations. It carries on a variety of activities such as making crime prevention movies under the supervision of the National Police Agency for use in training local crime prevention units. It designs and distributes crime prevention flyers, posters, handbooks, and even billboards, and publishes a monthly crime prevention newspaper circulated widely among prefectural and local crime prevention associations.

Funding comes from a variety of sources, including membership fees from prefectural federations and private business firms, and donations. Substantial payments are also received from the proceeds of legalized wagering on motorboat and bicycle racing; in some prefectures, the motor boat racing association has supplied crime prevention demonstration vans. There is no subsidy from the national government. However, prefectural and local crime prevention associations receive some funds from prefectural and local governments.

The premier crime prevention event is the annual national awards ceremony, which is usually held in a large downtown Tokyo hotel. Volunteers make the trek to this meeting from all over Japan. Awards go to citizen volunteers who have made outstanding contributions to crime prevention in their communities. "Last year we presented seventy-five such awards," said Kei Sakai, a retired police officer in charge of affairs at the federation.

Tokyo office personnel includes a director, a chief executive, a second secretary, two section chiefs, and three female secretaries. The majority of the staff were former police officers. When we asked Sakai if he had ever been asked for a briefing by a public official from the United States, he said:

> I can't recall that we have ever had an American before. However, we've had law enforcement officials from Indonesia, Malaysia, and

Singapore here asking about Japanese crime prevention programs to aid
them in their fight against crime in their countries.

Asked to express an opinion on possible reasons for Japan's phenomenally low crime rate, our hosts listed seven points:

• Japan's police system is probably better than those in most coun-
tries. It is nationally coordinated.
• Japan has a homogeneous population, with no significant racial
minorities.
• The neighborhood crime prevention organization enjoys wide-
spread citizen participation.
• There are strict gun controls.
• The population in general has a respect for law.
• Police have direct communication with the citizenry and enjoy a
large measure of public trust.
• The Japanese family system also contributes.

When asked about any crime problems facing their country, our
hosts were equally frank and succinct:

Japan's number one problem today is juvenile delinquency. There have
been three peaks in our delinquency—1948, 1951, and now a new wave
of delinquency is beginning in 1981. We are concerned with such
things as classroom violence, use of stimulants such as paint thinner,
and lack of self discipline. Parents seem to be losing their traditional authority over their offspring. Teachers are also losing their authority. Perhaps there has been too much prosperity and even too much democracy.

Public Education Campaigns

There are five highly publicized nationwide public education programs
in Japan every year that are particularly noteworthy. A large amount of
newspaper, television, and radio publicity is always generated by these
campaigns, and the programs themselves feature movies, lectures,
symposia, exhibitions, community, neighborhood and PTA discussion
groups, and writing and speech contests. The Japanese are very committed to these campaigns and seem to be exceptionally successful in
focusing public attention on them. For instance, every fourth Friday is
crime prevention day all over Japan.

One of the most dedicated supporters of the crime prevention program was a member of Japan's royal family, the late Prince Takamatsu, younger brother of the late Emperor Hirohito. Prince Takamatsu's untimely death in 1988 deprived the Ministry of Justice and its program of perhaps its most faithful and certainly its highest-ranking booster.

Every year, crime prevention gets off to a fast start with the "End-of-the-Year Crime Prevention Campaign," which runs from December 11 to January 7, during the traditional *Oshōgatsu,* which includes the New Year's holidays. That campaign is followed three months later by the "Spring Crime Prevention Campaign" from April 16 to May 15, and when summer rolls around, Japan's dedicated crime fighters present the "Summer Crime Prevention Campaign," a national effort sponsored by the Ministry of Justice from July 2 to August 20. This program has been held annually since 1951. In autumn, from October 11 to October 20, comes the campaign developed and sponsored by the National Police Agency and carried out by all local departments. By the time this campaign finishes, crime prevention workers are already preparing for the end-of-the-year campaign, which starts the cycle all over again on December 11. Throughout the year, crime prevention volunteers continuously monitor and observe conditions in their communities, assist in maintaining good order, and provide juvenile guidance.

The structure of crime prevention in Salem, and Oregon in general, pales in comparison with this well-established pyramidal organization scheme. Although a basic crime prevention course for police officers and citizen volunteers is offered at the Oregon police academy, there is no state-level person or agency responsible for assisting in establishing and overseeing crime prevention programs. A staff person at the police academy formerly maintained liaison with local crime prevention groups in addition to his full-time duties as an instructor at the academy, but this person has recently retired and has not been replaced.

The only statewide organization in the field is the Crime Prevention Association of Oregon (CPAO), a private, voluntary group of crime prevention professionals, law enforcement officers, interested citizens, and security personnel from private industry, who have banded together to share methods and techniques and to foster advancement of the preventive approach to crime and delinquency. The CPAO is active, functioning, and nationally recognized. It holds quarterly meetings all over the state, conducts a wide variety of crime prevention training programs, serves as liaison with local crime prevention groups, and holds well-attended annual statewide conferences and training sessions.

Traffic Safety

To be successful, both crime prevention and traffic safety involve a large measure of public education, cooperation, and support, and both involve some of the same approaches in generating publicity and community support. One of the most effective broad-based campaigns is Japan's Traffic Safety Education Campaign (*kōtsū Anzen Undō*), held twice yearly in spring and autumn. We have observed traffic safety education campaigns in the United States, but this is one of the most successful that we have witnessed anywhere.

In Japan, crime prevention and traffic accident prevention appear to be equally important to the government and to the citizenry. Both are the subject of twice-yearly campaigns. The Traffic Bureau is among the five top bureaus in the National Police Agency, with programs including traffic planning, enforcement, and regulation throughout the country carried out by special traffic police (*kōtsū Keisatsu*). As with the crime prevention association, the traffic safety associations (*kōtsū anzen kyō*) are also organized at the local level in cooperation with each local police station, through the prefecture, and ending in an umbrella organization at the national level. There are 1,300 such local organizations across the country, and forty-seven at the prefecture level. Their activities include:

• Conducting a nationwide traffic safety campaign twice a year, in spring and autumn, under co-sponsorship with the national government. All campaigns feature slogans that are highlighted in all publicity. "Watch for Pedestrians!" "Protect Our Junior Citizens!" "Watch for Bicycles and Mopeds!"

• Conducting official commendation ceremonies for persons who have made a significant contribution to traffic safety during the preceding year.

• Providing "on-the-street" traffic safety guidance.

• Sponsoring various meetings and distributing pamphlets to promote traffic safety.

The National Police Agency also conducts social gatherings for traffic police (*kōtsū keisatsu kondan kai*) at the local level, to obtain opinions and special input on fundamental problems regarding activities of the traffic police from a wide range of citizens. Those invited include scholars, traffic experts, labor union representatives, and representatives of women's organizations.

The traffic safety guidance volunteers (*kōtsū shidōin*) are citizens involved in traffic safety activities (other than police personnel)—about 500,000 nationwide. Engaged mainly in traffic safety guidance "on the street," many belong to infant traffic safety clubs, PTA groups, or traffic safety associations in cities. On occasion, they can be observed teaching groups of schoolchildren how to cross streets and walk safely on narrow roads, and related matters.

Another duty is serving as traffic police monitors. This program was established by the police in order to secure feedback from the public on the effectiveness of traffic safety administration and control measures. An estimated 24,000 private citizens all over Japan send in some 68,000 traffic reports annually.

Comparing Crime Prevention in America and Japan

The most significant difference between crime prevention in America and in Japan is in organizational structure. Although citizen participation in both systems is purely voluntary, the American system is in reality a nonsystem compared to its Japanese counterpart, which is vastly more structured—a mammoth pyramid, to be exact, that begins at the neighborhood level and climbs step by step, building block by building block through the district, municipality, prefecture, and finally joins its forces at the national headquarters in Tokyo.

In the American "nonsystem," probably less than 25 percent of neighborhoods are organized, there is usually no statewide crime prevention organization of municipal entities, and there is no organization of state units at the national level. Of course, there is the admirable Crime Prevention Association of Oregon, the National Crime Prevention Council, and National Crime Prevention Coalition in Washington, DC, mentioned elsewhere. These organizations perform myriad invaluable services that in some ways approximate their Japanese counterparts. Nevertheless, the American structure does not come close to functioning like the Japanese pyramidal system, with networking and directing all crime prevention programs outlined above in their respective districts, beginning at the neighborhood level and then progressing through city (*shi*), county (*gun*), and prefecture (*ken*) to the national level; with coordination being carried out at each level in much the same manner as in Japan's nationally coordinated police and criminal justice systems.

It should be noted here that quite early in our study we discussed the causes and effects of the recent national trend toward imposing significantly more severe criminal sanctions in American criminal courts. It should not come as a surprise, therefore, that a similar national trend has likewise been claimed with respect to sentencing juvenile offenders. A recent article published in the *American Bar Association Journal* reported that an increasing number of youths are being transferred to the adult criminal justice system for prosecution as adults, and at an earlier age. The writer cites various statistics and statements by several juvenile delinquency specialists to support his claim.[1] The article quotes, among others, Robert Shepherd, Jr., director of the youth advocacy clinic at the University of Richmond School of Law:

> The trend [toward more severe sanctions for juvenile offenders] has been fueled partly by the public's misperception of a dramatically escalating youth crime rate, when in reality serious juvenile crime is about the same or even lower than it was ten or fifteen years ago. Nearly every poll you read shows that people think juvenile crime is exploding, and it's not true. We're getting more kids in secure facilities for lesser offenses.

Equally disturbing, the "Survey of Youth in Custody, 1987" compiled by the Bureau of Justice Statistics of the U.S. Department of Justice, found that minority youths—African-American, Hispanic, and others—comprised more than half of the youths in custody in publicly run detention facilities. The same survey reports that more than 60 percent used drugs regularly and almost 40 percent were under the influence of drugs at the time of their offense.[2]

According to a 1989 report of a task force of the National Council of Juvenile and Family Court Judges, an increasing number of U.S. juvenile and family court judges are now turning to a new problem-solving technique, alternative dispute resolution (ADR), which is similar to Japan's *Chōtei-in*. American judges have found that nonjudicial mediators are better able than the courts to resolve minor delinquency and status offense cases.

The *Criminal Justice Newsletter*[3] reports that after studying ADR programs across the nation in which probation officers or others help juvenile offenders, their families, and victims to reach a consensus on how the offender can make restitution, solve family problems, or otherwise resolve a case, the panel of judges concluded that in terms of the quality of results, formal adjudication often is not as effective as mediation-based programs.[4] "Family dysfunction is at the heart of many matters referred to court," the panel declared, and the ADR programs may be more flexible in addressing the entire range of family problems, as opposed to focusing solely on the charges against the youth, thereby reducing long-term dependence on the court. Said panel member Robert W. Page, a family court judge in Trenton, New Jersey:

> I have a dream of a court where the smallest room, and least utilized, is the courtroom, where the parties have attempted to get through all the other rooms first, where the courtroom is not the preferred room to resolve disputes.

Notes

1. *American Bar Association Journal* 76 (April 1990): 60, 63.
2. "Survey of Youth in Custody, 1987" (Washington, DC: Bureau of Justice Statistics, U.S. Department of Justice, September 1988).
3. *Criminal Justice Newsletter* 20, 12 (June 15, 1989).
4. See also the discussion of VORP (Victim-Offender Reconciliation Program) in Chapter 9 infra. For a comparison with Japan's alternative dispute resolution methods see Takeo Kawashima, "Dispute Resolution in Japan," in *The Social Organization of Law*, D. Black and M. Mileski eds. (New York: Academic Press 1973).

13

Problem Areas in Crime Prevention

Youth Gangs

Activities of youth gangs on the west coast of the United States, and media reports of such activities have increased considerably during the past few years. In Los Angeles and San Francisco, police have conducted regular "sweeps" to get gang members off the streets. Oregon's largest newspaper, *The Oregonian*, and area television stations have reported that two notorious drug-dealing African-American youth gangs from the Los Angeles area, the "Crips" and the "Bloods" have surfaced in Portland.

In 1987, there were 387 gang-related homicides in Los Angeles alone. In 1988, a total of ninety-three people reportedly died from gang violence, some of them innocent bystanders, according to the Associated Press. In one such incident, a young woman of Japanese ancestry was fatally wounded by a stray bullet while walking along the sidewalk in a hitherto peaceful Los Angeles area shopping district.

On April 24, 1988, Salem's daily newspaper, the *Statesman-Journal*, reported in a wide-ranging feature article that although there were several youth gangs in three northside Salem high schools, there were no indications of unlawful activities by gangs. But on August 18, 1988, Portland recorded its first gang-war-related homicide, a young male alleged to have been a member of the "Crips."

Salem police are on the lookout for possible invasion from Portland, fifty miles to the north, of "Crips" or "Bloods," since members of these gangs have recently been observed in the Salem area. (These observations happen to parallel reports of Tokyo juvenile delinquents appearing in the Kawagoe area.)

The largest Salem gang is known as the MMPs, which stands for "mean master poppers." In the April 24 *Statesman-Journal* article mentioned above, fourteen MMPs posed for a group portrait, all wearing dark glasses to conceal their identities. Through their spokesman and leader they disclaimed any connection with drug dealing or any propensity to commit violent acts. However, several have been arrested mainly for traffic violations, and police are keeping a suspicious eye on them. Police report that two other youth groups, the "Lords of Darkness" and the "Hobbs," have also become established in Salem, and several Oriental youth gangs are reportedly operating in and around Portland. These latter gang members appear to be predominantly from Southeast Asian countries. They concentrate on "car clouts" (thefts from motor vehicles) and may also extort money from Southeast Asian immigrants living in the area and their business establishments. Similar groups of Asian youth—some believed to be immigrants from Hong Kong, and possibly from Taiwan—have reportedly been active for several years in San Francisco, Los Angeles, and Seattle. Some have been tried and convicted of serious crimes, including extortion, robbery and homicide.

In Kawagoe, where traffic offenses are the most numerous infractions, and there is a small amount of glue sniffing and paint thinner abuse among young persons, some law enforcement personnel believe that an influx of Tokyo juveniles has recently brought some of their misconduct patterns to the smaller city, contributing to the delinquency of local youth. As detailed earlier, Kawagoe has had some problems with hot rodders (*bosozoku*) and motorcycle gangs. Although the road traffic law was changed ten years ago, temporarily controlling the problem, it nevertheless persists.

The police report that a surprising 68 percent of Kawagoe's total reported criminal violation arrests are of juveniles, the highest rate in Saitama Prefecture. (Salem police report that only 26.2 percent of crime arrests involves juveniles.) Theft accounted for 78.1 percent of juvenile delinquency arrests in 1981, most typically shoplifting, followed by thefts of motor bikes and bicycles. According to a special survey conducted by the Ministry of Justice in Tokyo on juveniles' motives for committing larceny, reported in the Summary of the White Paper on Crime 1985 (p.8), 64.3 percent did so for financial gain, 28.3 percent for pleasure and 0.8 percent on account of poverty.

Racial and Ethnic Minorities
and Immigrant Groups

A study of racial minorities in the offender population by "The Sentencing Group," a Washington, DC–based organization that promotes prison reform, was released February 27, 1990. It reported that 23 percent of all males twenty to twenty-nine years of age currently incarcerated in jails or prisons or on parole/probation were of African-American ancestry. By contrast, the parallel figures for Caucasian and Hispanic offenders were 6.2 percent and 10.4 percent, respectively.[1] According to 1980 Census Bureau figures, African-Americans comprised only 14.3 percent of the total U.S. population. Thus, African-Americans constitute a disproportionately higher percentage of offenders than their percentage within the population would indicate.

This is by no means a new problem. It has concerned American criminologists, penologists, sociologists, and anthropologists for decades. Speculation as to the underlying causes or reasons for this disparity in African-American criminal behavior or criminal processing of African-Americans has centered on the following:

• Longstanding and deep-rooted racial discrimination in America in education, employment, job training, and law enforcement.
• Frequent low-economic status, lack of job skills, a higher instance of substance abuse, and disintegration of families and neighborhoods.

It is impossible to overemphasize the seriousness of the problem, and it should be noted that some of these so-called "causes" may actually be the result or effects of prejudice and discrimination, rather than causes. It is unquestionably of major importance in crime prevention, and should be of vital concern to all Americans, not only because of its devastating social consequences, but because of its enormous financial cost.

As noted at the outset in our discussion of the cost-effectiveness of crime prevention, crime costs America more than $45.6 billion annually for operating the federal, state, and local criminal justice system—and this figure does not include the immense financial losses of crime victims. It has often been pointed out that it costs more to keep an offender in prison than to send the individual to college, even in these times of skyrocketing tuition costs.

Two promising programs to help correct this special problem are the Perry Pre-school Head Start, a long-term effort described in Chapter 1, and the House of Umoja, originally established in Philadelphia in 1969 by an African-American couple, Sister Falaka Fatah and David Fatah. House of Umoja is an antigang program that provides a home for African-American youths at risk of joining gangs, emphasizing African values and culture and designed to help youth finish school and get jobs. ("Umoja" is Swahili for unity.) The length of residency is typically between one week and one year. There are now twenty-three Umoja houses in the Frazier district of Philadelphia.

An Umoja house is presently being established in Portland, Oregon. As a result of generous financial contributions from a Portland manufacturer of athletic equipment and a local savings institution, the group acquired an abandoned building plus two adjoining residences for the project. The house is expected to begin actual operation by the summer of 1990. The Fattahs will be the parents-in-residence, remaining in Portland for two months or two years—however long it takes to find suitable local "parents" to take over.

Japan has not experienced crime by racial or ethnic minorities to any extent because, as noted earlier, of its largely homogeneous population (97 percent ethnic Japanese) and historic strict government control of immigration. Recently, however, a small influx of foreign immigrant workers has been permitted. Also, in 1985, Japan took the unprecedented step of agreeing to absorb 10,000 Indochinese refugees. All this—a total of 12,915 immigrants in 1987—appears to be altering the crime picture. According to the latest available "1988 Official Summary of the White Paper on Crime," immigrants are increasingly coming to the attention of the Japanese police, some of them for committing criminal violations.[2]

A similar phenomenon (crime committed by recent immigrants) also occurred in American history, but on a much larger scale, beginning in the late 1800s until about 1920, following periods of peak immigration to the United States.[3] Irish immigrants began arriving in great numbers from 1850 to 1890. The Chinese started coming as contract laborers in the late 1800s and continued until their immigration was halted by the Exclusion Act of 1902. Italians and other mid-Europeans arrived in large numbers from 1900 to 1920 and again between 1920 and 1940. Jewish immigrants came from various countries during the same periods. Some of the new arrivals reportedly turned rather quickly to earning their living by engaging in illegal activity. Some became involved in serious violations of American criminal laws.[4] If one were to speculate about what triggered such behavior, the list of possible contributing factors should probably include the economic pressures felt by immigrants and the absence in their new environment of the kinds of informal social controls that had kept them on the path of rectitude in their native lands.

One extreme example of Irish-American criminality was the "Molly Maguires," an unusually violent terrorist society. Eleven of the group were eventually tried, convicted, and executed for murdering coal mine officials and police in Pennsylvania. The criminal activity of Chinese-Americans consisted mainly of operating illegal gambling parlors and using intimidation to extort money from fellow Chinese immigrants, and lethal gang "wars," commonly turf battles between rival tongs (quasi-fraternal organizations). The gambling activity sometimes involved payoffs to local officials. The "syndicated" criminal activity among Italian-American groups has become notorious, publicized by extensive portrayal in the print media as well as in television and motion pictures. Jewish underworld figures have attracted far less media attention, possibly because of their smaller numbers.

In due course, the antisocial behavior of these new immigrants subsided and all but disappeared (except for today's dwindling numbers of gangsters of Italian, Sicilian, or Jewish ancestry) as the immigrant groups gained improved economic status, were assimilated, and became established in their adoptive country. As Stephen Steinberg sums it up in *The Ethnic Myth*:

> That crime in immigrant communities was primarily a response to economic disadvantage, and not a product of deeper cultural abnormalities, is easier to see now that these groups have attained middle-class respectability. To realize this should make it easier to avoid confusion of social class with culture and ethnicity when considering the problems of minorities today.

Organized Crime: Japan's *Yakuza*

No profile of crime in Japan would be complete without some discussion of Japan's gangsters, the so-called *Yakuza* or *Bōryōkudan*. While the two terms are often used interchangeably, "Yakuza" is apparently the popular term, while "Bōryōkudan" (literally "violence-prone groups") is mostly used in official police publications and statistics. Sanseido's "New Concise Japanese-English Dictionary" defines the word "yakuza" as "worthless, useless, good-for-nothing." Taiseido's "Romanized Japanese-English Dictionary" provides an identical definition except it adds: "a good-for-nothing [fellow]."

Japanese people familiar with these gangster groups say that they have existed in Japanese society for several hundred years. Some private citizens we interviewed averred that present-day gangsters date back to the Edo period (1615–1868). Some Yakuza even claim to have Samurai origins; the Yakuza would then predate American gangsters by a very long time, although the American might well argue that some of the U.S. gangster fraternity trace their origins to the Sicilian Mafia or Cosa Nostra. Yakuza are believed to have three different origins:

- Gamblers' groups (*Bakuto*).
- Street stallmen groups (*Tekiya*).
- Racketeer groups (*Gurentai*).

The gamblers and street stallmen, with a strong feudal-type rank system, possibly originated in the middle of the Edo period (eighteenth century). According to police and other observers, each group has its own membership, territory, and origin, with its own boss (*kumichō*), office, and members. Sometimes one group has a "godfather" relationship with the boss of one or more other groups.

The Yakuza have a custom of body tattooing and cutting off a finger. Brutal punishments such as cutting off fingers, expulsion, or lynching are inflicted on those who violate the group's strict rules. It is not a criminal offense to be a member, but an estimated 90 percent of the members have criminal records. In 1981, for example, 8 percent of penal code offenders were members. During the same year, the number of members arrested under the Nerve Stimulant Control Law totaled 10,935, or approximately 50 percent of the total drug offenders. In 1981 police reported 2,452 Yakuza groups, with an active membership of 103,263 throughout Japan.

Crimes committed by Yakuza range from smuggling drugs and illegal firearms, gambling, loan sharking and racketeering, to insurance fraud and extortion. Crimes that accompany Yakuza operations may include assault and homicides, many of which are committed during turf conflicts between competing groups. Japanese gangsters can be surprisingly ingenious in finding and developing unlawful methods for raising needed operating funds, according to reports carried in the American press. One method devised by some Yakuza leaders is apparently unique to Japan: it consists of buying a few shares of stock in a corporation and then using the shares to extract "protection" payments from the corporation for not disrupting annual stockholders' meetings, or for not exposing corporate secrets or law violations, or for "persuading" recalcitrant minority stockholders to refrain from raising objections or disruptive behavior at stockholders' meetings. A recent and new illegal group of Yakuza are the *jiageya*. The jiageya are racketeers who pressure small landowners to sell their property to them at a low price so that it can then be traded on Tokyo's speculative real estate market at a high price.

The number of suspects of stimulant drug offenses cleared by police who were Yakuza members has been increasing since 1975, totaling 11,096 in 1982, an increase of 161 over the previous year. In 1982, 50.685 kilograms of stimulant drugs were seized from members, 47.4 percent of the total. The proportion of Yakuza offenders among the total number of cases cleared by police was only 6.6 percent, but in special classes of offenses, the percentages were remarkably higher— 59.8 percent for intimidation, 54.7 percent for gambling, 39.4 percent for extortion, and 32.6 percent for homicide.[5]

In 1981, police seized 1,027 handguns from Yakuza; most of these are believed to have been smuggled from Southeast Asian countries and the Philippines. The number of guns seized from members in 1982 was 1,767, which set a new record; 326 bullets were fired by members, also a record. Forty-four persons were killed, and ninety-six were injured by these bullets.[6]

There have been persistent reports that Bōryōkudan groups have recently secured footholds in Hawaii and the Los Angeles area, where they prey upon legitimate businesses run by Japanese nationals and Japanese-Americans.

Kawagoe police consider themselves fortunate that only one crime family group operates within the city, the *Sumiyoshidan*, and so they do not have to deal with intergang warfare, as several other cities do. Ostensibly engaged in legitimate businesses, the Sumiyoshidan is believed to be involved in such illegal activities as drugs, gambling, bookmaking, loan sharking, and the like.

The National Police Agency believes that the drugs being smuggled into Japan have been manufactured illegally in South Korea, Taiwan, Hong Kong, and adjacent countries. The bulk of these drugs (heroin, LSD, hashish, and cannabis) are thought to be part of the drug traffic controlled by Japanese organized crime groups, and to constitute their biggest source of income.

Only one example of the Sumiyoshidan's so-called "legitimate" activity came to our attention—control of concession stalls along the parade route for Kawagoe's famed annual fall festival (*Matsuri*). Although most of these stalls seem to be located on the public streets, the Sumiyoshidan charges each stall operator 10,000 yen for "protecting" him and his stand from interference, including would-be competitors. According to one private informant, failure to pay the required protection fee might result in a visit from Sumiyoshidan representatives, followed by serious damage to the stall of the operator who refused to pay.

This practice is apparently common knowledge and accepted without question by the police and all concerned. One long-time American resident observed that the main difference between American and Japanese gangsters is that in Japan they exist openly, for all to see. Unlike their American counterparts, they do not shun publicity; in fact, they seek it, even boldly displaying the gang's name on a large sign in front of their headquarters. Some observers interpret this as a desire for fame and public acceptance. Still, the police are ever watchful of the Yakuza and do not hesitate to arrest and prosecute when the gangsters go too far in their activities.

An event of potentially major significance in the long history of the Bōryōkudan occurred on August 23, 1990, according to a feature article datelined Tokyo in the *Portland Oregonian*.[7] On that date the Japanese police suddenly staged simultaneous raids on the offices of Japan's largest gangster organization, the Yamaguchi *Gumi*, and arrested 20 gang members. Said Superintendent Shigeyuki Yamaguchi, deputy national chief of the organized crime squad of the National Police Agency: "We are going to crush them."

The reason behind the raids, according to the article, was that in the past month the Yamaguchi *Gumi* had been linked to 22 violent gang-related incidents, including several in Tokyo, traditionally the territory of the Sumiyoshi *Dan*, the same gang that holds sway in Kawagoe. Other reasons include: the accidental killing in late June 1990 of a sixty-six-year-old man who was apparently mistaken for a rival gang boss, and the Yamaguchi Gumi's refusal to surrender the gang member believed to have killed the man, as tradition reportedly demands. An additional reason given was the decision of the Yamaguchi *Gumi* to end its long-standing cooperative relations with the police as clandestine tipsters (*Kikki Komi*) in assisting the police in solving serious crime by underworld figures.

According to Superintendent Yamaguchi (no relation to the gangster family) the police are also drafting a proposed new law that would, for the first time, make it a crime to be a member of a Bōryōkudan.

There are, to be sure, many Yakuza members in Japanese prisons. As of February 1, 1988, a total of 621 were reported incarcerated in Fuchu Prison, a maximum security institution near Tokyo. A recent study by the Ministry of Justice of the age levels of Yakuza members within Japanese prisons reported that 28 percent were in their twenties, and 33 percent were in their forties. In a similar survey taken ten years earlier, the figures were roughly reversed: 39 percent were in their twenties and 16 percent were in their forties.

If the number of younger gangsters in prison is decreasing, it could indicate that the Yakuza may be having difficulty recruiting young men to perform the type of criminal acts that often lead to arrest, conviction, and imprisonment. Further, the increases in the number of older gangsters incarcerated might mean that these older members are doing more of the nefarious and risky work themselves, instead of pushing it off on their younger lieutenants. Many law-abiding Japanese as well as the police are hoping that this trend will continue, with the eventual result that the Yakuza will disappear from the scene entirely.

Gang warfare between groups is not uncommon, with fatal consequences to some of the participants, although it is apparently rare for members to kill or injure a private citizen. There have recently been reports in the American press of extensive damage to private property in the Kobe area from stray gunfire as a result of turf battles between rival gangs. One gangster group's errant marksmen were described in the American press account as the Japanese version of the American movie, "The Gang That Couldn't Shoot Straight."

Modern-day Yakuza sometimes identify themselves with right-wing political groups. According to Walter L. Ames,[8] who devoted a considerable amount of his time to studying these gangster groups, up to 70 percent in the western region are of *burakumin* origin, traditionally outcasts in Japanese society. Ethnically Japanese, the burakumin have been stigmatized for centuries because of employment in such supposedly unclean occupations as slaughtering of animals, leather working, or sewage disposal. They constitute roughly 2 percent of the population and always reside in segregated areas or ghettos.

The gangster groups stand out as a curious anomaly in Japan's otherwise law-abiding and well-regulated society that criminologists agree is one of the most crime-free nations in the world. Perhaps, like their American counterparts, these gangsters have not only survived but prospered because they meet some portion of society's need to patronize the services they provide.

Drugs and Crime in America

The nature and extent of the drug problem in the United States and the correlation between drugs, alcohol, and crime have been documented in a number of sources.[9] According to the Bureau of Justice Statistics, most violent offenders (53 percent) and property offenders (56 percent) were under the influence of alcohol or drugs during commission of the offense for which they were charged.[10] The National Institute of Justice reported that 78 percent of state prisoners and 75 percent of all jail inmates reported having used drugs. In both cases marijuana was the drug most often used.[11] According to a study sponsored by the Department of Justice in 1987, from 53 to 79 percent of all males arrested for serious offenses in twelve major cities showed positive in voluntary tests for recent drug use (70 percent in Portland, Oregon). Most of those who were tested were charged with such crimes as burglary, grand larceny, or assault.[12]

Use of drugs has been virtually a nationwide epidemic. The National Adolescent Health Survey,[13] conducted since 1975 under the auspices of the University of Michigan, discovered the following in the fall of 1987, among some 11,000 eighth- and tenth-grade students in both public and private schools:

• Fifteen percent of eighth-grade students reported having tried marijuana and of those, 44 percent reported first use by grade six. Thirty-five percent of tenth-grade students reported having tried marijuana, with 56 percent of these reporting first use by grade eight.
• Twenty-one percent of both eighth- and tenth-grade students reported trying various inhalants (glues, gases, sprays). Sixty-one percent

of the eighth grade students reported first use by grade six; 78 percent of the tenth-grade students reported first use by grade eight.

• Of those students who have tried cocaine, 62 percent of the eighth-grade students reported first trying it in grade seven or eight. Seventy-six percent of tenth-grade students first tried it in grade nine or ten.

• Over half of last year's high school seniors had tried an illicit drug, and over a third had tried an illicit drug other than marijuana.

• Although overall drug use among young people showed a gradual decline, the United States still has the highest rate among the world's industrial countries.

According to the most recent survey by the same research group—the 15th Annual National Survey of American high school seniors taken by the Institute for Social Research, University of Michigan—the long-term trend away from the use of marijuana, cocaine and other drugs continued in 1989.[14]

Among the findings reported from that survey are the following:

• *Marijuana*: Current use of Marijuana, defined as any use in the prior 30 days, is down from a peak of 37 percent in 1979 to 17 percent in 1989 among high school seniors, and among college students the decline between 1980 (the earliest year for which college data is available) and 1989 was from 34 percent to 16 percent. The proportional drop in daily marijuana use has been even greater in both populations.

• *Cocaine*: Cocaine use, which remained at peak levels throughout much of the Eighties, began an important decline in 1987 and 1988 that has continued into 1989. Among high school seniors the proportion who are current users of cocaine fell by more than half, between 1986 and 1989, from 6.2 percent to 2.8 percent. An even larger proportional drop in current use has been observed among college students over the same interval—from 7 percent to 2.8 percent.

• *Crack*: Crack (the smokable form of cocaine that comes in chunks or rock form) has not shown a large decline as did powdered cocaine, but the investigators report that the movement seems to be in the downward direction. Among high school seniors, the proportion having used any crack in their lifetime fell from 5.4 percent in 1987 to 4.7 in 1989, and the proportion using any in the past year fell from 5.4 percent in 1987 to 4.7 in 1989, and the proportion using any in the past year fell from 3.9 percent in 1987 to 3.1 percent in 1989. Current—use in the past 30 days—has remained fairly stable over this interval at 1.3 percent and 1.4 percent, respectively.

Declines in crack use were also observed among the college students and the total sample of high school graduates 19 to 28 years old in the 1987–89 interval.

Causes of the Trends: "We think that the forces leading to the continued downward trends in marijuana and cocaine are much the same as they have been in the past." Lloyd D. Johnston, Principal Investigator of the study adds: "That is, a heightened concern about the health and other effects of these drugs. The proportion of seniors and young adults in their twenties concerned about the adverse consequences of cocaine use—particularly experimental and occasional use—continues to increase, as does the proportion concerned about the use of crack cocaine specifically." Of the seniors surveyed, 54 percent now see "great risk" of the user harming himself physically or in other ways even if he uses powder cocaine only once or twice, and 63 percent now feel that way about experimenting with crack.

Changes in reported availability have not accounted for the downturns, since the proportion saying they could get cocaine or crack "fairly easily" actually has increased and because a very large proportion of these age groups continue to say marijuana is "readily available" to them.

"The broad trends we are seeing are due almost entirely to a change in demand, not supply," Johnston comments. "This reduced demand is attributable largely to the important changes occurring in the attitudes, beliefs, and social norms of our young people."

Treating Drug/Alcohol Abuse in Salem

The damaging consequences to the social structure of dangerous drugs and narcotics-related crime needs no emphasis. It is clear to anyone that the availability of illegal drugs, despite seemingly vigorous enforcement of antidrug laws, is far more serious than "hot rodders" and "cruisers." Most law enforcement officers are of the opinion that the major cause of the increase in crime in the Salem area has been the flow of illegal drugs into the community. Some estimate that up to 50 percent of crime of all types is directly or indirectly related to drugs. Salem police have recently created a Special Street Crimes Unit to deal with drugs, and to a lesser extent, prostitution problems, which are presently concentrated just a short distance north of the Portland Road section, where cruisers formerly gathered (see Chapter 5).

According to Attorney General Dave Frohnmayer, increasing quantities of Mexican tar heroin are finding their way to the Salem area. Frohnmayer estimates that there are around 1,000 heroin addicts in and around Salem, and concurs in the general assessment by Salem police that there is a close correlation between drugs and other crime, especially burglary and shoplifting.

The preeminent public agency for treating drug and/or alcohol abuse in the Salem area is the Marion County health department. In addition to a director, the department is staffed with two drug-alcohol counselors for adults and three full-time and one part-time counselor for juveniles. The basic mode of treatment is group counseling, and the department conducts a weekly adolescent outpatient group that meets for fifteen weeks. It also conducts an intensive outpatient group three times a week for six weeks, once a week for four weeks, then once a month for the balance of a year.

In addition, the department operates a methadone program; methadone, a heroin substitute, is the treatment of choice for most long-term heroin addicts, according to Roger Applegate, director of the Marion County program. Applegate describes the program as follows:

> We mix a combination of education, counseling and group programs. With about 80 percent of our youth abusers, the primary drug is marijuana. The remaining 20 percent are using stimulant drugs.
>
> With our methadone referrals, the majority are engaged in crime to support their habit. We require those in the methadone program to work toward becoming drug-free.
>
> Methadone patients seldom become involved in crime while in the program. We find that about a 30 percent recovery rate is about standard in the whole drug-alcohol abuse field.

Applegate recommends expanding the youth services team concept as the most effective way to obtain early recognition and treatment of the young abuser. He also believes that drug education programs should begin in the elementary grades. He theorizes:

> Drug addiction seems to resemble a disease process in many ways. It works on the individual like a disease. The addict goes through the same basic process as an alcoholic goes through.

Typical of the services rendered by private nonprofit drug and alcohol rehabilitation establishments is the facility operated by the White Oaks Rehabilitation Center, which operates a detoxification center, a residential treatment center for adults, and an outpatient treatment program for families. White Oaks reports a 35 percent success rate for its residential treatment program for adults. An almost universal finding for juvenile abusers is that they have no family support structure as they wrestle with their abuse problem. White Oaks is presently treating thirty young probationers from juvenile court, approximately thirty-five inmates from the Oregon State Correctional Institution (usually younger adult offenders), and thirty others. They report that almost 100 percent of the drunken driver court referrals are hard core alcoholics and drug abusers.

In *Thinking about Crime*,[15] James Q. Wilson wrote that the main effect of all conventional law enforcement efforts to reduce heroin use is to drive up the price of the product, and therefore have not only failed but might in fact contribute to the problem: the increased cost of the drug leads to the commission of even more crimes and the corruption of even more police officers. "We have not" writes Wilson, "learned how to reach deeply into the lives of such [drug-addicted] persons—we can alter prices, change penalties and provide counseling, but we cannot create character."

Drugs and Crime in Japan

In Japan, stimulants (mainly amphetamines), cannabis (hemp and marijuana), and narcotics and opium are classified as dangerous drugs. From our inquiries, it appears that drugs are not a serious problem in Kawagoe. Kawagoe police are very vigorous in enforcement of antidrug laws. Most of the drugs are reported to be amphetamines and barbiturates, with hard narcotics not presently seen in the area.

The National Police Agency, on the other hand, reports that there is significant traffic in drugs in Japan and that this traffic seems to be increasing despite rigorous enforcement efforts. Penalties are severe. Possessing, selling, or receiving cannabis draws up to five years. Smuggling cannabis "for profit" can bring life imprisonment; the sentence for trafficking in narcotics is three to fifteen years, or up to life imprisonment.

According to national statistics, in 1982 more than half of all female prisoners and one-fourth of all male prisoners in Japan had been convicted of drug-related offenses. The average age was in the thirties. Drug abuse in Japan appears to have come in two waves: the first came in 1945, and subsided in 1956; the second started in 1970 and has been increasing steadily every year.

In Japan, as in Oregon, judges sometimes suspend the execution of sentence for users of marijuana and other so-called soft drugs, but not for hard drugs. A study by the Research and Training Institute of the Ministry of Justice, however, revealed that in 1976, 25.1 percent of those receiving a suspended sentence in stimulant drug cases later had their suspension revoked.

For information on how and why individuals start using drugs, a study made at Japan's Fumoto prison is worth noting.[16] When asked, "What was your reason for using drugs?" Japanese prisoners serving sentences for drug violations responded:

- Curiosity—38.7 percent.
- To ease pain from illness—33.9 percent.
- To keep awake while gambling—14.5 percent.
- To combat boredom while working—6.5 percent.

About their motives for selling drugs, they responded:

- To earn a livelihood—34.1 percent.
- To earn money to support a drug habit—15.9 percent.
- To raise money for a gangster group—6.8 percent.
- To comply with a request from an influential person—5.5 percent.

Treating Drug Offenders

In the mid-1950s, the Narcotics Control Law was amended by the introduction of a compulsory hospitalization system, including medical treatment and counseling for confirmed addicts. Originally, drug abusers were sent to eight special regional hospitals, but the current practice is to treat them in regular mental hospitals. The maximum length of hospitalization is seven months.

According to Kazutaka Ichikawa, director of the Narcotics Division of the Ministry of Health and Welfare, the drugs currently being abused in Japan are stimulants, cannabis (hemp and marijuana), and organic solvents.[17] Stimulant drugs constitute the biggest problem, and there does not appear to be significant abuse of cocaine, heroin, or LSD. According to this report, one-third of stimulant abusers are in their thirties and one-fourth are in their forties, while those under twenty-four constitute about 30 percent of the total. The male-female ratio is about eighty-two to eighteen, according to Ichikawa, but there has been a growing increase in the number of female abusers. Second-time offenders have increased from 37 percent in 1979 to 50 percent in 1985.

Organic solvents have been abused primarily by adolescents. In 1984, more than 50,000 persons were "guided" or arrested, 80 percent of them under the age of twenty.

Japanese authorities believe that group therapy has been most successful in dealing with drug offenders, particularly young people. During therapy sessions, video presentations have also proved effective. If continuance of these treatment groups can be assured, say the authorities, there is a good chance that rehabilitation of offenders will succeed.

Medication treatment alone has been found insufficient to cure dependency. Not surprisingly, in an encouraging number of cases, family pressure and change of living environment have been effective in stopping an individual's drug abuse.

The rate of repeat offense for drug abusers is approximately 43 percent. In other words, some 57 percent stopped abusing drugs, or were not rearrested for a drug offense.

Special treatment is available for convicted drug abusers on a trial basis in a number of correctional institutions. As far as we learned, there is no special aftercare for drug offenders discharged from penal institutions, although some may be sent to a rehabilitation aid hostel with other ex-offenders. Two kinds of treatment programs are used for stimulant drug prisoners: the so-called general programs and differential programs, which vary according to different types of stimulant drug abusers.

General treatment includes:

• Investigation to determine the prisoner's problems. A special questionnaire is used to determine the prisoner's motivation for abusing drugs, frequency of abuse, etc.

• Commencement of physical rehabilitation, since most addicts are physically depleted by their abuse.

• Lectures on the serious physical and mental effects of drugs; this may be presented in the form of live lectures as well as by films.

• Discussion and reporting phase, focusing on the prisoner's past conduct and its pernicious effect upon the prisoner's family and associates.

• Lectures on the whys and wherefores of antidrug laws.

• Counseling concerning the prisoner's plans after release. Prisoners are requested to prepare individual life plans including specifics on how they intend to avoid drugs and become law-abiding citizens.

Differential treatment, predicated on the type of stimulant abuse involved, includes these types of individuals:

• Those who had already committed other crimes before they became drug abusers. Most in this category belong to gangster groups. Here the treatment method is to improve their environment, especially relations with their family and associates, and to teach the prisoner about the adverse effects of drugs.

• Individuals who used the drug in order to withstand long hours of work, especially all-night workers. Treatment methods for this type of abuse are vocational training, development of regular habits, and ridding them of false notions about the necessity of using drugs on their jobs.

• Individuals who had experienced personal problems, such as insolvency, unemployment, and the like before they started using drugs. Most have a defeatist attitude toward their lives and used drugs to provide excitement in an otherwise drab existence. Treatment methods for this type include physical rehabilitation, education on the physical and legal consequences of their addiction, and strengthening their work ethic.

• Abusers who had family problems such as divorce, separation, and so on before they started abusing drugs. Most have poor family relationships. Many used drugs to seek pleasure in order to distract themselves from their stress and loneliness. They started using drugs for excitement and to forget their personal problems. Treatment methods for this type seek to improve the abuser's relations with his or her family or to secure a suitable alternative living situation for the abuser following release.

Notes

1. "One in Four Young Black Men in Jail, on Probation or on Parole," *Oregonian* (Portland, OR), February 27, 1990, p. A11.

2. Government of Japan, Ministry of Justice, Research and Training Institute, "Summary of the White Paper on Crime" (Tokyo: 1988), p. 11.

3. Maurice R. Davie, *World Immigration, with Special Reference to the United States* (New York: Macmillan, 1936); United States Bureau of the Census, "A Century of Population Growth" (Washington, DC: Government Printing Office, 1909).

4. See U.S. Immigration Commission, *Immigration and Crime,* vol. 36 (Washington, DC: Government Printing Office, 1891); Senate Document, vol. 18, 61st Congress, 3rd Session, 1910–11; Steven Steinberg, *The Ethnic Myth* (New York: Atheneum, 1981), pp. 116ff; Bob Considine, *It's the Irish* (New York: Doubleday, 1961), p. 70; L. Cordasco, ed., *Studies in Italian American Social History* (Totowa, NJ: Rowman and Littlefield, 1975).

5. Government of Japan, Ministry of Justice, Research and Training Institute, Tokyo, "Summary of the White Paper on Crime" (Tokyo: 1986).

6. Ibid.

7. "Japanese Police Crack Down on Organized Crime, Raid Offices," *Oregonian* (Portland, OR), August 23, 1990, p. A6.

8. Walter Ames, *Police and Community in Japan* (Berkeley: University of California Press, 1981).

9. M.D. Anglin and George Speckart, "Narcotics Use and Crime, A Multi-sample Multi-method Analysis," *Criminology* 26, 2 (Spring 1988): 197; John Carver, "Drugs and Crime: Controlling Use and Reducing Risk through Testing," in *Research in Action* (Washington, DC: National Institute of Justice, 1986).

10. "Profile of State Prison Inmates, 1986," Bureau of Justice Statistics Special Report (Washington, DC: Government Printing Office, 1986).

11. "Annual Report, Fiscal 1986," Bureau of Justice Statistics, (Washington, DC: Government Printing Office, 1986).

12. "Drug Use Forecasting," National Institute of Justice (Washington DC: Government Printing Office, 1988).

13. "Illicit Drug Use by American High School Seniors, College Students and Young Adults," Institute for Social Research, University of Michigan News Release, Ann Arbor, Michigan, January 12, 1988.

14. "Drug Use Continues to Decline According to University of Michigan Survey: Cocaine Down for Third Straight Year," University of Michigan News Release, Ann Arbor, Michigan, February 13, 1990.

15. James Q. Wilson, *Thinking About Crime* (New York: Basic Books, 1983).

16. United Nations Asia Far East Institute for the Prevention of Crime (UNAFEI) Report for 1981, Resource Material Series No. 20, Fuchu, Tokyo, Japan.

17. "Report of the International Seminar on Drug Problems in Asia and the Pacific Region," United Nations Asia Far East Institute for the Prevention of Crime (UNAFEI) Report for 1986, Resource Material Series No. 31 (pp. 293, 300ff), Fuchu, Tokyo, Japan.

14

Underlying Causes of Crime
and Delinquency

Crime and delinquency are predominantly urban phenomena. Most modern criminologists agree that the causes of crime and delinquency are multiple, exceedingly complex, and often interrelated. Just as there are many causes, solutions lie not in any one direction but in many. According to the *Encyclopedia of Crime and Justice*, there are at least five different theories of crime causation—biological, economic, political, psychological, and sociological—each with several individual variations.[1]

Biological theories stress genetic factors. Economic theories convey the image of the criminal as a rational, calculating human who chooses his own life-style. Political theories hold that any behavior is criminal only because that is how the government defines and punishes antisocial behavior, personality problems, and so-called criminal personalities. Sociological theories stress that society itself, its social organization or social structure, is the primary causal factor, that worldwide socioeconomic changes are the root cause of the problem. According to the *Encyclopedia*,

> It is futile to argue about the superiority of one or another of the five types of theories . . . . each has advantages for particular problems and purposes . . . . the best preparation for effectively using any type of theory is awareness of the potential uses of the others.
>
> The choice of the causal theory determines what is looked at and what is overlooked in explaining particular crimes.
>
> The various types of theories . . . are more likely to complement than

to contradict each other . . . . [Although] one theory may be most useful for a particular category of crime or criminal . . . the other theories contribute more to our understanding of another category.

Near the top of the list of causes in both Japan and the United States is social change—the massive social changes that these two societies have undergone in the last forty to fifty years, including:

- Rapid urbanization and high population mobility.
- Poverty (in the United States).
- Inflation.
- Family breakdown and inadequate parenting.
- The school dropout effect.
- Unemployment (in the United States), particularly of youth.
- Drug and alcohol abuse and lack of respect for authority (again particularly in the United States).

Additional factors that are peculiar to the United States are:

- Easy availability of firearms.
- Acute shortage of jail space to incarcerate offenders.
- Racial discrimination.

All of these factors, and doubtless others, have contributed to the rise in both crime and delinquency.

Affluence and Crime

In analyzing published commentary dealing with the underlying causes of crime, one of the most often-repeated shibboleths is that crime is caused by poverty. Those who subscribe to this school of thought postulate that if everyone had good housing and enjoyed a decent standard of living, crime could be greatly reduced, if not virtually eliminated.

Opponents of this view include two eminent British thinkers, Lord Justice Sir John Widgery of the Court of Appeals, and criminologist Leon Radzinowicz. In a speech before the 1968 annual convention of the American Bar Association in Philadelphia, Widgery declared that "Anyone who thinks that better housing, the relief of poverty by itself will bring a decrease in crime is, I venture to say, in for some kind of disappointment."[2] On the basis of his field studies in Great Britain, Radzinowicz concluded that providing good housing and a decent living standard did not necessarily result in reducing crime.

Other researchers have claimed that their studies show that, with the exception of Japan, nations with the highest standards of living have higher crime rates than the poorer, less developed nations.[3] Japan appears to be an exception to the general rule that as the gross national product of a country increases, crimes tends to increase.

Some American experts have pointed out that several industrialized countries, including the United States, had less crime during the world-wide Great Depression of the 1930s when thousands were thrown out of work, than during the recovery years that followed. Also weighing in on the side of those who hold that crime is not necessarily caused by poverty is Japan's Ministry of Justice in its Summary of the "White Paper on Crime, 1984":

> Thefts, which used to be attributed to poverty, have been increasing in number in spite of Japan's economic and material development. Increase in the number of thefts is actually the main contributing factor to the overall increase in the number of offenses in Japan.
>
> Moreover, studies show that in many cases, the economic conditions and other personal factors of theft offenders, including their family backgrounds, are not clearly distinguishable from those of ordinary citizens. This illustrates one of the characteristic features of recent crime and delinquency: i.e., the so-called generalization of crime and delinquency.
>
> On the other hand, although the number is rather small from an international point of view, there is still an increasing tendency in the commission of heinous offenses and drug offenses, particularly those involving stimulants. These findings seem to reflect the pathogenic side of an affluent society.
>
> As to the family situations of delinquents, eighty percent have their natural parents and nearly ninety percent middle class, upper class families in terms of economic conditions. From these statistics, it may be possible to say that delinquency proliferates amongst almost all of the social classes.

Japan in Transition

Present-day Japan is in many ways a society in transition. Nowhere is this more evident than in its younger generation. According to some social critics, the new breed of young Japanese (called "the new humans," *shin ningen*) are woefully lacking in the true "Japanese spirit" (*Yamato damashii*). For example, Hakuhodo, a research group established by a leading Japanese advertising agency, characterized the new breed as follows:

> They do not want to make deep commitments because they do not want to accept the responsibilities that commitments require. . . . They do not have a historical perspective. They know nothing about World War II, postwar recovery, "oil shocks," etc. . . . The thought of not having enough money to spend bothers them. Unlike their elders, who equated not having money with having to struggle to survive, Japanese young people today often equate it with the possible loss of friendships.

A similar view is expressed in an editorial in *Japan Echo,* a respected journal of "informed opinion"[4]:

> The fact is that today's young people have rejected that ethic (self-sacrificing loyalty and true grit) and all that goes with it. To them, the generation that sacrificed leisure and personal fulfillment for the corporation or some other "greater good" is an object of pity, not admiration. They are determined to enjoy life, not to prove themselves by climbing one rung higher than the next person.
>
> They see work essentially as a way of earning a living—enjoyably, if possible—and do not depend on it as a source of fulfillment, which they can find in a multitude of places outside the workplace, pursuing hobbies, socializing with friends, and so forth.
>
> The main factor behind this new attitude is the very economic prosperity that the older generation worked so hard to achieve. Comparatively speaking, today's young people have been brought up in the lap of luxury by parents attentive to their every material need. Unlike most members of the previous generation, they generally have few siblings—one on average—with whom to share this attention. Such an environment can hardly be expected to foster either selflessness or driving ambition.

Peter Tasker, an English writer living and working in Japan, describes the "new humans" as follows[5]:

> In Japanese eyes [the] values [of the "new humans"] are deeply subversive of the most cherished national self-image. Loyalty, self-sacrifice,

perseverance—to the new humans these concepts make no more sense than the tenets of state Shinto.

According to Akiyuki Nosaka, one of Japan's most respected modern novelists, new humans can be characterized as "apolitical, egotistical, inarticulate, blindly conformist, lacking in enterprise, illiterate, cowardly, bigoted, clumsy, and stupid."

Yet Japan's new humans are really different. The attitudes of the young are the most sensitive indicators of the changes their parents have wrought, and post-war Japan has experienced change on a momentous scale.

Throughout, the guiding light has been a special kind of mass pragmatism which has required the sacrifice of individual satisfactions for the economic good of the group. When that is no longer necessary, what is supposed to replace it? No one knows, least of all the new humans, but it is they who must find the answer.

Several Kawagoe officials and private citizens echo the view that Japan's recent prosperity is having an adverse effect on the attitude of young people toward fundamental moral values including honesty, integrity, and respect for authority. They believe that this was at least in part responsible for their country's soaring juvenile delinquency rate.

There is also a substantial segment of today's Japanese society, particularly the older generation, who feel strongly that the steady increase in juvenile delinquency is due to too much democracy and too much democratization; they equate crime and delinquency with permissiveness. This is, of course, tied to the dramatic changes in Japanese society brought about as a result of World War II and the Allied occupation of Japan. The opinion, however, was expressed to us on only two occasions, presumably not to hurt our feelings. Nevertheless, it surfaces from time to time, particularly in letters to the editor columns in the Japanese press, and it is an important part of the whole equation.

Youth and Crime

Oregon Data

According to a study by the state department of education, until recently Oregon had the second largest number of youth in the nation in secure custody. Alcohol was a factor in half of 113 deaths of teenagers in automobile accidents during 1980, and 25 percent of students who entered schools left before graduation. In addition, the Oregon Department of Education published the following statistics in September 1986[6]:

• *Youth in poverty*: over the past two decades, about 5 percent of Oregon families with children under eighteen have been below the federally defined poverty level. In 1980, females were the sole head of the household in 37.7 percent of families.

• *Drug and alcohol abuse*: Oregon's rate of monthly and daily marijuana and cocaine use is higher than the national rate for twelfth-graders. It is estimated that 8,000 adolescents in Oregon have significant alcohol problems, and more than 12,000 suffer from illicit drug abuse: a Salem police officer recently reported that 92 percent of the graduating seniors at Salem's high schools have tried alcohol, and 50 percent reported weekly use; 50 percent have tried marijuana, and 30 percent are weekly users.

• *Youth unemployment*: a dropout has a one in three chance of being unemployed in Oregon, as compared with a one in eight chance for an enrolled or graduated sixteen- to nineteen-year-old. Forty-nine percent of black students who dropped out were unemployed in 1980. (Not to be overlooked is the widespread lack of basic job skills common to this group.)

• *Working mothers*: conservative estimates are that in Oregon at least half of all mothers of children under the age of six have now entered the labor force. The percentage is even higher once the child reaches school age. A total of 212,496 children under the age of nine are affected by the return of the child's primary caregiver to the workplace. Nationally, according to "Youth Indicators, 1988," a report just issued by the U.S. Department of Education, one-sixth of white children, one-fourth of hispanic children, but more than half of all black children live in single-parent homes.[7]

• *Youth crime and delinquency*: studies in several cities outside Oregon tend to confirm what Oregon law enforcement officials have long maintained out of personal, on-the-street experience—that is, that a small number of youth are responsible for a disproportionate amount of crime. In a study conducted in Philadelphia entitled "Delinquency in a Birth Cohort," researchers found that 6 percent of the children born in the same year committed more than 50 percent of the offenses attributable to all youth born that year.[8]

Table 14.1

Juvenile Offenders Detained in Kawagoe between 1981 and 1986

Age	1981	1982	1983	1984	1985	1986
Over 15	588	653	622	784	710	710
Under 14	106	193	165	134	207	111
Total	494	846	787	918	917	821

Japanese Data

Although Kawagoe is statistically a low-crime area, it has the highest juvenile delinquency rate of any city in the prefecture. Police report that in 1986, out of 2,167 reported crimes in the city, 68 percent of the arrests and clearances were of juvenile offenders. (In Salem, the comparable figures were 18,695 and 26.2 percent, respectively.)

The most common juvenile offenses were shoplifting and bicycle and motorcycle thefts. Table 14.1 shows the figures for detained juvenile offenders between 1981 and 1986.

According to the National Police Agency, "There are many juveniles who abuse drugs such as paint thinner and stimulant drugs . . . . the number of juveniles who use stimulant drugs has sharply increased. Among all abusers of stimulant drugs, more than one in ten is a juvenile."[9]

For a variety of reasons, virtually all juvenile crime is increasing throughout Japan. Toshiho Sawai, a national government official, addressing a United Nations Asia Far East Institute conference at Fuchu, Tokyo, Japan in 1983, enumerated some causes:

• Excessive and widespread materialism, instead of traditional Japanese values.
• Urbanization causing weakening of family function which used to foster, control, and educate children.
• Isolation brought on by concentration of population in cities and causing the breakup of the traditional sense of community.
• Impairment of socializing effects of the educational process because of overconcentration in middle schools on preparing students to pass senior high school entrance examinations.
• Isolation, which has increased the effect of peer pressure to commit delinquencies in a collective manner.

Youth Crime Assessments

In order to obtain input from Salem and Kawagoe youth, as well as from the adult population, on control and prevention of crime and delinquency, we submitted two questions to samplings of high school students ranging in age from fifteen to eighteen:

- "In your opinion what are the causes of youth crime and delinquency?"
- "What should be done to correct the problem?"

Salem Answers

The most frequently assigned cause among respondents in Salem was unfavorable family environment and poor parenting. In second place was peer pressure, drugs, and alcohol. Running in third place was boredom, frustration, lack of youth activities and youth recreational facilities, and disrespect for authorities. In fourth were search for excitement, too little spending money, and poverty. Then came the unlikelihood of punishment, lack of feelings of guilt, inability to cope, school pressures, revenge, and lack of motivation to engage in constructive activity.

There was a much wider range of opinion when it came to suggestions on how to remedy the problem. The most frequently assigned remedy was better parenting. Close behind was providing for heavier penalties, especially for drug dealing and drug use. Said one boy: "I favor a life sentence or deportation for repeat drug dealers. This would help the drug problem somewhat."

Next in popularity came a recommendation to require crime prevention education in schools. Also popular were more youth activities and recreational facilities, more youth counseling, and improving the legal system (penalties are too even). Also mentioned were such other excellent suggestions as:

- Place more juveniles on probation instead of unconditional release.
- Provide more jail space.
- Patrol school hallways and lunch areas.
- Have schools place more emphasis on reinforcing positives rather than negatives.

- Foster self-discipline.
- Eliminate plea bargaining in juvenile cases.
- Set stricter curfews.
- Provide more athletic programs.
- Improve youth-police relations.
- Establish citizen patrols in neighborhoods.
- Increase penalties for delinquent behavior.

Three individuals were of the opinion that nothing could be done to correct the problem.

Kawagoe Answers

To our surprise, the most frequently assigned cause given by Kawagoe high school students (103 answers from students in two high schools—100 percent) was practically identical with the first cause listed by the Salem students—namely, bad family environment. This included a lack of communication, parents' indifference to their children's behavior, too much indulging of children by parents, a bad relationship with parents, divorce of parents, and both parents working.

Other causes suggested by respondents were:

- Bad companions (39 percent).
- Lack of self-discipline (32 percent).
- Unsatisfactory school situation (27 percent), including too-strict school regulations, and overly standardized education.
- Society shortcomings (21 percent); these included too-education-oriented society, decline in public morals, too-materialistic society, too-affluent society, antisocial TV programs, and too-easy availability of alcohol and cigarettes through vending machines.
- Teacher inadequacies (18 percent); included in these answers were lack of enthusiasm, no attempt to understand students, failure to recognize students' individuality.
- Feelings of personal isolation (5 percent); examples given were a lack of any person to talk with about his or her problem.
- Curiosity to experience adult behavior (5 percent).
- Rejection by adults (4 percent).
- Lack of a hobby (4 percent).
- Frustrations in daily life (4 percent).

Among the suggestions of Kawagoe respondents for correcting the problem were:

• More communication with family members (40 percent), including more time to communicate with each other at home, especially communication between parents and children.
• Good friends (25 percent).
• Develop self-discipline in order to be able to reject the temptation of delinquent behavior (22 percent).
• Have something to be able to concentrate on, such as a hobby, sports, etc. (16 percent).
• Make the school system better (16 percent); four answered, ". . . not to enforce too-strict school regulations"; six answered, "We need more communication with teachers."
• Parents should place more trust in their children (9.7 percent).
• Improve social circumstances (7 percent).
• Eliminate family problems. Examples of this included the recommendation that parents not fight with each other at home (5 percent).
• Parents should discipline their children and warn them not to engage in delinquent behavior. They should guide their children (6 percent).
• Parents should pay closer attention to supervising their children's education (5 percent).
• There is a need for someone to talk with about personal problems.

Parental Responsibility

When a child becomes a criminal, is it always the parents' fault? The answer is a resounding, "No!" according to Stanton E. Samenow, a clinical psychologist who took part in an eight-year study of criminals at St. Elizabeth's Hospital in Washington, DC. Says Samenow:

> Crime resides with the person and is caused by the way he thinks, not by his environment. . . . Criminals think differently from responsible people, and . . . these thinking patterns show up in early childhood. If we are to combat crime in this country, what must change is the way the offender views himself and the world. Focusing on forces outside the felon is futile. Only when we understand the criminal mind can we be effective in changing some of these people.

Criminals come from all kinds of families and neighborhoods. Most poor people are law-abiding, and most kids from broken homes are not delinquents. Children may bear the scars of neglect and deprivation for life, but most do not become criminals. The environment does have an effect, but individuals perceive and react to similar conditions of life very differently.[10]

Environmental Factors

In an effort to keep alcohol out of the hands of juveniles, Oregon's liquor laws prohibit the sale of beer, wine, and other alcoholic beverages to anyone younger than twenty-one. Sale of hard liquor to adults is permitted on licensed premises only. Stores, restaurants, and night clubs are subject to heavy fines if they sell to minors.

In Kawagoe, until recently there was no restriction on the sale of beer and sake (rice wine) from vending machines to anyone of any age. Such sales are now prohibited after 11:00 P.M. Cigarettes can be obtained from vending machines in both cities, although minors are prohibited from buying cigarettes in Oregon. In Kawagoe, sexually oriented magazines may also be purchased from vending machines; that is not the case in Salem. Although there are several so-called "adult" bookstores (in some cases, over strenuous neighborhood objections), minors are prohibited from frequenting such establishments and proprietors are subject to stiff fines if they allow minors to enter.

The Japanese recommend environmental changes as a means of increased crime prevention:

• Better urban design to facilitate visual observation and security of both residential and business areas.
• Better outdoor lighting for streets, residential and business areas, and other places of active public use.

What Have We Learned?

We have gained a great many insights into the prevention and control of crime and delinquency in two widely disparate cultures. It is apparent that cultural differences do not mean that methods and techniques proven successful in one may not be transferable to another. In fact, there is much we can learn from one another.

Prevention is clearly the wisest long-term solution to America's crime problem. We need to expand its use significantly. By starting with young children and continuing through the years of formal education, we can begin to bring America's mammoth and multifaceted crime problem under control. America should look at such Japanese techniques as the kōban system, character education in the schools, improved correctional practices, a shortened summer school vacation, and handgun control.

Although Japan and Kawagoe have significantly lower crime rates than the United States, they might profitably examine Salem's strengths, such as its neighborhood crime watch program, parenting education, drug abuse education, youth service teams, antidropout programs, anticruising ordinances, and victim-offender reconciliation project.

In general terms, the fact that Japan is blessed with a significant number of informal social controls and core Japanese values of duty and self-discipline that have existed over hundreds of years contributes significantly to that country's low crime rate. The United States is a much younger society with a totally different heritage—one of individualism, inalienable rights, and fundamental freedoms. There is no better illustration of this difference than the controversy and media *blitzkrieg* currently generated by gun enthusiasts and the National Rifle Association over attempts to pass laws requiring registration of handguns, or for that matter putting any limitations on the largely unrestricted purchase and possession of pistols, revolvers, and even military assault rifles.

There is a price to be paid in human life and human misery as a result of the virtually unrestricted purchase and possession of handguns. A 1984 California study reported in the *Journal of the American Medical Association* that treatment of gun-related injuries in the United States costs at least a billion dollars annually in medical costs, excluding doctors' fees, with taxpayers footing most of the bill. Says Michael Martin, a professor at University of California Medical School and lead investigator for the study:

> I hope this study will help elected officials realize that the issue of firearms restriction is not simply one of individual rights, since the taxpayers pay the vast majority of the costs associated with firearms injuries. . . . I think people generally think of firearms restriction as only

a political issue. I hope this study makes it clear it is also an important economic issue.[11]

In 1985, according to the Japanese Embassy in Washington DC, there were a total of forty-six handgun deaths in Japan.[12] During the same period in the United States, there were 7,548 handgun murders, according to the Uniform Crime Reports of the U.S. Department of Justice.[13] On a per-capita basis, there are fifteen times as many police officers killed on duty in the United States annually as in Japan. Americans must realize that if we are going to continue our present philosophy, whereby the rights and freedoms of the individual are paramount, we must be prepared to accept a higher crime and delinquency rate than that of a more regulated society such as Japan.

Many Americans, particularly city dwellers, are understandably vexed by crime in their cities and neighborhoods. Frequently they are looking for simple answers and one-shot panaceas, but as we have tried to point out, there are no easy, magic solutions. We must avoid false expectations. Any assumption that a well developed, integrated approach to control and prevention of crime and delinquency will eliminate all crime and delinquency would be highly unrealistic. Similarly, a belief that an improvement in the standard of living and housing will substantially solve the crime problem for all time to come is probably illusory. As we have seen, although general economic advancement may prevent crime and delinquency in certain forms, it is likely to generate new forms of the same problems.

Notes

1. Daniel Glaser, "Crime Causation: The Field," in *Encyclopedia of Crime and Justice*, Vol. 1, Sanford H. Kadish, ed. in chief (New York: Free Press, 1983), pp. 307–08. The discussion in the following paragraphs draws heavily from this article, and all quoted material is reprinted with permission of The Free Press, a division of Macmillan, Inc.

2. Lord Justice Sir James Widgery, "American Bar Association Speeches, 1968" (unpublished), Cromwell Library, American Bar Foundation, Chicago, IL.

3. Proceedings of the Third United Nations Congress on Prevention of Crime and the Treatment of Offenders, Stockholm, 1965.

4. "Japan's Young Generation," *Japan Echo* 16, 1 (Spring 1989): 60.

5. Peter Tasker, *The Japanese* (New York: E.P. Dutton, Talley Books, 1989) pp. 98–99.

6. "At Risk Youth: Planning Document for the State Board of Education and

the Oregon Department of Education," Oregon Department of Education, Salem. OR. September 1986, pp. 7–8.

7. "Youth Indicators, 1988," Department of Education Report (Washington, DC: Government Printing Office, 1988), p. 21.

8. Marvin Wolfgang, Robert Figlio, and Thorsten Sellin, *Delinquency in a Birth Cohort* (Chicago, IL: University of Chicago Press Chicago, 1972).

9. "The Police of Japan," National Police Agency Tokyo (1982), p. 43.

10. Stanton E. Samenow, *Inside the Criminal Mind* (New York: Times Books, a division of Random House, 1984), pp. 5, 13ff.

11. Michael J. Martin, Thomas K. Hunt and Stephen Hulley, "The Cost of Hospitalization for Firearms Injuries," *Journal of the American Medical Association* 260, 20 (November 1988): 3048–50.

12. Letter dated October 23, 1986 from the Embassy of Japan, Washington, DC, to Ms. Susan Whitmore, Handgun Control Inc., Washington, DC. The "Summary of the White Paper on Crime" does not contain this information.

13. "Crime in the United States," Uniform Crime Reports (Washington, DC: Government Printing Office, 1986), p. 10. It should be pointed out that the Uniform Crime Report figure represents persons *murdered* by handguns only. It would presumably not include persons accidentally killed by handguns or handgun suicides.

15

Implications for the United States

It is appropriate at this point to offer a Japanese expert's perspective on crime prevention in America. After describing Japan's crime prevention programs, Kazuhisa Suzuki, a young crime prevention specialist interviewed at the Ministry of Justice in Tokyo, talked about U.S. programs with which he was quite familiar:

> You in America inaugurate many fine programs. If you will forgive me for saying so, where you seem to go wrong is that you don't give those programs a decent chance to prove themselves. When your experimental programs do not produce the expected results in just a year or two, you cut off the funding or switch to something new. We feel that you just don't give some of your promising programs a chance.

America's policy makers—especially local, state, and national elected officials—would do well to heed this discerning observation of what is perhaps the major flaw in much of America's recent social engineering. Americans too frequently do not take the long-range view in government policy making. And the same can probably be said about the private sector, where we manage the nation's business and industry, as well as in our individual and family lives.

Japan has always been known for its ability to learn from other countries, adapting its borrowings to fit its own culture patterns and value systems. The Japanese became legendary for taking American inventions in business, management, or production, improving on them, and ultimately creating their own innovations. Japan has never been too proud to learn from the West. America should not be too proud to learn from Japan, especially in such a critical area as the prevention and control of crime.

We have seen that Japan's lower crime rate is due to many factors, including the greater effectiveness of its pervasive network of informal social controls, whereas the United States relies almost entirely on formal legal controls—the criminal codes, police, prosecutors, and courts. In addition, Japan is happily free from the broad social unrest, racial unrest, widespread traffic in drugs, experimentation with substance abuse, and a host of other pressing social ills currently plaguing America. The Japanese criminal justice system deters, not because of the severity of punishment but rather because of the certainty of that punishment. Not only do Japanese police catch more of their lawbreakers, but far fewer escape punishment.

The solution to America's growing crime and delinquency problem lies not in any one direction but in many. It calls for more than merely stronger, more punitive responses such as more police, more jails, and longer sentences. Just as there are many sources of crime, so are there many sources of crime prevention. Many individuals and public and private agencies continue to seek solutions to the problems. Some work toward heading off delinquency, others toward reducing opportunities to commit crime. All should be part of any effective crime prevention program.

Ways and means must be found to generate more citizen involvement in crime prevention. Increasing citizen involvement in the Japanese mode may well be the way that U.S. cities must go to reduce crime. With cutbacks in federal assistance to state and local crime prevention and control, there is a greater need than ever before for citizen volunteers.

What Is Needed

A Comprehensive Plan

The crime and delinquency problem in America is statewide and nationwide, and it must be attacked with comprehensive statewide and nationwide plans developed by institutional and citizen leadership. Just as there is no single cause, there is no single solution.

Experimentation

The principal centers for innovation and action in developing useful delinquency prevention tools appear to be at the local level, particularly within individual communities. Experimentation should be encouraged with delinquency prevention programs suited to the needs of a community and the type of delinquent behavior being encountered because, as we have observed, there is no general solution or set of strategies that will prevent all delinquency. All programs should be carefully thought out and have an effective, even if only rudimentary, evaluation mechanism attached. Several studies, for example, raise serious questions about the efficacy of counseling services in preventing recidivism in both adult offenders and juvenile delinquents.[1]

Volunteers

As in Japan, American programs using volunteers in probation and delinquency prevention have generally yielded positive results. The key to success seems to lie in the interpersonal relationship between the volunteer and the juvenile. Effective use of volunteers can also be made in education and vocational training programs.

Earlier Intervention

A child must be taught at an early age that there are painful and predictable consequences of delinquent behavior. At present we are far from doing an adequate job of crime prevention education in schools. Ways and means must be found to instill self-discipline and to inculcate respect for authority. We must do a better job of identifying predelinquent youth, and intervening early before the pattern of delinquency becomes firmly established. The sooner potential offenders are recognized, the better the opportunity for cure and the lower the cost in tax dollars.

Education Programs

Education must be a critical part of any crime prevention program, whether national, state, or local. Comprehensive crime prevention programs should start in kindergarten and continue through all grades in all schools. Special emphasis should be given to kindergarten through grade six, with programs integrated into communitywide prevention programs so that every citizen gets a clear and consistent message from every source that individual law breaking is unacceptable behavior. The crime prevention message should be delivered by parents, siblings, peers, schools, employers, fellow employees, churches and synagogues, print and electronic media, and society at large. Ideally, prevention programs should focus not only on keeping youths from criminal conduct but on building their self-esteem through increased opportunities to attain social competency skills and success in the school environment. Such teaching methods can have a long-lasting effect not only on the prevention of crime but on the ideal of self-actualization as well.

The education department of each state should establish methods for evaluating the effectiveness of crime prevention programs, and should establish and promote standards for both school and class size. According to a national survey funded by the National Institute of Education performed in July 1985 by the Center for Social Organization for Schools at Johns Hopkins University, there is a definite correlation between school size and school disorder. The study found that larger schools experience more disruption because a smaller proportion of the students are generally engaged in meaningful activities.[2]

Other studies, including research done at the University of Illinois at Urbana-Champaign, have reported a similar correlation between class size and antisocial behavior in the classroom. This study also found that reducing class size and school size, along with restructuring the role of the homeroom teacher to provide more guidance functions, can have a positive impact on antisocial behavior.[3]

As the focal institution for individual and social development, schools should require these courses, from kindergarten through twelfth grade:

• Expanded Parenting Education—There is increasing recognition that the major force in preventing crime and delinquency is better-quality parenting. It would be difficult to overestimate the importance of parenting failure as a cause of crime and delinquency. We believe a compulsory course in family responsibilities and parenting is called for, including instruction on the sometimes disastrous effects of teen-age marriage. Too often these marriages have a high failure rate, a high fecundity rate, and a high school dropout rate. The award-winning "family health" curriculum taught in Oregon's Eugene-Springfield and Medford high schools is highly recommended.

• A Comprehensive Long-Range Citizenship Education Course—

Instruction in the rights, responsibilities, and accountability of the individual is critical in a democratic society. We see the process of learning to respect not only the rights of others, but to respect authority and the law, as one of the best ways to attack the crime and delinquency problem and to develop responsible citizens. This is the strategy behind the Japanese character education courses that start in the primary grades. (It does not appear, however, from our studies in Japan that the curriculum content in the United States should necessarily be the same as that taught in Japan.)

• Expanded Drug Abuse Education—Many criminal justice officials in the forefront of the nationwide battle against drug traffic are of the opinion that drugs are responsible for at least half the crime in the country. Only a small part of the total traffic in drugs is being interdicted, and there is a need for stepped up drug-abuse education at all levels of society to discourage drug use and thus reduce the number of buyers. Also, the value of using carefully selected ex-drug addicts to describe their lives as drug abusers should be considered. This could be made a part of an existing drug education program. Accordingly, schools should step up their existing programs, as well as seeking new approaches.

All states should enact drug-free workplace laws, conduct drug education programs for all employees, and include drug testing and counseling where appropriate.

Schools should also consider a program using selected ex-offenders or minimum-security incarcerated offenders, both male and female, to describe to students how they progressed from juvenile delinquency to the state prison, what it's like to lead a life of crime, and how it feels to spend time behind bars. Suggested titles for such a program could be:

• You decide.
• It's your life.
• Personal decision.

The North Carolina crime prevention director describes its shock program, called "Think Smart," in these terms:

> They [ex-offenders] talk for fifteen or twenty minutes on what they did to get arrested, why they committed the crime, life in prison, and their

plans for the future. Corrections staff selects the inmates for training. A correctional or law enforcement officer accompanies them to school presentations.

We started with male inmates but are now training youthful offenders and women. It is very sobering for kids to hear a prison inmate. "Think smart" reached 168,000 kids in 1987 compared to 62,000 in 1986.

Another program of this type is "Scared Straight," which was the subject of a documentary film shown on national television. Scared Straight features a shock-type presentation administered by hardened criminals at the Rahway State Prison (New Jersey) to a small group of would-be young toughs. It is intended to shock young offenders into going straight and has an undeniably powerful impact. Although the "Scared Straight" program has its strong supporters in police and educational circles, others think that it may be a bit too strong in content and of questionable value in reducing recidivism.[4]

The Salem police Crime Prevention Unit has experimented with using ex-offenders as presenters in neighborhood burglary prevention programs, with mixed results. There is one possible side benefit of programs using offenders and ex-offenders: North Carolina reported that the program may have caused the offenders themselves to rethink their past conduct and may provide a means of motivating the offenders to rehabilitate themselves and thus reduce recidivism.

Along this same line, but in a decidedly noncrime mode, some schools have tried a program using a carefully selected young mother to describe what it's like to be a teenage mother and to describe some of the problems she encountered trying to make her own way and provide for her baby without help from the child's father. This program could be made a part of the parenting education course in high school.

We believe that schools should shorten the summer vacation to one month in order to expand the curriculum as recommended. This would have the added benefit of decreasing the excessive amount of idle time of school-age youth. The present three-month summer vacation is an anachronistic holdover from our agricultural past.

Community Action

It is a fact that communitywide, community-based efforts are more effective than federal or state governmental program directives, and a range of activities can be accomplished within individual communities. Neighborhood and community groups—including existing organizations, social service agencies, churches, synagogues, schools, city and county governments, and law enforcement agencies can devise and carry out comprehensive, multidisciplinary crime prevention efforts.

Youth Involvement

Ways and means must be explored to involve more youth in designing and carrying out crime and delinquency prevention programs and projects. Too often, youth are treated as mere recipients of anticrime programs, not partners in finding solutions to problems. This is often also true of in-school programs. We believe that young people have real potential for leadership in reducing crime and delinquency. Experience has shown that if adults act out of such a belief, following through with appropriate behavior, relationships form based on mutual trust. In fact, parents should begin the process at home by involving children in discussions of important family decisions. Adults in policy-making positions must develop the capacity to hear and understand what is being said by youth, many of whom have worthwhile ideas on current social problems (see Chapter 14).

For instance, communities should develop volunteer service training programs for junior and senior high school students. Such activities allow youngsters to make a difference directly, giving them the sense of a stake in their communities, a sense of accomplishment, of belonging, and of civic responsibility.

In delinquency prevention as well as in crime control, America needs to commit to a proactive, preventive strategy of programs that will address the problems of youth with special needs. Although the great majority of American youth manage to adjust themselves to their society, there are many who for various reasons do not. At any rate, from all indications the current method—the individual treatment approach that attempts to remedy individual maladjustments after misbehavior patterns have become firmly established—simply does not work.

Increased Police Visibility

One of the most effective components of any crime prevention program is police presence. What a help it would be if there were an indelible impression of police presence at all times, places, and incidents of potential crime and delinquency!

With use of the kōban system, foot and bicycle patrols as well as patrol cars, the Japanese police have a much higher visibility, thus contributing to Japan's famous "safe streets" and lower crime rate.

A noteworthy development in the study of crime prevention strategies occurred in October 1988, when the Milton Eisenhower Foundation sponsored a study trip to Japan by representatives of twelve major U.S. municipal police agencies and community action representatives. The foundation asked the delegation to evaluate the Japanese police system to determine if U.S. cities could adopt Japanese programs and strategies to American policing in the areas of police training, community services, and early intervention. Captain Thomas Potter, of the Portland Police Bureau, says:

> We observed their communication centers, police academies, police stations, and kōbans. We walked with kōban foot patrol officers as they walked their beats, made home visits, and stopped a variety of citizens. We rode with patrol car officers as they drove around police station boundaries, and talked with volunteer citizen groups about crime prevention, traffic safety, and neighborhood concerns.

Among Potter's recommendations are the following:

- Establish closer community ties.
- Develop training more oriented to public service and community relations.
- Provide more opportunities for creative experimentation.
- Sponsor youth orientation programs to build trust between officers and young people.
- Develop a police volunteer bank to engage in proactive programs such as mentoring and role model programs.
- Implement problem solving by police in patrol, investigations, crime, and fear reduction.

Captain Potter was elevated to the position of Chief of Portland's Police Bureau on November 19, 1990. As chief he continues to implement that department's five-year plan to convert to "community policing" which he drafted in 1989 under the direction of former Chief Richard Walker, whom he succeeded.

Problem-oriented Policing

For the most part, American police are traditionally "incident oriented," instead of "problem oriented." Generally, when a crime incident occurs in the city or the county, a call comes in for police help and a squad car is sent to the scene. Problem-oriented policing is based on the premise that, together with citizen cooperation, corrective police strategies can reduce the incidence of crime in the community. Numerous ongoing programs across the country and overseas support the strategy.[5] To become more effective, police agencies should engage in more problem-oriented policing, working more closely with community groups and social service agencies.

According to a feature article, "Cops Under Fire," in the December 3, 1990 issue of *U.S. News and World Report*, some law enforcement experts believe that "police and politicians made a major mistake in promoting 911 numbers with the promise of immediate response. 'With that kind of increase in the tyranny of 911 [New York's 911 calls increased from 2.7 million in 1980 to over 4 million in 1989, as reported earlier in the same article], cops lost the time to take any initiative or get to know the community,' says University of Maryland criminologist Lawrence Sherman. So police work has come to be almost exclusively reactive. Some departments are trying to change that through 'community policing,' which takes cops out of their cars and puts them back on the foot beat, getting to know their neighborhoods while emphasizing precrisis problem solving. But weaning the public off 911 will be tough—almost as tough as getting the public to develop a better appreciation for what cops are asked to face."[6]

Statewide Anticrime Coordination

In the American political system, public agencies tend to go separate ways in finding solutions to crime problems. Japan, on the other hand, has a nationally coordinated police system with decentralized administration at the prefectural (state) level. An integrated approach is the only answer to the crime problem of Oregon and other states. A crime control coordinating council is necessary, under the personal leadership and direction of the governor or attorney general, to coordinate the work of police, prosecutors, courts, corrections, parole and probation, the public schools, welfare, and city and county officials so that all may work together. Most of these agencies and officials are conducting crime prevention, either primary or secondary, of one sort or another, but there is no coordination and no centralized direction.

The crime control coordinating council would, first of all, provide leadership at the state level to develop, plan, and carry out a long-range, statewide effort, implemented by local crime prevention councils, that would mobilize state, county, and local agencies and experts in an all-out attack upon the rising tide of crime and delinquency. The council would also stimulate local citizens in the most vital and effective of all crime prevention efforts—citizen action.

The 1989 Oregon legislature passed a law drafted by the American author of this study, creating an Oregon crime prevention resource center in the executive department. The law provides, among other things, that the center shall:

• Develop, plan, and carry out a comprehensive long-range integrated crime prevention program implemented by local crime prevention councils.

• Provide a mechanism to support, unify, promote, implement, and evaluate crime prevention efforts.

• Act as a clearinghouse for crime prevention efforts.

Centralized Criminal Justice Planning

A single state criminal justice agency should coordinate all planning. The present system in Oregon with criminal justice planning spread between four or five different agencies (Oregon criminal justice council, corrections division, crime analysis center, state police, juvenile services commission, and juvenile justice advisory committee) has not worked out satisfactorily. An example of its inadequacies is seen in the present prison and jail space crisis, where we have scores of criminals being turned loose because there are no jails or prisons in which to incarcerate them. A coordinated criminal justice plan would have anticipated this problem and brought it to the attention of the legislature.

A crime prevention agency should be created in state government with a staff trained in community action who could assist local communities in setting up and carrying out a comprehensive, long-range, integrated year-round attack upon crime and delinquency. The program would be implemented at the county and city levels by community crime and delinquency prevention councils.

In addition, a clearinghouse should be set up in that agency for collecting and disseminating crime prevention information and techniques so that successful ideas can be relayed and instituted in other communities.

Revitalizing Neighborhood Watch Programs

Too few neighborhoods have functioning crime watch organizations. Crime watch is an excellent crime prevention program, but it suffers from a lack of citizen participation. Nationally, crime watch programs have an average life of eighteen months. New ways must be found to revitalize these programs. They might include small expense payments to citizens who perform the time-consuming job of recruiting participants. The Japanese make such payments in certain cases.

Additionally, local and statewide media should dedicate a portion of their time or print space to crime and drug abuse prevention announcements, and local industry groups, such as hotel/motel owners, retail merchants, car dealerships, car rental agencies, and so on, should cooperate with local enforcement to help the police combat criminals who use their services.

Handgun Control

Stronger handgun control laws are mandatory at the local, state, and national levels. Japan, like most countries, has had such laws for many years; no one there possesses a handgun, except police officers. What is needed in the United States is a law requiring registration and licensing of all handguns and handgun owners, and stipulating punishment for unlicensed possession. There is no constitutional bar to requiring gun owners to register their guns and to obtain a permit to possess them.

State Correction System

State corrections systems should study Japanese correctional methods, including:

• Investigating Japanese behavior modification methods for "turning around" inmates through work, counseling, guidance, rewards, and withdrawal of privileges.

- More physical education programs for inmates.
- Advisability of a separate institution for traffic offenders.
- Expanding vocational education programs.
- Investigating Ohio and Japan systems for manufacture and sale of prison-made goods with profits applied to cost of operation.
- Establishing a no-smoking rule inside all correctional institutions.

Probation and Parole

State and local authorities responsible for probation and parole supervision should give serious consideration to Japan's enormously successful voluntary probation and parole officer program. A number of states and political subdivisions are already experimenting with such a program. The responsible authorities, instead of simply continuing to "beef up" apprehension and punishment of repeat offenders, need to develop proactive aftercare supervision strategies that emphasize offender control through treatment, both within and outside the probation and parole system. Among other strategies, treatment should include offender improvement in the areas of substance abuse, employment, and family relationships.

The use of electronic ankle bracelets to monitor the movements of probationers and parolees holds some promise, but these devices are still in the experimental stage, and they are very expensive.

At present, the most feasible alternatives to expensive confinement in jails and prisons include:

- More intensive personal supervision and monitoring.
- Job training.
- Mandatory work or community service.
- Restitution payments to victims.
- Reimbursement payments for cost of supervision.
- Random drug and alcohol testing.
- Immediate incarceration or reincarceration for violations of conditions.

More Government Leadership

> For if the trumpet gives an uncertain sound, who then will prepare to the battle?
>
> —St. Paul's First Letter to the Corinthians

Crime prevention programs are something of a stepchild at virtually every level of government. There must be more leadership in crime prevention from our government leaders. That necessarily includes strong financial backing of successful programs, and there is also a need for public recognition of volunteers.

Legislatures should enact comprehensive reporting acts for firms engaged in the manufacture, sale, and distribution of precursor chemicals (a chemical that is essential in the manufacturing or processing of a controlled substance), with criminal penalties for nondisclosure.

From a historical point of view, it is instructive to note proposals made thirty years ago (February 16, 1960), when, as Oregon Attorney General, I called a statewide conference at the state capitol in Salem to address the then growing crime problem. More than a hundred sociologists, educators, police, psychologists, juvenile court judges, and religious, civic, and business leaders gathered to examine the nature, extent, and underlying causes of crime in Oregon; to evaluate the crime prevention efforts; and to make recommendations for improved crime prevention action at city, county, and state levels. These are some of the preliminary findings and suggestions received from those in attendance at the conference:

- There is a need at the state level for study, leadership, action, and coordination to develop an overall program to head off young potential offenders before they start treadmilling in and out of our courts, jails, and prisons.
- There is a great amount of knowledge and skill among our trained and experienced professional people that we are not now putting to use.
- Young offenders form the core of the crime cancer. At the same time they offer the greatest prospect for successful treatment in any crime control program.
- Youth from all types of home environments and economic groups are affected. Vandalism and delinquency in well-to-do neighborhoods are not uncommon.
- Use of automobiles figures in an alarmingly high number of cases of antisocial or criminal behavior in youth.
- Our present methods for early detection of potential delinquents in schools, health clinics, and youth groups are inadequate.
- Present programs by existing agencies directed toward problem

families that most need counseling and guidance are inadequate.

• We must develop new methods to reach and provide moral and ethical training for predelinquent children who have little or no family or religious training in this area.

• The efforts of numerous public and private agencies dealing with offenders and providing protective services are not properly coordinated.

• There is a serious need in most communities for a better vocational and apprenticeship training program for unacademic youth.

• Industry, labor, and public agencies should join forces in working out an aggressive work-opportunity program for ex-offenders on probation or parole.

• All public and private social action groups should be working harder at developing public pressure in forcing a cleanout of obscene books on our newsstands, TV programs, and antisocial movies, etc., which serve as how-to-do-it crime kits for our impressionable predelinquent youth.

• Juvenile delinquency may double in the next ten years.

• There is a close relationship between juvenile delinquency and a high divorce rate, broken homes, and the breakdown in family life.

• There is a low ebb in morality because of World War II, the Korean War, the lack of religious training, and insufficient desire for spiritual instead of material values.

• There is a need for mental health emphasis to get at the root of problems.

• An intensive research program aimed at the underlying cause of crime is needed.

• Many children are not taught respect for their parents, which as a result carries into the schools and to law and order.

• The church and the school must do more than they are now doing to prevent delinquency and crime.

Greater Coordination among Volunteer Agencies

Salem is fortunate in having a large number of volunteer agencies and volunteers engaged in delivering a wide range of indirect auxiliary crime prevention services. Even so, greater collaboration and coordination is needed to address community needs and to prevent duplication of effort and working at cross purposes. A community services coordinating council representing all agencies and organizations is the logical step.

A Legislative Crime Prevention Package

Ultimately to form an integrated approach to crime prevention and control, many measures require careful consideration at various levels—neighborhood, city, state, national, and international. What we believe is urgently needed for Oregon, and no doubt other states as well, is the development of a comprehensive plan as part of the process of statewide development. Policy options should range from management of juvenile behavior problems within the family itself to custodial treatment of the hardened criminal.

A central authority in state government should be created to conduct criminal justice planning, possibly under a state crime control coordinating council. Such a planning authority would prepare a comprehensive, long-range state-level plan under the personal leadership of the governor or attorney general. This would insure better coordination and cooperation among all the components of the criminal justice system. In addition, in due course it would cause police, prosecutors, judges, and all other officials in the justice system to be less parochial in their outlook and approach to the problem. We should establish, by statute, a crime control coordinating council, comprised of all local and state agencies involved in the criminal justice process, and we should establish by statute a crime prevention agency in state government to supervise and coordinate all crime prevention units in carrying out a state plan and to act as a central clearinghouse for crime prevention techniques and information. We should enact new legislation or strengthen existing legislation to accomplish the following:

• Authorizing forfeiture of assets of drug dealers, imposition of stiff fines in addition to imprisonment, and imposition of stiff fines for tax evasion on illegal income.
• Requiring registration and licensing of all handguns and handgun owners and punishing unlicensed possession.
• Requiring productive work for all prison inmates.
• Authorizing employment of citizen volunteer probation and parole officers, and providing for insurance coverage and expenses.

• Authorizing greater use of civilians in domestic relations and juvenile court matters as court counselors and court conciliation commissioners.

In short, America must look at other societies in Europe and the Far East, including Japan, and heed the valuable lessons to be learned from their approaches to preventing and controlling crime and delinquency.

Is America's "Get Tough" Strategy Working?

An important question is just how effective are the more severe criminal penalties recently enacted by U.S. legislative bodies, along with the current sentencing practices of the courts designated to implement the penalties? Do longer prison sentences imposed in American courts have the desired effect of reducing crime? Are they producing the opposite effect? Do they have any effect at all?

Serious doubts are now being heard about whether these policies and practices may be adversely affecting America's "war on crime." As pointed out earlier, the American criminal justice system is frequently rated as the most punitive of any major industrial country in the free world. Why, for example, should the United States have nearly ten times as many offenders behind bars as Japan?

Over the past twenty years, U.S. prison populations have increased 250 percent, and they have tripled since the end of World War II. America is convicting and sentencing criminal defendants faster than it can build prisons to house them. The attendant costs of these construction programs border on the astronomical. Yet, at the same time, as more offenders are being sent to prison, U.S. crime rates are still increasing. According to the Federal Bureau of Investigation Uniform Crime Reports, U.S. crime peaked about 1980, declined for a few years, and now has increased for the past four years. The brief downturn of the early 1980s is generally believed to have been due to the aging of the post–World War II "baby boom" generation.

The federal courts and a few states—notably Minnesota, Washington, and Oregon—have recently adopted "sentencing standards and guidelines." These moves were devised to reduce sentencing disparities and to bring sentencing decisions in line with prison capacities. It is still too early to assess the effect of these measures.

Studies by American criminologists such as Don Gibbons, W.G. Nagel, Michael Gottfredson and Travis Hirschi[7] postulate that longer prison terms are in reality counterproductive; they are not deterrents to crime, but in fact have the opposite effect. The authors point to America's sky-high recidivism rates and the social costs of imprisonment, and argue that long-term incarceration has neither rehabilitated nor deterred most of those sent to prisons from committing new crimes when released.

As noted earlier, criminologists specializing in juvenile delinquency have taken this same view of punishments now being imposed by juvenile courts—namely, that minimal intervention or leaving delinquent youth alone, wherever possible, may be the better policy.

On the opposite side of this discussion are ranged a significant number of national, state, and local political figures, particularly during partisan political election campaigns. There are also some respected criminologists, such as James Q. Wilson and Richard J. Hernnstein,[8] who see strong sanctions as necessary to stem America's tide of crime. A 1978 Gallup national public opinion survey on the issue of capital punishment reported that 62 percent of those surveyed favored capital punishment while 27 percent were opposed and 11 percent had no opinion.[9]

Japanese jurists usually prefer to sanction offenders with a fine and/or a minimum term, believing that lighter sentences encourage rehabilitation and that long sentences tend to harden prisoners and propel the offenders deeper into the criminal subculture, causing a higher likelihood of future criminal behavior. A similar policy is favored in a number of countries on the European continent, including Norway, Sweden, Denmark, the Netherlands, West Germany, Austria, and Switzerland.[10]

Correctional administrators have frequently pointed out that severe overcrowding in jails and prisons places a tremendous burden on both inmates and staff, and sometimes leads to institutional violence. Numerous federal courts have ruled that overcrowded conditions can constitute "cruel and unusual punishment," in violation of the U.S. Constitution.

Research has shown that not *all* offenders, but *most*, typically discontinue their crime-prone behavior patterns after reaching their thirties, if not earlier. Unfortunately, there will no doubt always be a class of violent, habitual offenders whom society must incarcerate for extended periods of time because public safety and protection of the public against violent offenders must be the paramount consideration. However, the time is long overdue for governmental leaders and policy makers at the local, state, and national levels to reexamine American law enforcement strategies, including the present "get tough" sentencing policies, and to determine if offenders are in fact being sentenced for longer terms than circumstances warrant. It may be high time for radical changes in national crime strategies, especially in the area of sentencing philosophy and practices

A Final Word

As we confront the problem of crime and delinquency and the task of how to prevent and control it, the threshold question is: Who should do the job, "the government" or "the people"?

Addressing this question in his testimony before the congressional select committee on children, health, and families on March 9, 1988, John A. Calhoun, executive director of the National Crime Prevention Council, a nonprofit volunteer organization dedicated to leading the fight for community crime prevention, said:

> The answer is government *and* community—parents, schools, police, business owners, churches, social workers. We do the job together because none of us can do it separately.
>
> The answer is, both must do the job. Communities will not restore and renew themselves by executive fiat; but some government role—federal, state, local—is critical, for only government can assemble certain types of resources and exert certain moral and legal authority.
>
> Americans can be educated to take effective action to prevent both personal and property crimes.
>
> The government must provide certain tools to enable its people to be fully functioning citizens. But the government cannot create citizens. The community, through its leaders, must do that. The burden is on each of us.
>
> Unless we help our young people develop a sense of stake in their communities and their futures, there may be neither communities nor future.[11]

Obviously, there are important historical, ethnological, and cultural differences between the United States and Japan that enter into the crime rate equation. Nevertheless, some of Japan's methods, techniques, and strategies are certainly worth considering—perhaps even borrowing—by hard pressed American communities searching for new approaches to preventing and controlling crime and delinquency.

Notes

1. R. Martinson, "What Works? Questions and Answers about Prison Reform," *The Public Interest* 35 (Spring 1947): 22–54; R. Fishman, "An Evaluation of Criminal Recidivism in Projects Providing Rehabilitation and Diversion Services in New York City," *Journal of Criminal Law and Criminology* 68 (1977): 283–305.

2. Denise Gottfredson and Nancy Karweit, "Research Report No. 43, School Size and Disorder" (Baltimore, MD: Johns Hopkins University Center for Social Organization of Schools, 1985); Denise Gottfredson, Nancy Karweit, Nancy and Gary Gottfredson, "Research Report No. 37, Reducing Disorderly Behavior in Middle Schools" (Baltimore, MD: Johns Hopkins University Center for Research on Elementary and Middle Schools, 1989).

3. Report of the Governor's Select Committee on the Impact of Drugs on Crime, Education and Social Welfare" (St. Paul, MN: State Planning Agency, October 1989).

4. Steven Lab, *Crime Prevention Approaches, Practices and Evaluations* (Cincinnati, OH: Anderson Publishing Co., 1988), pp. 136–37.

5. R. Trojanowicz and B. Bucqueroux, "Community Policing: A Contemporary Perspective" (Cincinnati, OH: Anderson Publishing Co., 1990); Jerome Skolnick and David Bayley, "Community Policing: Issues and Practices Around the World," U.S. Department of Justice, National Institute of Justice, Issues and Practices (May 1988).

6. "Cops Under Fire," *U.S. News & World Report*, vol. 109, No. 22, December 3, 1990, pp. 32, 35.

7. Don Gibbons,"The Limits of Punishment as Social Policy" (San Francisco, CA: National Council on Crime and Delinquency, 1987); W.G. Nagel "Balancing Offender Needs and Public Safety," Proceedings of the American Corrections Association (College Park, MD: 1980), pp. 245–46; Michael Gottfredson and Travis Hirschi, "Why We're Losing the War on Crime," *The Washington Post*, September 10, 1989, p. A3.

8. James Q. Wilson and Richard Hernnstein, *Crime and Human Nature: The Definitive Study of the Careers of Crime* (New York: Simon and Schuster, 1985).

9. Gallup Report No. 150, Sept. 1978, Princeton, NJ, p. 21.

10. *Encyclopedia of Crime and Justice*, Sanford H. Kadish, ed. (New York: The Free Press, 1983), vol. 2, pp. 485–89; Richard Terrill, *World Criminal Justice Systems* (Cincinnati, OH: Anderson Publishing Co., 1984), p. 171.

11. Testimony published March 9, 1988, in Congressional Report entitled "Youth and Violence: The Current Crisis" (Washington, DC: Government Printing Office), pp. 83–196.

Appendix A

Summary of Findings

In terms of crime prevention strategies, the following measures have been found effective in Japan:

- The kōban system of police substations.
- Reinforcement of police patrols and effective police deployment.
- Special countermeasures against specific offenses and high-risk groups.
- Improvement of police-community relations.
- Improvement of public participation in crime prevention and control through community organization.
- Crime prevention associations and traffic safety associations.

Some crime prevention strategies found effective in Salem are:

- Special street crime task force.
- Differential police response.
- Special countermeasures against youthful auto cruisers.
- Improvement of police-community relations through a police-community liaison committee and neighborhood crime watch, the Land Trac computer system, and vehicle tracking.
- Crime watch liaison with garbage haulers.

In the United States, crime prevention is everyone's concern, but no one's responsibility. While a number of state, local, and private organizations carry on some prevention activities, for the most part crime prevention remains a byproduct rather than a goal. More important, there is a complete lack of coordination, even among state agencies working on the problem, since there is no centralized responsibility for crime prevention, which is the best means of attacking deviant behavior at a cost that amounts to only a fraction of what the American criminal justice system is now costing every taxpayer.

Some studies of the dimensions of active criminal careers have estimated that a juvenile offender who becomes an adult career criminal will cost society between $100,000 and $200,000 before he or she is finished. If the United States were to spend even 2 percent of the time, effort, and money now spent in catching and punishing offenders, to develop, plan, and execute a crime prevention program, the crime rate would not only be reduced, but the country would be money ahead in the long run. It is costing the state of Oregon an estimated average of $14,600 a year to maintain an inmate in a state correctional institution. If a statewide crime prevention program resulted in preventing half a dozen persons from reaching MacLaren School (a juvenile training school for boys) or some other correctional institution, it would easily pay for itself in two years.

In short, we are satisfied that in terms of dollars and cents as well as in human costs, crime prevention is cost-effective. First and foremost, the long-term nature of the prevention approach must be recognized. Because the problem is statewide, it needs to be attacked with a comprehensive state plan developed by institutional and citizen leadership under the direction of the governor and the attorney general. A coordinated planning process is required.

A better job simply must be done of "heading off" predelinquent youth before the pattern of delinquency becomes firmly established because delinquent behavior is often cumulative. At present, virtually all our resources and efforts are devoted to trying to catch and punish offenders after the pattern of delinquent behavior has been set, at which point it is simply too late to change the behavior patterns of most of the offenders milling through our courts, jails, and prisons. Too often, policy makers in positions of authority over the criminal justice process and the legislature have targeted the effects rather than the causes of crime and delinquency. In other words, too often the emphasis has been on the end result rather than on the causes of crime and delinquency.

Traditional social controls to counter antisocial behavior in American society such as the family, the neighborhood, churches, the policeman on the beat, and so on, no longer suffice, and in some cases, have all but disappeared. For the future, the schools are the best hope for replacing the training and nurturing too often absent from the home and family.

Ways and means must be found to generate more citizen involvement in crime prevention. For example, the YMCA's big brother-big sister program is severely handicapped by a lack of citizen volunteers. And Salem's neighborhood watch program is faltering badly, with only 25 percent of neighborhoods participating. Increasing citizen involvement of the kind seen in Japan may well be the way U.S. cities must proceed in order to reduce crime. It would not be an exaggeration to say that the entire criminal justice system of Japan is based largely on citizen volunteers.

The kōban system and foot patrolling should be considered, particularly in high-crime areas. One of the best success stories for this approach is in Santa Ana, California, where crime was reduced by 50 percent with a modified version of Japanese-style techniques. Other success stories have been reported from such widely separated cities as Detroit, Michigan, Baltimore, Maryland, Flint, Michigan, Seattle, Washington, Houston, Texas, and now Portland, Oregon.

Ways should be found of securing better coordination among private volunteer social welfare organizations offering various types of crime prevention-related services, many of which are funded by the United Way. In fact, because of their broad scope, United Way organizations may well be in the best position to take the lead in plans to foster and enforce, if necessary, centralized coordination of efforts to avoid the present overlapping and lack of a coordinated approach.

Appendix B

Implications for Japan

It is appropriate here to consider whether some American crime prevention ideas might merit consideration in Japan, as well as in other countries struggling with the same daunting problems. With Japan's crime rate only a fraction of America's in practically every category except juvenile delinquency, it is perhaps presumptuous to make recommendations of methods and techniques employed in the United States. Nevertheless, we believe that a significant number of innovative programs in America and in Oregon should be of interest to Japanese authorities responsible for public safety in their jurisdictions. Accordingly, the following are methods, techniques, or strategies examined in this book that could be considered for possible adoption or adaptation in Japan and other nations:

- Technical Advances
Land Trac (Chapter 5)
Vehicle Tracking (Chapter 5)
Electronic Report Scanner (Chapter 5)
- Tactical Advances
Special Street Crimes Unit (Chapter 5)
Differential Police Response (Chapter 5)
Youth Service Teams (Chapter 7)
Neighborhood Crime Watch (Chapter 5)
Crime Watch Liaison (Chapter 5)
- In General
Use of Volunteers (Chapter 5)
Use of Police Reserves (Chapter 5)

Use of Police Cadets (Chapter 5)
• Education
School-Police Liaison (Chapter 7)
Block Homes Program (Chapter 7)
Perry Pre-School Project (Chapter 1)
Head Start (Chapters 1 and 9)
Colorado School Project (Chapter 1)
Rape and Molestation Prevention (Chapter 7)
Parenting Program (Chapter 7)
Student Representation (Chapter 7)
Resolving Student Disputes (Chapter 7)
Youth Employment (Chapter 7)
School Size and Class Size (Chapter 15)
Antidropout Programs (Chapter 7)
A Variety of Innovative Educational Programs (Chapter 7)
• Juvenile Court
• Social Welfare
Support Enforcement Unit (Chapter 6)
• Community Action Techniques (Chapter 9)
Mothers Against Drunk Driving (Chapter 9)
YWCA/School Teen Parents School (Chapter 9)
YMCA Big Brother/Sister Program (Chapter 9)
Victim-Offender Reconciliation Program (Chapter 9)
• Special Problem Areas (Chapter 13)
Anticruising Ordinances (Chapter 13)

Glossary of Selected Japanese Terms

Bōhan-in A neighborhood crime prevention patrol volunteer
Bōhan Kyōkai A crime prevention association
Bōhan renrakusho A neighborhood crime prevention contact point
Bōryōkudan Official term for gangster
Bushidō Moral code of the Samurai
Chōnai kai A neighborhood association
Chōtei-in A court-appointed mediator
Chuzaisho A rural police substation
Danchi A large-scale apartment complex
Denwa konner A police telephone consultation corner
Dōtoku kyōiku Classroom moral/character training
Fuzoku eigyō A business affecting public morals, e.g., pinball parlors, night clubs, turkish baths
Fukushibu City welfare office
Gaijin Any foreigner (literally an outside person)
Gakkō-keisatsu renraku kyōgikai School-police liaison committee
Haji Shame
Himawari musume Special crime prevention policewomen
Hashutsusho Technical term for kōban
Hodōin A crime prevention street worker, sometimes paid
Hogoshi A volunteer probation/parole officer
Ijime Student bullying
Issei A first-generation (immigrant) Japanese-American
Jichikai A self-governing federation of renakushō
Jidan Informal dispute resolution
Jūdō A form of jùjitsu

220

Jujitsu Hand-to-hand combat technique
Katei hōmon Home visits by schoolteachers
Katei saibansho Family court
Keisatsu shidō Police "guidance" for wayward youth
Keisatsu sho A police headquarters; national police headquarters
Kikki Komi A police tipster
Kendō Fencing with bamboo spears
Kōban A neighborhood police substation
Kokka Kōan Iinkai National Public Safety Commission
Kōtsū Anzen Undō Traffic safety campaign
Kyogo-in A juvenile home
Meishi A business or professional card
Mombushō Ministry of Education
Mura hachibu "Shunning" by the neighborhood
Nikkyoso Japan Teachers Union
Nisei A second-generation Japanese-American
Ochikobore A school dropout
Omawarisan Popular term for a police officer (literally "Mr.
  Walkaround")
Oshogatsu Annual New Year's holiday
Pachinko A vertical pinball machine
Samurai Premodern warrior class
Sansei A third-generation Japanese-American
Seishin Japanese spirit
Seishōnen ka City youth guidance office
Sempai kōhei seidō Deeply rooted hierarchical system
Seto oya A foster home
Shihō kenkyūsho National Legal Training and Research Institute
Shimin sanka Community action by citizens
Shodō Calligraphy
Shōnen-in A juvenile training school
Shōnen Keimusho A youth prison
Shūshin Self-discipline instruction
Sōdan konner A police consultation corner
Yakuza Older term for Japanese gangster

Index

ROBERT Y. THORNTON was Oregon's Attorney General for sixteen years and is presently a senior judge of the Oregon court of appeals. Over the years he has made eleven trips to Japan, where he taught at Tokyo International University and appeared as a guest lecturer at Waseda, Rikkyo, and Hokkaido Universities, Waio College, the Ministry of Justice, the Asia-Far East Institute for the Prevention of Crime and Treatment of Offenders, and the Legal Training and Research Institute of Japan. For his contributions to Japanese-American understanding, in 1976 he received the Order of the Sacred Treasure from his Majesty, the Emperor of Japan.

Thornton is a graduate of Stanford University, George Washington University School of Law (J.D.), and the U.S. Army Japanese Language School. He has coauthored an annotated edition of the Constitution of the United States and has written numerous legal commentaries as well as articles on Japan's judges and riot control police. He was designer of the crime prevention resource center law passed by the Oregon legislature in 1989 and was recently appointed by the governor to the state crime prevention advisory committee.

KATSUYA ENDO holds a master of education degree from Keio University, a master of education degree from Seattle University, and a Ph.D. in education from International Christian University. Endo is currently an assistant professor of education at Tokyo International University.